Faces from the Flood

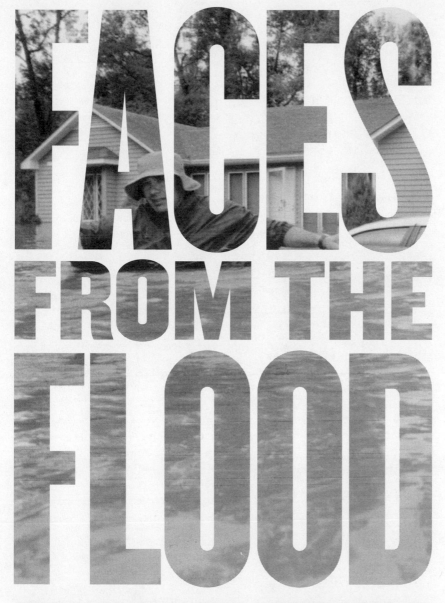

FACES FROM THE FLOOD

HURRICANE FLOYD REMEMBERED

Richard Moore and Jay Barnes

THE UNIVERSITY OF NORTH CAROLINA PRESS | CHAPEL HILL AND LONDON

Designed by April Leidig-Higgins
Set in Minion by Copperline Book
    Services, Inc.
Manufactured in the United States
    of America

All royalties from the sale of this book, after expenses, will be contributed to the American Red Cross and the Salvation Army.

The paper in this book meets the guidelines for permanence and durability of the Committee on Production Guidelines for Book Longevity of the Council on Library Resources.

Library of Congress Cataloging-in-
    Publication Data
Moore, Richard, 1960–
Faces from the flood: Hurricane Floyd
remembered / Richard Moore and Jay
Barnes.
p. cm.   Includes index.
ISBN 0-8078-2861-0 (cloth: alk. paper)
ISBN 0-8078-5533-2 (pbk.: alk. paper)
1. Hurricanes—North Carolina.
2. Floods—North Carolina.
3. Hurricane Floyd, 1999.   4. Disaster
relief—North Carolina—Evaluation.
I. Barnes, Jay.   II. Title.
QC945.M73 2004
363.34'922'09756—dc22   2003019660

cloth   08 07 06 05 04   5 4 3 2 1
paper   08 07 06 05 04   5 4 3 2 1

Page i: A young girl gathers canned food for her family at a Tarboro relief center after floodwaters swamped her home. (Photo by David Weaver; courtesy of the *Rocky Mount Telegram*)

Page iii: Larry Torrez wades through chest-deep waters near a home on South Hillcrest Drive in Goldsboro. In communities submerged by Hurricane Floyd, residents were forced either to wait patiently for rescue or to move about under treacherous conditions. (Photo by Brian Strickland; courtesy of the *Goldsboro News-Argus*)

Page v: Volunteers at the North Carolina State Fairgrounds in Raleigh load relief supplies onto a truck bound for Rocky Mount. People from across the state and the nation pitched in to help the victims of Hurricane Floyd. (Photo by John Rottet; courtesy of the *Raleigh News and Observer*)

Pages vi-vii: Floodwaters filled the streets of Bound Brook, New Jersey, after the passage of Floyd in September 1999. (Photo by Daniel Hulshizer; courtesy of Associated Press)

Page ix: Lonnie Smith, a twenty-three-year-old Marine stationed in New Orleans, drove more than a thousand miles toward Hubert to check on his family before floodwaters stalled his minivan on NC 258. Two fellow Marines used their truck to pull Smith from the flood. Driving in floods is hazardous, and well over half the fatalities attributed to Floyd in North Carolina involved motorists attempting to cross submerged roads. (Photo by Don Bryan; courtesy of the *Jacksonville Daily News*)

Page xv: Employees of Murphy Family Farms, along with friends and neighbors, float a group of dead pigs down a flooded road near Beulaville in the days following Hurricane Floyd. (Photo by Alan Marler; courtesy of Associated Press)

Page 217: Kayla and Kristen Graham examine a toppled oak tree one block from their home on Lenoir Avenue in Kinston. Though floodwaters caused the greatest destruction, high winds still created problems along the path of the storm. (Photo by Charles Buchanan; courtesy of the *Kinston Free Press*)

This book is dedicated to the thousands of North Carolinians who suffered during the great flood of 1999, and to the countless men and women who gave them comfort.

Contents

The passage of Hurricane Floyd through eastern North Carolina in September 1999 produced an epic flood that ranks as the most widespread, destructive, and deadly natural disaster in North Carolina's history. Sixty-six counties were declared disaster areas, damage estimates exceeded $6 billion, and there were fifty-two reported fatalities. More than sixty thousand homes were flooded, and of these, many were hit rapidly and unexpectedly. Hundreds of desperate victims had to be rescued from rooftops and submerged vehicles. Floyd tested our state and its people like no other previous experience.

Faces from the Flood is a recollection of Hurricane Floyd told in the words of those who endured it. It features three dozen firsthand accounts from those who experienced the flood, including victims, volunteers, heroes, scientists, and government officials. Their stories cover dramatic rescues, sorrowful losses, and uplifting displays of spirit and courage.

We began with the hope of selecting stories that would serve as representative examples of the ways the state's residents encountered Floyd. But for every person whose tale appears here, there are hundreds, if not thousands, of others whose experiences, though similar, were in their own way just as unique, just as deserving of being told. With this publication, then, we reflect on our state's greatest disaster through the lens of a few people's experiences, and in

Preface

On the morning after Hurricane Floyd swept through eastern North Carolina, Governor Jim Hunt and Richard Moore toured the affected area by helicopter. They witnessed this scene near Rocky Mount, where floodwaters poured into a rock quarry, creating "the largest waterfall that will ever be in eastern North Carolina." (Photo by Richard Moore)

In the days following the hurricane, volunteers at St. Paul's Baptist Church in Rocky Mount prepared food for rescuers and those who had lost their homes. (Photo by Rip Woodin; courtesy of the *Rocky Mount Telegram*)

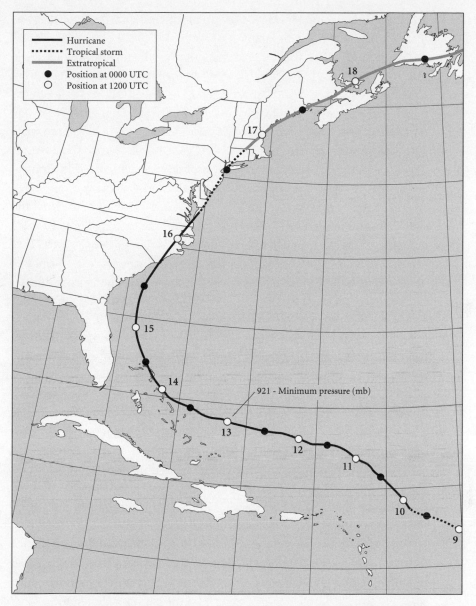

Best track positions for Hurricane Floyd, September 9–18, 1999 (NOAA/National Hurricane Center)

doing so, we hope to offer some appropriate and lasting tribute to what was many North Carolinians' finest hour.

We two authors had very different perspectives on Hurricane Floyd at the time it passed through the state. Jay, who was then director of the North Carolina Aquarium at Pine Knoll Shores, had grown up on the coast, in Southport, hearing stories of great hurricanes like Hazel and learning respect for the power of those storms. His interest in hurricane history had led him to write two books on the subject (*North Carolina's Hurricane History* and *Florida's Hurricane History*). Richard was North Carolina's Secretary of Crime Control and Public Safety. Appointed by Governor Hunt in 1995, he was our state's chief emergency management official, and in that capacity he oversaw the state's emergency response to the hurricane and the ensuing flood. Richard had his own unique experience with Floyd. Indeed, in one of the interviews presented later in this book he relates his dramatic encounter with the power of the storm, but it was his interactions with the people on the front lines—victims, heroes, relief workers, local officials—and his sense that their stories should not be forgotten that formed the real beginnings of this book.

To gather this collection of stories, we interviewed over fifty individuals from seventeen counties around the state. With the help of various government agencies, private charities, businesses, and media, we developed a list of interview candidates in the spring of 2002 and conducted our interviews between May and October of that year, most of them in person, but a few by telephone. We posed a few standard questions to start the interview process, but mostly we just invited these folks to tell their stories. Each interview lasted about an hour, though many could have gone on much longer. For some, reliving the disaster was emotionally draining. Many found themselves fighting back tears as they spoke of the devastation in their communities and shared their experiences.

The recorded interviews were transcribed and edited, after which we selected the ones we thought provided the best overview of the hurricane and carefully condensed and reedited those for clarity. To the interviews we added some of the most striking photographs from the period, acquired from some sixteen different newspapers, wire services, government agencies, and individuals. (For the benefit of future researchers, the original interview recordings and transcripts will be archived in the Southern Historical Collection of the Wilson Library, on the campus of the University of North Carolina at Chapel Hill.)

Hurricane Floyd and the ensuing floods produced many heroes—the tireless, the brave, the generous, the compassionate—and yielded a bounty of awe-inspiring deeds. *Faces from the Flood* offers only a snapshot, a mere sampling of North Carolinians' many and varied personal experiences with the storm and its aftermath. It can serve as a scrapbook of memories and a history lesson for future generations of hurricane watchers. But we also hope it causes readers to pause and reflect on the consequences, good and bad, of large-scale natural disasters and their impact on life in the Tar Heel State.

Richard Moore
Jay Barnes
June 2003

Previous page:
Donald Beaman looks out from the second floor of his barn on Beaman—Old Creek Road in Greene County as he waits for supplies. Although his wife evacuated their home becasue of flooding from Hurricane Floyd, Beaman chose to stay home to watch over his property with the family pets, two border collies. (Photo by Donna Hardy; courtesy of the *Kinston Free Press*)

In the years just before Hurricane Floyd, North Carolina residents were besieged by a cluster of destructive hurricanes. After decades of relative calm, the Tar Heel State was hammered by a sequence of storms beginning in 1995. The '95 season was a busy one—the second most active Atlantic season on record. Hurricane Felix threatened the Outer Banks that year, though it turned back out to sea just before landfall and spared the barrier islands a direct hit. In 1996 North Carolina was blasted by Hurricane Bertha in July, followed by the devastating Hurricane Fran in September. Fran was the costliest storm to hit the state up to that time, causing a whopping $5 billion in damages. Just two years later, Hurricane Bonnie made landfall near Cape Fear—the same general area where Bertha and Fran had come ashore—and brought more destruction to the Tar Heel coast. As the next hurricane season rolled around, coastal residents were on edge, wondering what future storms might swing their way.

As it turned out, the summer of 1999 was another busy one at the National Hurricane Center. Forecasters tracked a string of tropical storms across the Atlantic and Caribbean and struggled to keep up with an above-average number of dangerous and shifting hurricanes. Eight hurricanes formed in the Atlantic that year, five of which—Bret, Cindy, Floyd, Gert, and Lenny—became powerful category fours. Since 1886, when reliable weather records first began to be kept, such a thing had never happened.

North Carolinians also struggled that year, contending with a trio of storms whose cumulative impact on the state was epic. Beginning with the appearance of Hurricane Dennis in late August, continuing through the catastrophic floods of Hurricane Floyd in mid-September, and culminating in the lingering rains of Irene a few weeks later, 1999 entered the record books as the most deadly and destructive hurricane season in Tar Heel history.

In late August, just two weeks before Floyd swept up the Atlantic coast and through eastern North Carolina, another hurricane was vacillating just offshore. Hurricane Dennis was not especially powerful or destructive, but it teased and taunted forecasters and coastal residents for days while churning up the surf along the Outer Banks. Strong winds and high tides swept breakers over fragile portions of Hatteras Island, cutting off NC 12 and denying access to the lower parts of the island. Thousands of tourists and residents who had not evacuated were isolated for five days. Emergency management officials struggled to provide food, water, and medical treatment to those in need. The press soon labeled this Labor Day vacation spoiler Dennis the Menace.

Hurricane Floyd on September 14, 1999, as it swept through the central Bahamas on its way toward the U.S. mainland. At its peak, Floyd was as powerful as Hurricane Andrew and about the size of the state of Texas. (Photo courtesy of NOAA/National Climatic Data Center)

Hurricane Floyd
NOAA-15 AVHRR HRPT
Multi-spectral False Color Image
September 14, 1999 @ 1244 UTC

On September 1, Dennis was downgraded from a hurricane to a tropical storm as it drifted aimlessly just off Cape Hatteras. But storm-force winds continued to batter the coast from Cape Lookout to New Jersey. High tides swept sand into beachfront swimming pools at Nags Head, and severe beach erosion undermined and washed away cottages along the strand. Steady rains fell all across the eastern counties. Over the next two days, the drifting tropical storm turned and edged south, finally coming ashore near Cape Lookout on September 4. From there it tracked inland, weakening as it dissipated over central North Carolina throughout the following day.

Once Dennis had passed, skies over eastern North Carolina returned to normal, and Outer Banks residents began cleaning up the mess left behind. Water levels in rivers and streams throughout the eastern part of the state were high from the rains dropped by the storm, and their volumes were increased by scattered summer thunderstorms, including the localized heavy downpours so typical of that time of year. These rains refilled the creeks and ditches and set the stage for the arrival of the season's most potent rainmaker —Hurricane Floyd.

While Tropical Storm Dennis was still churning off the Tar Heel coast in early September, the tropical depression that would become Floyd was just

starting to spin off the western coast of Africa. Growing steadily in size and strength as it drifted westward, Floyd eventually became a large hurricane at 8:00 A.M. on September 10. It passed well above the vulnerable little islands of the Caribbean and north of Puerto Rico and Hispaniola, continuing to build steam as it bore down on the eastern Bahamas. Atmospheric conditions were just right to permit Floyd to intensify into a massive and powerful hurricane. Dramatic satellite photographs showed the monstrous storm at its meteorological peak on September 13. Barometric pressures dropped and sustained winds reached 155 mph—nearly category-five strength. At this point forecasters warned that Floyd was "as powerful as Hurricane Andrew, but three times its size."

The size and power of Floyd drew the full attention of hurricane forecasters in Miami, but it was the projected path that most concerned them. As the storm inched westward through the Bahamas, all eyes in the eastern United States focused on this awesome weather spectacle. Nightly news broadcasts

Residents and vacationers fled the Outer Banks as Hurricane Floyd turned toward the Carolinas on September 15, 1999. Floyd caused the largest evacuation in U.S. history—almost three million people left their homes to avoid the storm. (Photo by Drew Wilson; courtesy of the *Virginian-Pilot*)

began to headline Floyd's approach to the Florida coast. Even seasoned fore-casters who had witnessed the terrific destruction of Hurricanes Andrew and Hugo admitted they had never feared the approach of a storm like they did with Floyd. As the storm moved through the central Bahamas, it loomed big-ger and meaner than preceding storms, and it seemed destined to strike some portion of the Florida coast.

Evacuations began from Miami northward, and almost seventy emergency shelters opened across Florida's coastal counties. The warnings were taken se-riously, as almost 1.3 million Floridians packed up their cars and fled their

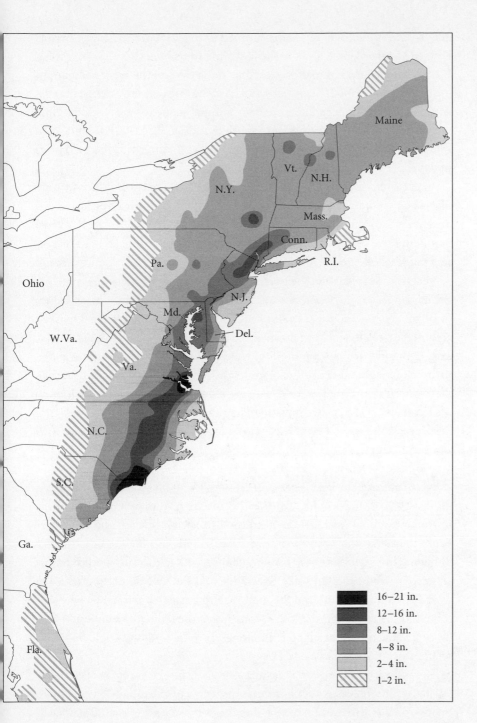

Total precipitation
from Hurricane Floyd,
September 13–17,
1999 (NOAA/Climate
Prediction Center)

16–21 in.

12–16 in.

8–12 in.

4–8 in.

2–4 in.

1–2 in.

homes. Interstate highways were jammed with traffic, NASA shut down its Kennedy Space Center, and for the first time in its twenty-five-year history, Walt Disney World in Orlando closed its doors. When the predicted path of the storm began to shift northward, hurricane warnings were extended up the Atlantic coast, and more and more communities launched evacuations. Hurricane Floyd was curving away from south Florida, and coastal residents from northern Florida to the Carolinas grew increasingly concerned with each news update.

As the hours passed, it became apparent that Floyd was going to miss Florida altogether. Its broad wind field swept the coast near Cape Canaveral on September 15, though the eye passed 110 miles to the east. A data buoy just beyond the eye recorded fifty-five-foot waves every seventeen seconds. Heavy surf pounded the beaches and wrecked fishing piers, but Florida was spared a direct hit from what had the potential to be its worst hurricane ever.

The danger was not over, however. Hurricane warnings were extended up through Georgia and the Carolinas as Hurricane Center forecasters worked around the clock to pin down the most likely landfall scenario. It was not an easy task. In South Carolina, hundreds of thousands of coastal residents grabbed their belongings and fled, pouring onto already crowded highways to escape the storm. Traffic moved so slowly and nerves were so frayed that some motorists left their cars to engage in fistfights on the highway median. Residents of the Charleston area had extra reason to worry: the menacing Hurricane Floyd was approaching South Carolina almost exactly ten years after the state's last great disaster—Hurricane Hugo.

Evacuees from Florida, Georgia, and South Carolina scrambled away from the coast as best they could, some fleeing hundreds of miles up Interstate 95. In North Carolina, evacuations from the Brunswick beaches and the Outer Banks went smoothly. Some people who had stayed on Hatteras and Ocracoke through Dennis decided not to take any chances with Floyd. They packed hastily and drove inland to places like Greenville and Rocky Mount, not knowing what was to come. In the end the mad rush to escape Hurricane Floyd, from south Florida to the Virginia coast, constituted the largest evacuation in U.S. history. Some estimates suggested that nearly three million people fled their homes along the southeast coast.

Floyd continued to spin northward as it passed the Georgia coast on September 15, but forecasters could see that its broad turn was not sharp enough to miss land. North Carolina was going to get the storm. The good news was that the hurricane had weakened considerably as it made its turn toward the Carolinas. Winds dropped from 140 mph to 110 mph throughout the day on the 15th. Because of the storm's drop in intensity, the much-feared storm surge would be less destructive. But Floyd was still a huge storm—so large that its outer rain bands extended from New York to Florida. Heavy rains began falling across eastern North Carolina a full day before the storm arrived.

At 3:00 A.M. on September 16, Floyd made landfall near Cape Fear and swept inland across North Carolina's coastal plain. The center of the storm tracked along the New Hanover County beaches, over New Bern and Washington, and back out to sea off the coast of Norfolk, Virginia. From there it accelerated past the Delmarva Peninsula and up the New Jersey coast. Its forward speed increased to 34 mph. The once mighty hurricane then took on extratropical characteristics and buffeted coastal New England with hard rains and heavy surf. Within two days it merged with a large low-pressure system over the North Atlantic and was no longer a distinct storm.

At the time Floyd made landfall in North Carolina, reconnaissance aircraft reported maximum sustained winds of 105 mph, though no coastal reporting station could verify winds that extreme. The lowest barometric readings in North Carolina were taken at New River Air Station near Jacksonville (28.32 inches) and the Wilmington airport (28.34 inches). The New Hanover County Emergency Operations Center recorded a peak wind gust of 130 mph, and there were a few unofficial reports of even higher gusts. Trees and power lines came down in numerous locations, shingles were snatched from the roofs of coastal cottages, and signs were toppled, but overall wind damages along the North Carolina coast were far less severe than had been feared.

Floyd's drop in intensity just before landfall was especially fortunate for barrier island residents in Brunswick, New Hanover, Pender, and Onslow Counties. Storm surges that could have measured more than sixteen feet in a category-four hurricane instead averaged less than ten feet. The greatest tidal surge, on Oak Island, was measured by the Corps of Engineers at 10.4 feet. The rolling tide buckled fishing piers, undermined beachfront cottages, and filled streets with sand along this hard-hit stretch. Oak Island town officials later reported that 40 homes were destroyed and 290 more were heavily damaged by the tide. Not since Hurricane Hazel in 1954 had this part of old Long Beach been beaten up so badly by a storm. High waters six to eight feet above normal also filled Pamlico Sound and backed up the Neuse and Pamlico Rivers. Though Floyd was a dangerous storm that delivered destructive tides, winds, and tornadoes to more than a dozen coastal counties, local officials and emergency planners were still breathing a sigh of relief that first day, thinking that they had dodged a bullet with this category-two hurricane.

But as everyone would later learn, it was the excessive rainfall that would make Floyd memorable. These rains, which in some areas lasted for more than sixty hours, fell over a region already saturated by previous storms. Heavy downpours marked the western side of the storm track, and because the rains had begun well before Floyd arrived, the overall storm accumulations included some record-breaking totals. At Wilmington, 13.38 inches fell on September 15, setting a new one-day record for that location, and the storm total was a remarkable 19.06 inches. The National Weather Service reported that rainfall totals averaged between 14 and 16 inches across many inland counties. Areas that received the most rain were in Brunswick, Bladen, Duplin, Wayne, Wilson, Greene, Pitt, and Edgecombe Counties.

When Floyd's rains first began to fall, the soils of eastern North Carolina were like a sponge saturated by earlier showers, especially those of Tropical Storm Dennis. Creeks and ditches were already filled to their brims, and the added rain was more than they—and the rivers into which they fed—could stand; their waters rose rapidly, overflowing banks and spreading into streets and neighborhoods. The river flooding was a serious danger not only in North Carolina, but throughout the mid-Atlantic region over which Floyd passed. New rainfall records were set in Pennsylvania, New York, and Connecticut. Heavy rains in Virginia, Pennsylvania, and New Jersey created dangerous flash floods. Six new river high-water marks were set in New Jersey, where flooding on the Raritan River submerged the entire town of Bound Brook under fifteen feet of water. Officials there later described it as the "single largest disaster to ever affect the state of New Jersey."

But nowhere did Floyd have a more disastrous impact than in eastern North Carolina, though the magnitude of the catastrophe was not understood at first. Especially dangerous were the flash floods that swept through the Tar, Neuse, and Northeast Cape Fear basins. Many early flood victims, in areas where the water rose quickly and silently, were taken by surprise; some were asleep in their beds and were awakened by the feel of water lapping at their backs. Others did not see the worst of it until days after the storm had passed, when rivers that had been steadily climbing finally crested.

With soils already saturated and rivers above flood stage, the excess waters had nowhere to drain and backed up into homes, farms, and businesses and over highways. Road bridges buckled under the rush of water, and low-lying sections of highways crumbled and were swept away. Dams burst, hog lagoons spilled over their levees, and scores of water and sewer treatment plants were submerged. Hog, chicken, and turkey operations were especially hard hit, as the floods drowned thousands of animals whose carcasses would drift for days. Entire neighborhoods were covered by raging torrents that trapped families in the upper floors of their homes. Many eventually retreated to their attics and roofs to await rescue by boat or helicopter. Motorists were washed off roadways; the fortunate ones were rescued from the tops of their cars, while others succumbed to swiftly moving currents. Along the storm's path and across at least a dozen Tar Heel counties, a flood of epic proportions held the entire population in its grip.

The day after Floyd's passage through North Carolina, as the sun emerged, the breadth and magnitude of the disaster started to become apparent. Aerial views showed farmlands and forests in numerous down-east counties that had been transformed into lakes. Meandering creeks and rivers that normally measured only thirty to fifty feet across had spread beyond their banks to reach widths of more than a mile. As assessments of the affected areas accumulated, it became clear that Floyd was a disaster unlike any ever experienced in eastern North Carolina. No one in places like Rocky Mount, Tarboro, Greenville, Goldsboro, Snow Hill, and Trenton could recall flooding at this level within living memory. The water had reached unimaginable levels and was still rising. The media was quick to report the National Weather Service's observation that Floyd had left a five-hundred-year flood in its wake.

Reporting stations along the Neuse, Tar, and Northeast Cape Fear Rivers confirmed all-time record flood levels in the days following the storm. The Tar River crested in Rocky Mount at 32.35 feet, more than 17 feet above flood stage. In Greenville, it reached 29.72 feet on September 21 — more than 16 feet above flood stage. The Northeast Cape Fear River also set a new record at Chinquapin, where the river crested at 23.51 feet on September 18.

At Kinston the Neuse crested at 27.71 feet on September 23 — more than 13 feet above flood stage and more than 3 feet above the peak levels reached after Hurricane Fran. Kinston and much of the Neuse basin suffered severe flooding for weeks. The river was still above flood stage when Hurricane Irene brought more rains a full month after Floyd's passage. In all, at least nine U.S. Geological Survey monitoring stations in North Carolina registered new river flood records, as did one in Virginia, six in New Jersey, one in Delaware, and two in

Pennsylvania. Of the more than two hundred stream gauges monitored in North Carolina, twenty were destroyed by the massive movement of water.

During the first hours of the flood, rescue personnel sped into action to pull people out of submerged homes and sinking vehicles. Volunteer firefighters, sheriffs' deputies, local police, and ordinary citizens in dozens of communities responded to the threat of flooded neighborhoods with fishing boats, Jetskis, and backhoes. Coast Guard and Marine helicopters hoisted families off of rooftops and out of trees. Some communities had more advance warning and were able to evacuate before waters reached dangerous levels. But the severity of the flood caught many off guard, including emergency managers and town officials who had not expected to have to implement swift-water rescue operations in the streets of their own towns. By midafternoon on September 17, nearly 1,500 stranded residents had been plucked from their rooftops by rescue teams.

Though thousands miraculously escaped the flood, the greatest tragedy of Hurricane Floyd in North Carolina was the heartbreaking loss of 52 lives. Over half of those fatalities were people who were attempting to drive on flooded streets and highways and who died when their cars were swept into deep ditches. Fifty-two is the number of deaths reported by the state medical examiner,

Wilson County Rescue Squad member James Watkins used his Jet-ski to save a paramedic and two National Guardsmen from floodwaters on Airport Boulevard in Wilson. Their 2½-ton military truck was swept into a creek by surging water crossing the road. (Photo by Keith Barnes; courtesy of the *Wilson Daily Times*)

though the National Hurricane Center's official count was 56 deaths in the United States as a direct result of the hurricane, including thirty-five in North Carolina and more than a dozen in Virginia, Pennsylvania, New Jersey, Delaware, New York, Connecticut, and Vermont. Regardless of which figure is used, Hurricane Floyd's toll was still the largest of any U.S. hurricane since Agnes swept from Florida to the Northeast in 1972, killing 122.

The economic impact of the disaster was also staggering. Just three years after Hurricane Fran delivered a multibillion-dollar blow to the state, North Carolina faced an even greater financial burden imposed by the floods of Floyd. Damage estimates vary depending on whom you ask, but in general Floyd is considered to have cost the state at least $6 billion.

Even before Hurricanes Dennis and Floyd sent the region's rivers flowing beyond their banks, residents of North Carolina's largely rural eastern counties were already grappling with a multitude of problems. Economic woes had befallen farmers whose crops had long been the lifeblood of this region of the state. Tobacco prices had recently been cut by half, and prices for cotton, soybeans, corn, and other crops had fallen off dramatically. Other sectors of the economy were also suffering as jobs at small manufacturing plants and textile mills disappeared rapidly. Though cities in the central and western parts of

Mary and Budd Gray were rescued from their home in Kinston by Tim Lawson and Brad Byrd of the Lee County Rescue Team. The Grays waited until floodwaters neared their door before finally deciding to leave their home. (Photo by Francisco Kjolseth; courtesy of the *Charlotte Observer*)

the state were making great gains, many North Carolina counties east of I-95 had been hit with what economists called a "triple-whammy": loss of jobs, falling crop prices, and an eroded tax base. Even before the flood, economic and political leaders were talking about the ever-widening economic gap between rural eastern North Carolina and the rest of the state.

While the rural economy was suffering, the social fabric of the region was also feeling the strain. New challenges confronted small communities in which the population was declining and government support was limited. A fast-growing Hispanic population was largely underserved, and other longstanding issues of race continued to thwart progress in the troubled economies of small communities in the east. Then came the floods, and these same communities suddenly faced dramatic new hardships that dwarfed their earlier woes. Many who lost everything they had during Floyd had been economically disadvantaged even before the flood. To make matters worse, many of the poorest residents were the ones who lived in floodplains. It was said that the disaster took the most from those who had the least.

With more than 63,000 homes flooded and a quarter of a million people displaced, one of the greatest challenges facing emergency managers was how and where to house those who had lost their homes. Small cities of travel trailers sprang up around the hardest-hit areas to accommodate homeless families. Very few of these had flood insurance, and most had no choice but to wade through the task of filing for federal assistance. Some accepted government-

Rainfall Accumulations from Selected North Carolina Stations:
Accumulation Periods Ending at 8:00 A.M., September 18, 1999

Reporting Station	County	4-Day Total (in.)	21-Day Total (in.)
Goldsboro	Wayne	9.00	17.96
Greenville	Pitt	12.86	22.24
Kelly	Bladen	19.01	22.78
Longwood	Brunswick	16.52	19.73
Lumberton	Robeson	9.82	11.27
Roanoke Rapids	Halifax	12.10	17.87
Rocky Mount	Nash	15.65	23.99
Tarboro	Edgecombe	12.99	17.81
Wilmington	New Hanover	19.05	25.72
Wilson	Wilson	10.73	19.59

Source: National Climatic Data Center.

sponsored buyouts aimed at reducing the likelihood of so many people's ever being flooded out again. Meanwhile, scores of church groups and volunteers poured into eastern North Carolina to begin the long and grueling task of tearing out and rebuilding mud-encrusted homes. The cleanup and recovery was a massive, complex, and painful process that would last for years. But through it all, the true spirit of North Carolina's people shone brightly.

Floyd's impact on the state, as illustrated in the following statistical summary, establishes it without question as North Carolina's single greatest disaster:

- 66 counties declared disaster areas
- Total damages estimated between $5.5 and $6 billion
- 52 deaths reported by the state medical examiner
- 63,000 houses flooded
- 7,300 houses destroyed
- 86,954 people registered with FEMA for aid in the first five months after the storm
- More than 12,600 low-interest loans approved by the U.S. Small Business Administration
- 12,830 claims, totaling $141 million, paid by FEMA in national flood insurance, even though fewer than 13 percent of homes in the affected areas were covered
- Over $19 million raised from private sources for the Hurricane Floyd Relief Fund

Hurricane Floyd: Record Floods at NWS Forecast Points

Date	Location	Flood Stage (ft.)	Old Record	New Record
9/17/99	Neuse River near Clayton, N.C.	9	20.12	20.67
	Tar River at Louisburg, N.C.	20	25.34	26.05
	Tar River near Rocky Mount, N.C.	15	23.67	32.35
	Nottoway River near Sebrell, Va.	16	24.43	27.01
	Christina at Coochs Bridge, Del.	9	13.12	13.92
	Millstone River at Blackwells Mills, N.J.	9	18.68	20.97
	North Raritan River at Raritan, N.J.	10	15.51	18.78
	Rahway River at Springfield, N.J.	5.5	9.76	10.67
	Raritan River at Bound Brook, N.J.	28	37.47	42.13
	Raritan River at Manville, N.J.	14	23.80	27.50
	Saddle River at Lodi, N.J.	5	12.36	13.94
	E. Brandywine near Downingtown, Pa.	7	13.40	14.74
	Brandywine Creek at Chadds Ford, Pa.	9	16.56	17.15
9/18/99	Cape Fear River at Chinquapin, N.C.	13	20.16	23.51
	Fishing Creek near Enfield, N.C.	16	17.72	21.65
9/20/99	Neuse River near Goldsboro, N.C.	14	26.21	28.85
	Tar River at Tarboro, N.C.	19	31.77	41.51
9/21/99	Tar River at Greenville, N.C.	13	22.07	29.72
9/23/99	Neuse River at Kinston, N.C.	14	23.26	27.71

Source: National Weather Service/U.S. Geological Survey.

North Carolina Hurricanes, 1990–1999

Date	Name	Landfall Category	Maximum Wind	Pressure in N.C. (millibars)	N.C. Deaths	N.C. Damage (unadjusted)
August 1993	Emily	3	111 (g)	982	0	$13 million
July 1996	Bertha	2	108 (g)	973	2	$1.2 billion
September 1996	Fran	3	115	954	24	$5.2 billion
August 1998	Bonnie	2/3	115 (g)	964	1	$480 million
August–September 1999	Dennis	TS	110 (g)	984	0	$100 million
September 1999	Floyd	2	105	981	52	$6 billion

Note: TS = tropical storm; (g) = gust

- More than 30,000 hogs, 2.4 million chickens, and 700,000 turkeys counted among the agricultural losses
- 235 Red Cross shelters, housing a population of almost 50,000, open at the peak of the crisis; more than 1.3 million hot meals served
- 1,400 roads and highways closed because of high water
- Between 50,000 and 75,000 cars damaged by floodwaters
- 40 dams failed; another 61 damaged
- At least 50 hog lagoons and 24 municipal sewage plants submerged
- More than 1.5 million customers without electricity for some period of time
- More than 2,000 people rescued from flooded areas

Chronology of Hurricane Floyd and the Flood of 1999

Tuesday, August 24, 1999:
Tropical Storm Dennis forms some 225 miles southeast of the Bahamas.

Monday, August 30:
Hurricane Dennis, packing winds of 105 mph, moves to within 70 miles of the North Carolina coast. Steady rains begin to fall across the coastal counties.

Wednesday, September 1:
Hurricane Dennis is downgraded to a tropical storm as it drifts erratically off the coast of Cape Hatteras. Large waves and severe erosion batter the Outer Banks, ultimately overwashing NC 12 and isolating hundreds of residents on Hatteras Island.

Saturday, September 4:
Tropical Storm Dennis finally turns and comes ashore near Cape Lookout. It tracks inland and dissipates over the central region of the state, spreading heavy rainfall across a broad area. Ocracoke receives more than 19 inches of rain for the week, while reports from other stations range from 6 to 10 inches.

Tuesday, September 7:
Tropical depression that will become Floyd is first detected in the eastern Atlantic, some 1,000 miles from the Lesser Antilles.

Monday, September 13:
Hurricane Floyd reaches its meteorological peak about 300 miles east of the

central Bahamas, with a barometric low of 27.20 inches and maximum sustained winds of 155 mph. A hurricane watch is issued for Florida's southeastern counties and is later extended northward and upgraded to hurricane warning. Massive coastal evacuations begin in Florida and eventually extend up the East Coast through Virginia—the largest evacuation event in U.S. history.

Wednesday, September 15:
Hurricane Floyd moves toward North Carolina as a category-two storm, unleashing heavy rains along much of the U.S. East Coast. Wilmington, North Carolina, sets a new twenty-four-hour rainfall record of 15.06 inches.

Thursday, September 16:
Floyd makes landfall near Cape Fear at 3:00 A.M. and delivers a ten-foot storm surge to Oak Island. The storm center tracks across eastern North Carolina and southeastern Virginia. Flash floods caused by heavy downpours begin affecting several river basins, forcing thousands of residents to flee their homes. Heroic rescues begin in the predawn hours and continue throughout the day. Most of the fifty-two fatalities reported in North Carolina occur on this day.

Friday, September 17:
Rescue operations continue for a second straight day in several eastern counties. By midafternoon, nearly 1,500 stranded people have been picked up by helicopter. The Tar River in Rocky Mount crests at 32.35 feet, an all-time record high.

Saturday, September 18:
Search-and-rescue teams continue to fan out across submerged communities in search of the missing. Emergency shelters fill to capacity, and relief stations offering food and clothing are at peak demand.

Monday, September 20:
President Bill Clinton tours the flood-ravaged areas of North Carolina and stops to meet with residents in Tarboro. The Tar River crests in Tarboro at the same time, reaching a new record level of 41.51 feet.

Tuesday, September 21:
The remnants of Tropical Storm Harvey move across portions of North Carolina, bringing an additional three inches of rain to some flooded areas. The Tar River crests in Greenville at 29.72 feet, establishing a new record for that location.

Thursday, September 23:
The Neuse River crests at 27.71 feet in Kinston, establishing a new record for that location.

Friday, September 24:
Special disaster mortuary teams round up floating coffins dislodged from grave sites near Princeville.

Sunday, September 26:
Flood waters begin to recede in Princeville.

Tuesday, September 28:
Over a two-day period, portions of eastern North Carolina receive up to eight inches of additional rain from a passing low-pressure system.

Wednesday, September 29:
Classes resume at East Carolina University. The Reverend Jesse Jackson visits Princeville and tells residents, "Sometimes God takes us low just to lift us up."

Thursday, September 30:
Two weeks after Hurricane Floyd made landfall, more than 8,000 North Carolinians remain without electricity.

Sunday, October 3:
A six-hour telethon sponsored by the North Carolina Association of Broadcasters raises $2.2 million for hurricane relief. Ultimately Governor Jim Hunt's Floyd Disaster Fund raises over $19 million.

Tuesday, October 5:
Governor Hunt travels to Washington, D.C., to convince Congress to provide $5.5 billion in aid for North Carolina. Congress will end up providing less than half of the amount initially requested by Hunt.

Saturday, October 9:
Eight-year-old Brandon Davis becomes the flood's forty-ninth fatality in North Carolina. He is killed when his father attempts to drive on a flooded road where a bridge had washed away.

Monday, October 18:
Hurricane Irene skirts the North Carolina coast and delivers an additional four to six inches of rain over many of the already flooded eastern counties.

Monday, November 8:
Benjamin Harrison becomes the last of the fifty-two fatalities recorded in North Carolina when his body is found in a Nash County quarry.

Friday, November 19:
Sixteen homes in Farmville are purchased as part of FEMA's buyout program, the first of thousands of such purchases of flood-prone properties.

Monday, November 22:
The Princeville town council votes three to two in favor of rebuilding the town's dike. FEMA had offered to buy out the entire town, but this vote led the way toward reconstruction of the dike in an effort to preserve the community intact.

Tuesday, November 23:
Governor Hunt establishes the Hurricane Floyd Redevelopment Center and names Billy Ray Hall as director. Hunt also calls a special session of the General Assembly, which leads to the appropriation of $836 million in state-funded disaster assistance.

Tuesday, February 29, 2000:
FEMA reports that 86,954 people have registered for disaster assistance.

Friday, June 30:
Reconstruction of Princeville's dike is completed.

March 2001:
State officials announce that $821.6 million of the original $836-million state flood relief appropriation has been "spent, applied for, or otherwise obligated."

August 2002:
Thirty families are asked to leave their FEMA trailers near Tarboro, almost three years after Hurricane Floyd forced them from their homes. The government-funded trailers were initially intended to house flood victims for up to eighteen months, but the deadline for ending the program was extended several times.

Faces from the Flood

Richard Moore

As secretary of North Carolina's Department of Crime Control and Public Safety during Hurricane Floyd, Richard Moore was in charge of many of the key agencies that dealt with response and recovery. He traveled to the far corners of the flood, surveying the damage, consoling families that had lost their homes, and thanking volunteers and rescue workers. His leadership position gave him a unique view of the disaster and its lingering effects on our state.

When Floyd first appeared, we were already exhausted. We had just experienced one of the weirdest storms ever to come near North Carolina—Hurricane Dennis. It had toyed with us for weeks. It didn't actually do a tremendous amount of damage to our state, but it had worked the stuffing out of our small staff. Dennis wiped out Highway 12 on the Outer Banks and trapped about five thousand residents and tourists at Hatteras for about five days. We couldn't reach them or anyone on Ocracoke by any means. Not by phone, ferry, boat, ship, or road—it was a nightmare. The storm just sat off the coast and would not go away, whipping up the surf for days. Eventually it turned around, came back, and struck the coast as a tropical storm.

We had just stood down from our highest state of alert and started to let people go home to get some rest when Floyd appeared. I will never forget the fear I felt when I saw those early satellite images of this storm. The previous few years had taught me about how hurricanes look, and this thing was beautiful in a scary, macabre kind of way.

It was a perfectly formed storm, and it was massive. Originally predicted to hit Florida, it hovered between a category four and a category five—the most powerful kind. From the Keys through the Miami area, people began to evacuate Florida. As the Hurricane Center shifted the projected path northward along the Florida coast, a mass exodus of people moved up Interstate 95. Many of them eventually pitched camp in motels along the interstate in North Carolina. The projected path continued to inch northward, and for a while it looked like Floyd was going to take a track similar to that of Hurricane Hugo in 1989. It was predicted to come in around Charleston and quickly zip up somewhere between Charlotte and Greensboro. So we began to ready our people in that part of the state. I spent that Sunday afternoon doing one satellite feed after another warning central North Carolina to get ready for a potentially deadly knockout punch.

In the lead story on the national news, I described the storm as being big, fast, and mean, likening it to "Hurricane" Rubin Carter, the prizefighter. I was scared that we were about to witness a storm unlike any North Carolina had seen before. As it turned out, I was right, but for reasons different than I thought.

As Floyd drew closer, the projected track shifted again, further north and on a course closer to that of Fran. It was going to come barreling in some-where between Bald Head and Wrightsville Beach and slide up toward the Raleigh area. With Dennis weeks before and now Floyd, trying to stay ahead of these storms was unbelievably nerve-racking.

The winds dropped off dramatically in the twelve hours before impact. I can remember feeling this tremendous sense of relief around midnight, before landfall occurred. It was now somewhere between a category one and a two, which was something we felt we were ready for. Unless something really strange happened, we would have dodged yet another bullet. As that sense of relief came over our people, everybody let their guard down a little bit. We all tried to get a quick nap.

The next thing I remember was having a conversation with a climatologist from N.C. State who was monitoring rainfall in the river valleys, particularly the Tar-Pamlico and the Neuse. He was starting to see some really strange rain-fall numbers associated with this storm. We knew to expect a lot of rain dur-ing a hurricane, but some really abnormal things were going on. And of course this was after Hurricane Dennis had dumped quite a bit of rain in the previ-ous weeks. The ground was pretty saturated to begin with, and we really be-gan to be alarmed.

As the sun came up the morning after, we had accounts of some severe storm surge damage on Oak Island. But besides that, early reports were fairly positive. There was little structural or wind damage and no fatalities. So we did what we always do after storms—we got up in the air. Governor Hunt wanted to survey the damage to make sure that the state was putting all the re-sources that we had to bear to help our people. Equally important, the gover-nor needed to rapidly assess the situation to lobby Washington for critical fed-eral assistance. He always did this quickly and was very good at it.

As we got up in the air and left the Raleigh area, we really didn't see a lot. We worked our way down the Neuse and didn't see much in Goldsboro or Kinston. But we were getting reports that the rivers were swelling. Little did we know *how* they would swell. That was the toughest thing about Floyd that played out over the next two weeks—the fear created by this silent, deadly, creeping wall of water that just wouldn't quit. Very different from a tidal surge, where you brace for it and then it's gone. This was something that just kept coming and coming. No one could envision what was to follow.

I remember the helicopter pilot coming on the speaker telling the governor and me that he had just gotten a message from a private pilot who had just flown over Jones County. He said you just wouldn't believe it. We immediately flew down to Trenton, and what we saw was an eerie sight. It was a crystal-clear, sunny day, and the entire town of Trenton was gleaming in the sunlight. The strange thing about it was that the cars were in the driveways, the homes were all there, the roofs were intact, but the entire town was covered with what looked to be between two and four feet of water. It was almost like something out of a horror movie, where something comes through and kills an entire town. Even though it was midday, there was no sign of life. We didn't see any-one trying to drive, wading around, in a boat, or anything—it was complete and total stillness. We later found out that the town had safely evacuated that evening and morning. But Trenton gave us our first indication of what water was about to do to large parts of our state.

As we made our way back west along the Tar River, we started to see the sheer force and might of this unprecedented water event. After seeing extensive flood-ing around Tarboro and Princeville, we passed over a quarry on our way to Rocky Mount. The quarry had streams of water running into it from several different places, and they were all converging on one side. It created the most massive waterfall that will ever exist in eastern North Carolina. From the air it looked just like Niagara Falls. As we snapped photographs, I remember that you could actually hear the pounding water over the roar of the helicopter.

The next day we flew over the exact same spot and it was a small lake. The waterfall was gone. The quarry had filled up overnight with millions of cubic feet of water. For this small part of the state, the mighty force of the water was gone as quickly as it came.

By the end of September 17, the first day after, we had a good indication of what we were going to have to deal with. Based on our visual reconnaissance and the weather data we'd received, we knew we were going to see flood stages on the Northeast Cape Fear, the Tar River, and parts of the Neuse River that were beyond anyone's imagination. The highest water marks in people's mem-ories were about to be replaced by horrific new measures. We then knew that in the hours ahead we would have to do something we'd never imagined—large-scale swift-water rescue in eastern North Carolina. Flooding of biblical proportions was clearly on its way.

Obviously, our first priority is always to get people out of harm's way. The second is to maintain shelters to house and feed those that have been displaced. Through all our planning, in all our scenarios, we never dreamed that we would have to service these shelters exclusively by air. We never thought we'd have to haul porta-potties, supply hot food and cots, and move people around by air and air alone. In the days that followed, that's what we did.

Within forty-eight hours after landfall, eastern North Carolina was shut off from the rest of the world. We moved our National Guard forward command bases several times because of road flooding. There were large areas of Edgecombe, Pitt, and Duplin Counties and areas around Kinston and Goldsboro that could not be reached by vehicle. We had people trapped: people who had left their homes and couldn't get back, and people in shelters who were from out of state and could not leave.

So we began the greatest logistical challenge emergency management officials had ever encountered in North Carolina. We moved into a management phase of transporting food and supplies, locating missing people, providing adequate shelter, and rounding up porta-potties. It was a colossal effort. At the same time, we were asking people to help us help them. That meant just staying put.

Over the next few days, I became a constant presence in the media. Part of my job was informing the public of what was going well, what was not, and how they could help us. Almost overnight, everywhere I went I began receiving the gratitude of our people. During those days I went through the greatest peaks and valleys of my professional life. On one hand, to feel that gratitude and know that we were doing a great job, but also to see the complete destruction of our communities and the utter despair of our people. It was just a rollercoaster ride that I will never forget.

We went into the Chinquapin area of Duplin County a few days after the storm. I met a couple in their late sixties who were both terminally ill. I remember being there with them to face the reality that they would never again set foot in what had been their home for more than thirty years. It was really a low point. There was so much we were trying to do for people, but for some people, we would never be able to help them put their lives back together.

We learned the painful differences between water and wind damage. I think one of the reasons so many people will remember Floyd was that not only were there more than sixty thousand damaged homes, but people found out what flood damage does to treasured memories and keepsakes. When you have wind damage, you may have a tree on your house, maybe some water leaks in, and you may ruin some sheetrock or a piece of furniture. But when your home is flooded, you lose it all. You lose your grandmother's afghan, your wedding pictures, your baby photos, and your child's first-grade art projects. It's just all gone.

I spent a lot of time explaining to people what we could help with, and what we couldn't. When things were beyond our control and we could not help, that meant just standing there and sharing a good cry. Thanks to countless selfless and heroic acts, North Carolina did a remarkable job of rescuing its people from this silent killer. Lives were lost, but it could have been much, much worse. To see all our hard work pay off for our people may very well have been the pinnacle of my professional career.

Kurt Barnes has worked in water maintenance for the City of Rocky Mount for almost thirty years. But during that city's devastating flood, he was a true hero, swimming through strong currents near his home to ultimately save the lives of eighteen neighbors. He was later recognized with the 2000 Governor's Award for Heroism. He was interviewed in his Rocky Mount office in June 2002.

Kurt Barnes

That Wednesday, we all left work knowing that the storm was approaching. Instead of just hanging around here, everybody was just sent home, 'cause we were expecting a pretty bad storm anyway. So I went home and told my wife and kids that it would be safer if they would relocate, and I'd stay and watch the house.

So I was there at the house and the rain really came. Things started changing, ditches started filling up, and I started seeing more water than we normally did. At about three o'clock in the morning I remember seeing on TV that the storm was just about at the North Carolina–South Carolina line. I just felt something funny, so I got up and looked outside. There was water everywhere. It was two foot deep in the front yard. You could see it rise. I mean, you could see it coming up on the mailbox. It was just rising, like an inch every minute. You could just stand there and watch it rise. I knew we were in bad shape then.

So I walked to the end of the porch and looked across the street, and my neighbor about a half a block away was over there trying to contact me. His phones had gone out, and he was on his porch over there hollering. In that bad loud storm you couldn't hardly hear him. He was there with his wife and

Kurt Barnes stands in the front yard of his Rocky Mount home in June 2002. (Photo by Jay Barnes)

two teenagers. I spotted him over there, and we finally did make some kind of communication. I said, "I'm going to get us a boat!" He said, "You coming back, ain't ya?" And I said, "Yeah, I'm coming back!" When I turned to walk away, he yelled, "Hey, hey, don't forget me now!"

So while the water was about two foot deep in my front yard, I started moving stuff around in my house. You know, trying to get some of the stuff that I really had to. Get it up from down low and put it up high.

In just a few minutes I went back outside and checked, and the water was so high I was scared to leave. But I had to. I said, "Damn, I've got to go!" So I went and got a flashlight and got one of my little boy's life vests. I put that life vest on, and I put my raincoat over that and started trying to leave. Well, the water was so rough, so rapid coming down the street, I couldn't get out of there. It was now chest-deep in the yard. I tried leaving with that raincoat on, and that life vest, but there just ain't no way. That raincoat was like a parachute. So I stripped off the raincoat and tried leaving again with the life vest and flashlight. And I just couldn't do it. The current was just taking me. It was like trying to walk across a mountain stream, the velocity of water was just so rapid.

It was unreal how fast the water was rising. And I'll never forget it—I threw that flashlight back up on the porch, hung that lifejacket up in a tree, and went in a swimming mode. I swam across the street from my house. There was a real strong current coming down the street 'cause there was nothing in the way to break the flow. Once I got to the other side, I got hold of one of them pecan trees in the neighborhood and kinda just held on to it for a few minutes. And from then on, it was from tree, to bush, to telephone pole, to signpost. I grabbed anything I could get from one point to another.

It was terrible rain. There was probably thirty-, forty-mile-an-hour winds easy. Gusts were probably more than that. And that water was deep. Even if you could touch bottom, the water was still over your head. You could go down and bounce, but when you bounced up you had gone ten or twelve feet downstream. So I swam from tree to tree, and finally I got to a house that was

Ben Cullipher carries his son, Derek, while his wife, Jen, hauls a bundle of belongings as the family wades to safety in the flooded Duke Circle area of Rocky Mount. (Photo by David Weaver; courtesy of the *Rocky Mount Telegram*)

on the corner in the direction I was headed. I was tired, but I could see my Jeep way up at the top of the hill. I had parked on some high ground.

But when I got behind that first house, I got out of that wind a little bit. I swam right up on top of that guy's air conditioner. I could feel it under me. So I stayed there a couple or three minutes and really got my breath. And I remember thinking about my buddy. I thought, man, he's in a mess, 'cause this thing is out of hand. I really didn't know what the circumstances were for other people around there, other than I knew that water was going to be in a lot of people's houses.

So I sat there for a few minutes, and I looked over there at that Jeep, and I said, "Lord, if you'll just let me get over to that Jeep then I know I can help that boy." So I broke around the corner and pulled myself along the sides of the house. The water was coming down those streets unrestricted, and I mean it was terrible. The fastest stuff you've ever seen in your life. When I got back down on the side of the house again, I was hanging on to some telephone wires. I looked at that wire, and I saw that it went right on over to a telephone pole across that street. If I could pull this wire off this house right here, I could follow it across that street. I put my foot on the side of the house, and when I jerked that wire, next thing I know I'm on the other side of that street. Just like somebody on skis, it pulled me right around.

When I let go of the wire, I put my face in that water and swam as hard as I could. I just did make it to that pole. Things were floating by me—trash cans, big doghouses—the wind was howling, wires were popping all around me, I mean it was unreal. I kind of zigged and zagged up the street, from house to telephone pole. I mean I was swimming about as hard as a guy can swim. This wasn't no exercise swim, I was swimming for my life.

I finally got down close to where my vehicle was parked. There was one final current down a big ditch there, and it washed me up into some trees and bushes. I worked my way back out and finally got to my truck. I was so tired when I got to that Jeep, I could not leave. But I started thinking about my neighbor, and I said "I've got to go down there and get that guy."

I got in that Jeep and I took off. I had to go about five or six blocks to my father-in-law's house. I hooked up to my boat, and came burnin' it back down. I backed up until I was about two feet from that water. I unhooked my boat, pushed off, and the wind just floated me right on down. Just as I got into some trees, that boat fired up and I took off. I went wide open right straight to that guy's house. I was scared to death that they weren't even going to be there. But they were standing on the porch. They heard that boat and were looking for me. Each one of them had a black trash bag, with what little stuff they could put in it. The father of the family helped the kids get in. His wife was standing on the porch, and the water was shoulder-high to her. The water ended up getting into the chandeliers in that house.

But while we were sitting there loading up, one of the pecan trees right across the street blew over and hit the trees and wires. Well, the lights went out. I was scared, because I didn't know which way they had fallen, or how to get out around them. I was going to have to go under all them power wires and telephone poles to get out. So we took it easy and got out of there, and I shot that guy back up to my Jeep. But when we got them to high ground back where my Jeep was, I noticed my Jeep was in the water. That's how quick it was coming up.

I knew about this guy whose house we had passed, so I went back for him. When I pulled my boat up to get him, he came right out to the boat through his window. As we were getting him in the boat, I heard somebody hollering. Another family was trying to get our attention. So I carried him back to the bank and went tearing off back down there.

So there was this young couple with a baby, and this guy was partially paralyzed. But when I pulled up to his porch, there was another guy that worked for me. It was one of the scariest parts of the whole storm because his porch is four-and-a-half or five foot off the ground, and I drove that boat right up there on it. I'm about to freeze about this time, cold as I can be, scared to death, sitting in my boat up there on that porch, but I was more worried about them. It was the peak of the storm by then; I mean it was peaking out. It was as bad as it got.

What scared me so much was the mother with her three-month-old newborn baby. She walked around to get in the boat, and I said, "Let me have that baby." She handed the baby to me. We had no lifejacket for that baby, but I had a blanket. So just as she walked around, I'm trying to hold that baby, hold that boat, and get her in the boat, she walked right off that porch. The water was so deep, she didn't know where the porch ended. She just walked right off it. Well, when she did, she went out of sight. So I'm holding the boat, holding that baby, and I reached down in that water as far as I could with my other hand, and I felt her hair. She had a head full of hair. So I got a-hold of her hair and pulled her back up, and "Sssppppptttttttt!!!" She blew that water out. She was so glad somebody got that hair that she didn't know what to do. So I pulled her back up on the porch, and she was screaming. I yelled, "Get in the boat!" So I got her in the boat, and all the rest of them, and I said, "Y'all hold this baby and sit down in the bottom of this boat, and don't move." You couldn't hardly hear what I was saying, I mean the wind was howling, and wires were still popping. Then I carried them all back to the Jeep.

So somebody said there's another couple down there, and I can see the light. So I took off and rode right down the street with the boat and turned the corner. When I got there, he was standing on one of those wrought-iron corner railings that hold up the porch. His van had washed across the street and his car had, too. He told me later on that he had climbed all he could climb, and that he couldn't have held on another three or four minutes. He said he had held that flashlight as long as he could, but he just couldn't hold the light any longer so he dropped it and just held on. He was just glad we saw that light.

After I got him back, I felt like I had probably gotten most of the people out of there. But there was this guy with a pontoon boat that came in, and he was bumping into every tree and telephone pole. I told him he'd better get out of there before he got electrocuted. He said the Colberts are in their house up in the attic, and they can't get out. I knew the family, and I said I'd go in to get them, because he couldn't get between the trees, the bushes, and the poles. So I pulled my little boat in their yard with the Daughtridge boy. We couldn't get them to the door, so we jumped out of the boat and went in the back door. They had cut a hole in the kitchen ceiling, climbed up on the bar in the kitchen, and crawled into the attic. And then they wouldn't come out 'cause they were so scared. They were the only people in that damn neighborhood that had a swimming pool, but they couldn't swim well enough to get out, and they were scared.

So we finally coaxed them into coming out. We got them out of that hole in the attic, swam them through the kitchen, and then got them out the door outside. The water in that kitchen was at least six feet deep. I mean we didn't touch bottom when we swam them out. The water was probably only eighteen inches from the top of the door, and we had to duck down under that door to get them out. They put lifejackets on and we got them in the boat. And I'll never forget that the water was so high that the boat was rubbing up against the awning over the back porch.

But when we got the guy, his wife, and little kid in the boat, something stirred up a wasp nest that was under that awning. Although you couldn't see them, one of those wasps climbed on that little girl and stung her. She started screaming and hollering, and I thought a damn snake had bit her. But she just went screaming and hollering, and it just made things worse. She was probably about twelve. You couldn't hardly communicate 'cause the wind was blowing so hard and the rain was so loud. You couldn't tell what nobody was saying. When I saw her hand, I could tell she had been stung by a wasp.

Well, behind the house there was a dog in one of those dog pens, and it must have had about a nine-foot fence on it. There was probably about two foot of that fence out of the water—just enough that the dog couldn't get out. And he was in there treading water around and around. I said, "Whose dog is that over there? We've got to get that dog." And that little girl was screaming bloody murder from that wasp sting, but when I said something about that dog, she quit crying and didn't say another word about that sting. She said, "That's our dog!" So we took off over there to get the dog, and he was panicking. When we picked that dog up to put him in the boat he didn't bite us, but when we set him down in that boat, buddy he ate us up. He bit the guy with me and he bit me. Can you imagine? He was like a collie dog. He was wet and heavy, so it took both of us. And he bit that guy until he let go, and then turned around and bit me. Of course they grabbed him and calmed him down. I said, "Let's get out of here."

But the lady of the house said, "We've got two cats in that building." So I said, "Okay, let's get the cats." We pulled back up to this storage building and had to swim underwater through the doorway and come up on the other side. You could see those cats, walking around up in the rafters. I called them two cats, and both of them came right to me. I let go of the rafters, grabbed them two cats, and went right under the water. When I came back up on the other side, I was blowing water and them cats was, too. I threw the cats right in the boat, and that lady grabbed them. We got that family, the dog, and the two cats out of there.

When we finally got back to the Jeep, there was a big oak tree right there that was swaying, popping, and cracking in the wind. I told that boy, "Look, pull my Jeep up there out of the way. That tree's getting ready to fall." I was gonna head back out to do more searching. But just as I left the bank, I heard something went "Crrrrroousssshhh." That guy pulled my Jeep up right before that tree went down and would have crushed it. But he moved it just in the nick of time. Then I couldn't see nobody—it filled the whole end of the street. When we pulled off, you looked back and couldn't see nothing but that tree.

So we started doing a house-by-house search. One other couple that had been down there, they were the last two we rescued. They had a pull-down stairway and had climbed up in the attic. When we were beating on the houses, he came down. There was about five feet of water in that house.

They thought there were seventeen people, but actually it was eighteen people that we saved. Once we were convinced that everybody was out, I tried to go back to my house. When I got there, I pulled up to my porch and got out, opened the front door, and there was a current that just jerked it right open. I went in there to my two daughters' rooms, and everything in there had water in it, except the top dresser drawers on both their dressers. So I got a bag real quick, and I put that stuff in it, and went back and threw it in the boat. When I finally got back to check on my wife and kids, I told my wife, "Honey, we have lost everything." We stood there in the hall and pouted.

We had a unique neighborhood. All the people down there were real close. We knew everybody on a first-name basis, and they all had lived down there for a long time. We were real proud of the neighborhood we had, and the flood just devastated it. And it never recovered. In fact, everybody down there except three homeowners are out. They've demolished the homes.

Man, this city was a mess. In some areas, when that water came in it was so forceful that it washed cars all the way over from one side of the street to the other and they ended up cars on top of cars. I know that by Premier Ford and Advance Auto it was just like a dam broke when that water come through there. It washed the whole backside of that building out. My nearest neighbor had water twenty-eight inches deep in his attic. And several of the houses moved, came off foundations, and that kind of stuff. The water was about six inches below the rim on the basketball goal in my yard.

I went out to the dam on my birthday, about a month before Floyd. Some guys I work with asked me to come along with them. They rented a boat, and we got some ladders, ropes, and some harnesses, and we started checking the condition of the dam. I knew that dam wasn't in the shape that it should have been. And they did, too, 'cause every time they lowered them gates, that dam would go down. It wouldn't lower a foot or two foot or whatever, when they started it would just go completely down. It was very obvious there was a hydraulic leak in there somewhere. Well, when the storm came, I always had a lot of questions about the performance of that dam when they lowered it. I just felt like they lowered it at the worst time in the world for me and my area. I think if you were going to lower it, you should have lowered it when that storm was two or three days away. But for them to lower it seven o'clock on the night of the storm, I just don't know if I would have done that. Since that time, the city has spent I'm sure well over a million dollars to fix that dam. They also went in there with the Corps of Engineers, and they cleaned out all of them creeks and all that was backed up. I think we can handle a flood of that magnitude a lot better now. At least I hope so.

People were just tickled to death about getting out, patting me on the back, writing me letters and stuff. But it just didn't sink in until later on. For about a week and a half there, we were just steady working. Everybody in this whole city, the city workers, the firefighters, I mean everybody was just totally exhausted. People were sleeping on couches down here, and in chairs. As long as our families were safe, we were a workforce that was like an army.

My mom told me, "Boy, you don't know what all you did in saving them people. If you hadn't went out there when you did, them people wouldn't have made it." The neighbors are the ones who pursued the award that I got. They all got together and sent a letter to the governor, I think. It was something that I really didn't expect. I mean I'm proud of it, but I think I did what anybody else would have done. It was scary, though. It was luck that we got them out. I was just at the right place at the right time, and luckily things just worked out.

Diane LeFiles is director of community schools and public information for the Edgecombe County schools. Once the flooding began, she was asked to handle public information and media relations for Edgecombe County. She worked through countless details of the disaster and gained a broad perspective of its impact on her community. She was interviewed in her Tarboro office in June 2002.

Diane LeFiles

I was actually out of town when the hurricane hit and could not get home right away. The airport in Raleigh was closed, and then when the airport reopened, the roads were closed. So I was in a little bit of a panic to get home. I didn't know what I would be facing when I got here. We were actually in Las Vegas and were watching Tarboro on CNN, so I knew we were in big trouble.

It was Sunday afternoon before I pulled into town. My house was okay; we had a little roof damage. I went immediately to the emergency operations center, which is located in the county jail. I could not go directly there, because there were holes in the road, the roadways were covered with water, and I had to wind my way around to get there. When I walked in I found our county

manager, Joe Durham, and he asked if I would handle public information and media relations, because he knows that's what I do. So within thirty minutes, that's what I was doing.

The emergency operations center was working on a twenty-four-hour-a-day, seven-day-a-week schedule, and I don't remember if I went home that night or not. We would start at six o'clock in the morning, and generally things were quiet after about two A.M. That first few days, that first week, it was pretty intense around the clock. I didn't really sleep at the EOC, we just kept going.

Helicopters were landing on the site next door to the jail. The Air Force had set up a radar station to monitor all the helicopters, and they landed on the lawn. They made rescues at night, and they used flashing police car lights and portable generators to light the landing field.

We were in the jail, so early on the prisoners were transferred out and the jail became a bunkhouse. Volunteers and law enforcement agencies from across the state all bunked in the jail. We had the highway patrol and a law enforcement contingency in one room, we had National Guard people, and Social Services had a section. There were lots of agencies—it was like an alphabet soup. We had SERT and SORT and ARC, and I could tell you what they all mean,

but they were all different responders. In addition to groups like the Salvation Army, we had church agencies that came along a little bit later. It was an absolute beehive.

In the center of the room there were long tables with banks of telephones. Each table had probably about four telephones, legal pads, and pencils, and lots of paper. The phones just rang constantly. The telephone company came in early on and set up additional phone lines with numbers that rolled over, so that people that needed help, or people that wanted to offer help, could get through. And this operation center served as a hub for all of the communications that were coming in to the community. At this time, telephone lines to the general population were down, there was no water, and there was no electricity.

There was one cable TV station that was operating when the electricity finally did come back on, and that was a little local station out of Rocky Mount, WHIG. They were a little local station that just broadcasts on our cable, but they were the only ones operating, everyone else was down. The cable company was flooded, and the newspaper office was actually flooded. Cell phones were going crazy. The cells were up, but they were jammed, and that was a big issue. We used cell phones as much as we could, but they had limitations as we

After being forced from her home, Corenthia Garett styles Dajour Brown's hair on the floor of E. B. Aycock Middle School in Greenville. The school served as a Red Cross emergency shelter and housed more than 250 people following Hurricane Floyd. (Photo by Christopher Record; courtesy of the *Charlotte Observer*)

The Tar River spread beyond its banks in Edgecombe and Pitt Counties and reached record levels following the rains from Hurricane Floyd. (Edgecombe County Land Records/GIS; Pitt County Planning Department)

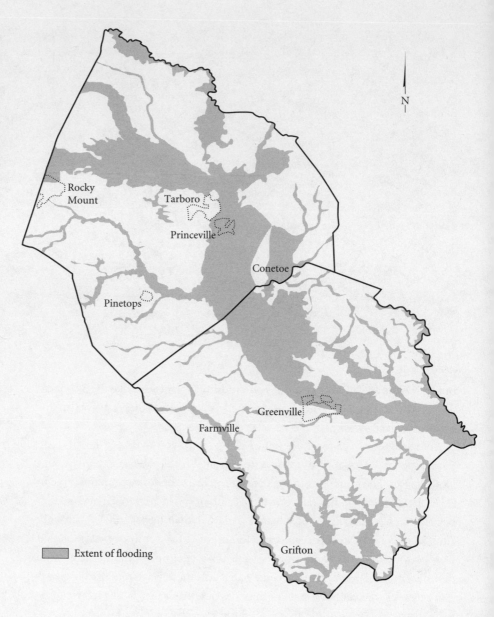

Rocky Mount

Tarboro

Princeville

Conetoe

Pinetops

Greenville

Farmville

Grifton

N

Extent of flooding

found out. People were calling from all over the country, checking on relatives, and telephones were really an issue. But thank goodness for cell phones, because that was a way to get beyond that gap.

The volunteers started showing up immediately. The National Guard and Coast Guard were absolutely wonderful. I would give a commercial for them anytime. For anyone who ever doubts the benefits of living in this country, I just say that you need one disaster experience to appreciate what's here for us.

All the real emergency calls went to 911. The calls we got were honestly a little less urgent. They'd say there were caskets floating, or what do I do about this, or when is the water going to come back on. Or I can't find my grandmother. Or we have this person at a shelter who is diabetic and we need to get medication over there quickly. The operations center was open for three and a half weeks.

Coupled with this, we had school issues. We have fourteen school buildings in the county, and two of those school buildings were completely underwater. The school in Princeville had eighty-eight inches of water inside. It was one cinderblock from the ceiling tiles. Muddy river water was in that building for well over two weeks, so it was completely destroyed. The other one was Patilla Elementary School over in East Tarboro. It didn't have quite as much water in it, about four-and-a-half feet. But anytime you have more than three feet of water in your building, then all your wiring, all your computers, everything is destroyed. All the important stuff is down below the light switches.

Tarboro High School served as the primary shelter site. Friday night, when the water started to rise, everyone knew that the high school was the place to go. So they all went. We had about three thousand people show up in the middle of the night with no electricity and no water. But that's where they went. School officials were there, local emergency people were there, the Red Cross, and others, and it was absolutely wall to wall in that school building. We had people with medical issues, and the library became a hospital room where they took care of people. The gymnasium was just sleeping bags, blankets, pillows, and people everywhere. There had not been time to set up a proper shelter. It all happened at once. And it was literally in the middle of the night.

We had a large group of Hispanic people who came, and we found that some were frightened by attempts to rescue them. They were frightened. They thought that law enforcement was coming to get them, to take them home for immigration. So their perspective on being rescued was a little different. And then they were brought into these shelters into a sea of people, and the language barrier was another issue. Their presence created another dimension for the shelter staff.

People were trying to bring pets into the shelter. I remember seeing this one woman who had a little Chihuahua inside her jacket, and she would cover that little dog up if anyone with a nametag went by. She was afraid that someone was going to make her take that dog out of the shelter. If it had been a German shepherd, they probably would have.

There were all emotions in the shelter. Children were frightened, but amazingly, people were very patient. They were not irritable, they were just grateful. There was just a lot of uncertainty, and a lot of tension. But it was not an angry tension, just a relief to be safe. And a lot of people expressed gratitude and pitched in. They wanted to be busy. So they would sweep, or they would help serve food, or they would look after the children. I remember seeing older people gather groups of children up to tell stories. Children's books came from somewhere, so they would gather those up and sit with the children, with paper and pencils, and tic-tac-toe, and little games to entertain the children would spontaneously take place. Later on, things became more organized, and there was actually a routine, but early on people just took care of each other. That was really heartwarming to see.

When the cots started arriving, it was amazing to see the families group themselves according to their addresses. If they lived up on Oak Street, for example, in house number one, number two, number three, they arranged themselves just like they lived geographically. So this neighbor was here and that neighbor was there. It was self-sorting, I guess you'd say. People actually established their own little space, where they had all of their family members and all of their stuff. Whatever they had accumulated from the donations were put around and under their cots, and they began to reestablish their possessions.

The churches were wonderful. Sunset Church of God opened their doors and housed a lot of the National Guard. They took in a lot of people, and they sent volunteers out into the different shelters. Really all of the churches contributed. Now there were some that were flooded. St. Luke over in Princeville was flooded, and the St. Luke here in town was also flooded. And Calgary Episcopal Church was flooded. The two St. Lukes churches are African American churches, and the Calgary Episcopal is predominantly white. Those churches all kind of banded together, and eventually had shared services. It was great to see them come together like they did.

The Salvation Army was primarily in charge of food. They brought in these mobile kitchens that were just amazing. They really know how to do that. They bring them in on trailers and they set them up, and the American Red Cross assisted with that as well. These are people who apparently go from disaster to disaster. They have their own travel homes and they filled up the parking lot at Tarboro High School. They are professional Red Cross volunteers, I guess you could say. Many of them were from other parts of the country and had seen wildfires, tornadoes in Oklahoma, they had seen floods, mudslides in California, just all over the place. It was nice to have people who cared, but who also had been through disasters enough to help us understand that we were going to get through this, too. For us it was terribly overwhelming, and I think that the Red Cross people, the Salvation Army, and others who had been through disasters before helped us understand that.

The National Guard, the Coast Guard, and others from the military were really the same way. They were lifting coffins out of the water with great respect, and very sensitive to the fact that someone loved the person in this coffin. I think we all saw another side of the military that was there. I'm very emotional about all of this.

I saw the government agents in our community work—no one punched a clock, no one kept a time sheet, everyone just did what had to be done. These were some of the heroes in Edgecombe County. Our county manager, our health department director, emergency management director, Mr. Freeman from the Department of Social Services, our law enforcement people, our sheriff, the chief of police, the mayor, the fire chief, I mean the list goes on and on. And yes, that was their job, either because they got elected or they got a paycheck to do those things. But they went far above and beyond. Jim Bayliss worked the whole time with a broken arm. He had a tree through the roof in his house, and his arm was in a sling, and yet he was there around the clock with no regard for his own home, which was a compete disaster. These folks all went absolutely above the call of duty.

I think that initially, when it all happened, the community really came together. In the emergency operations center, you could look around that room and you could not tell who the local people were, and who had come from somewhere else. They just meshed, and everyone did what they did best, and there were no egos. And I think that was probably the most wonderful part about the whole thing.

There were many other heroes. One person I can think of, who did this out of the goodness of her heart, was Ernestine Smith. Ms. Smith opened up her home to those who needed help. I don't know how many people were living in her house, or how long they stayed there, but I know it was at least a month, maybe longer. Her whole house was just wall to wall people. She just took people in, and I think that story was repeated over and over. They weren't total strangers; I think some of them may have been relatives, and then friends of relatives and neighbors of relatives. I don't know who all they were, but I do know she had a house full for a very long time.

Mary Williams had a home near Princeville along with her husband and son. They got the call telling them to get out, so they left. But then they went back to gather some critical things that they would need. Their son was in high school at the time. He went into his room to grab some important stuff and then they got in the car and drove away. By the time they left the second time, the water was becoming a serious problem. When they got to where they were going, their son said, "Mom I've got some of my stuff." When she opened up the bag, he had like ten pairs of shoes. Of all the things he could save, he got his shoes. I think that kind of symbolizes how we kind of panic, and your priority list isn't always right. They ended up losing everything.

In my first trip into Princeville after the flood, I went in a Humvee with a media group and the National Guard. It was totally silent—there wasn't a soul there. But we rode by this house, and on top of this house was all this clothing. It was really the strangest thing. Well, the National Guardsman told me this story about the man who lived in this house. He had these suits. They told him to get together everything he wanted to take with him and that they were coming to get him. So he got his suits and clothes, and he got on his roof. A helicopter came, but he was too afraid to get in the helicopter. Now the man is standing on his roof, surrounded by water which was coming up, holding all of these suits and clothes, and he wouldn't get on that helicopter. So when the helicopter left, it blew all the clothing across the roof and in the trees. They finally had to go get him in a boat. And the clothing was there for a long time, scattered all around.

One day I got a call from a woman named Wimberly Burton. She called me from Boston. She actually grew up in Rocky Mount but had not lived here in a long time. She said that she knew what had happened here, and that she and some friends were interested in being part of the relief effort. Well, this was probably about a month after the flood. The emergency operations center was closed and schools had reopened, but things were still not normal by any stretch of the imagination. She said she and some friends wanted to come down and visit.

By this time, I'd had probably hundreds of phone calls like that. Some actually happened, and others didn't. But this particular group did follow through. So we took them over to the Princeville School and showed them what had happened there, and just told them the story. They wanted to know what they could do to help.

We very quickly told them we did not need any more stuff. Now we were very grateful to have all of the donations of clothes and supplies, but what we really needed at that point was money. There were things that we had to buy that people could not give us. I was also concerned about some of our students, because out of eight thousand students in the county, we had fifteen hundred that lost everything—about twenty percent of the student population. A good number of them were high school students. And of that number, we had kids that were planning to go to college that now were not going to be able to go. If your family is in survival mode, there's no money for tuition.

So this group heard that and said, "Okay, that's the project we'd like to take. We'd like to help kids who want to go to college and make sure they have that opportunity." So they went back to Boston and went about raising money. They made a two-year commitment to help the junior and senior classes from all three of our high schools go to college. The money was for kids who had been flooded, and we had a list. So that's what they did.

I went up to visit them in Massachusetts, and we had a meeting at Endicott College. I met Dr. Richard Whiley, the college president. Not only did Dr. Whiley give us a thousand dollars as a personal donation, but he arranged for a four-year scholarship for one of our students from that graduating class. Now there's a young lady who is going to college on that scholarship. Not only that, but he did it for the second year, so we actually had two students receive full scholarships to go to school in Boston.

In the whole program, we had about thirty students who received money for college. It wasn't an organization, and that's what's so wonderful about it. It never incorporated, it was not a 501(c)3, it was just people who cared. They're just wonderful folks. Why would people in Boston care about what happens here? Theirs is just one of hundreds of stories like that.

Shortly after the water went down, this man showed up downtown with a tool belt. He was a telephone repair person. I think he was from the western part of the state. He drove his truck here by himself, showed up downtown, and went door to door reconnecting telephones. And he just did it. No one asked him to do it, and I don't know that anyone knows his name. But he came with his expertise and his time and helped us out. And there were probably dozens more like him.

So we just had all kinds of heroes.

If there is a silver lining here, it's that we had a large group of people that were living in substandard housing before the flood, that now have lovely places to live. It has allowed us to rebuild some parts of our community that we would never have been able to afford to rebuild. We are still struggling with that issue. Edgecombe County is an economically depressed county. We have one of the highest unemployment rates in the state. Floyd was a huge setback for this community. But we do have better housing for some people who really needed it, and we have two brand-new schools.

Rebuilding was accomplished by all different people. What I observed was that whatever your skills were, that's what you did. If you could fix telephones, you fixed telephones. If you could spoon soup, that's what you did. If you could handle the media, then that's what you did. Everyone did whatever they did best to help it all come together. It didn't matter where you lived, which side of the river you lived on, or whether you spoke English, people just pulled together. I think it made the community stronger that what it was before.

Lindy Pierce   Lindy Pierce is one of the countless volunteers who helped rebuild eastern Carolina after Floyd. Traveling with her church group from Dover, Delaware, Lindy made her first trip to Tarboro in June 2000 when she was only fifteen. Among her projects was the repair of the Mount Zion Primitive Baptist Church in Princeville. She was interviewed by phone in May 2002.

Youth in Action is a youth group that is nondenominational. We have kids from four or five different churches, and some students who don't attend church. I've been involved with it for five years. We started working for Habitat for Humanity every summer doing construction. We've been in North Carolina for the past two summers, and we're going to be heading down there this summer to do more work in Goldsboro.

We get all our money through fund-raisers that we do at two of the main churches, Christ Episcopal and St. Andrews Lutheran. We hold spaghetti din-

Lindy Pierce, a member of the Youth in Action church group from Dover, Delaware, has a mouthful of nails as she works to rebuild the Mount Zion Primitive Baptist Church in Princeville. (Photo by Bob Jordan; courtesy of Associated Press)

ners, silent auctions, pancake breakfasts, and receive a lot of donations. We're not sponsored by others; all the funds that we have we raise ourselves. Gary Knight and my mom, Amy Pierce, are the leaders of our group. Charlotte Webb is now director of the Northeast region of Habitat, and she was our North Carolina contact.

We had one of the bigger Habitat teams. We normally had between twenty and forty people. Last year was our biggest group. We took forty-one down, and this year I think we have thirty-six going down. The first year we were in North Carolina we had twenty-eight or twenty-nine. They normally have two or three construction foremen, but they're not there all the time because it's not their primary job. So they'd just give us written instructions and we'd just have to do it. We had about ten or fifteen that are about my age, and they've all done construction for at least four or five years, in different places, so we have some experience in a lot of different things. They just tell us what to do and we do it.

Most of the materials were donated. Every year we have leftover funds, and last year I think we gave them around twenty-four hundred dollars. They use those donations to get more lumber and supplies for the houses. All of the local volunteer foremen are local builders and contractors.

In June of 2000, we came to Tarboro and stayed at the armory. When we first got there, it seemed like all the houses around us had some kind of water damage. The houses had waterlines everywhere, which was not something we were used to seeing. We were building two new homes to replace two homes that were completely destroyed. I was kind of nervous at first, because we didn't really know what we were going to be doing, and what kind of construction we were going to be working on. But when we finally got the hang of it, we ended up doing mudding and siding on the walls inside. We framed another whole house, because we had a lot in our group—somewhere around forty I do believe—so it doesn't take us long to finish things. We built the two houses almost completely from the ground up, and by the end they were completely enclosed and everything. It was really a big accomplishment.

Believe it or not, roofing is actually my favorite. My friend and I finished a whole roof by ourselves. They bet us we couldn't do it, so we did the whole thing in two days.

The homeowners were so very, very grateful. They had a ceremony there for us, and two of the people that were going to be receiving the houses were there. An elderly lady from one of the families was very emotional about it, which made the rest of us emotional. I mean, the lady cried. She was so excited to see how far we had gotten. It was really heartwarming to see how happy these people were about the work we were doing for them.

When we went back in 2001, we repaired a historically black church. It was the first black church in North Carolina, I believe, and it had been completely covered in water—the only thing that had been left exposed was the steeple. Everything had to be repaired. The entire inside had to be gutted out and redone. You could see the waterlines all the way up to the top of the church. We had to redo probably twelve of the thirty stained-glass windows. My best friend and I worked on the belltower, which had to be completely refinished. There were no steps anymore, and everything was torn down or washed away.

Apparently, the church bell hadn't been rung in seven or eight years. When we finally got it to work, we had people coming from every direction down to the church when they heard it. They were all so emotional about their church being rebuilt and hearing the bell. It was kind of emotional for us too, 'cause we didn't know the story behind it at all. The people of the church sent us many, many letters and thank-you notes throughout the year as it was becoming completed. It looked so different from when we were there.

And we also helped a lady who lived down the street. She had a bench where her husband used to sit before he died, and there was a concrete slab there that was completely ruined. She was really old, like almost eighty-nine. She just wanted somebody to repair it, so she talked to some of our leaders. Five or six of us walked down there and rebuilt her concrete slab so she could walk out to her bench.

The area where Mount Zion was is primarily black. Here you have a huge group of primarily white teenagers coming in, and you would expect that there would be differences. But they were all very warm. They really were so receptive towards us, I mean, they brought us food and they asked us if we needed any help. Many of the people from the church would come every day to do what they could. There was the sweetest elderly man who would walk around to everybody with a water jug and ask them if they needed water, because he wanted his church to be finished. And the pastor came every day and said prayers with us in the morning. It was amazing, the reception we'd get from people who didn't even know us.

We do it all out of the goodness of our hearts. We do it because the Lord asks us to do things like that, and to help other people. If something like the flood were to happen to us, we'd want people to come and help us. If I didn't have a home to live in, I'd have to rely on other people to help rebuild my home.

I definitely want to continue doing this. I love working and helping people and seeing the gratitude they give in return. We're not really heroes, we're just doing the right thing. That doesn't make us heroes. We don't need thanks for what we do, because people always ask us what we get out of doing this, and we're not out to get something. We're out to help people, and that's all it is. Just helping others, instead of being selfish all the time, like regular teenagers.

Among those on the front lines of the disaster was James Mercer. As director of emergency services for Edgecombe County, he was at the epicenter of the flood and was in command during some of Floyd's most dramatic events. His efforts garnered him the Edward Foster Griffin Award, the state's highest honor for emergency managers. He was interviewed in his Tarboro office in May 2002.

James Mercer

As supervisor for all of the response and the recovery, I didn't see a lot of the things that were going on in the field. I had information, and I had reports. Most of the people that I deal with are department heads, fire chiefs, rescue

Brent Nash and Ricky Thompson use a canoe to check the damage to Thompson's business on St. James Street in the flooded downtown area of Tarboro. (Photo by Patrick Schneider; courtesy of the *Charlotte Observer*)

squad chiefs, mayors, and elected officials. Those are the people that I come in contact with on a daily basis. They were all out there in the field. They were the incident commanders. I was just the overall Emergency Operations Center (EOC) manager.

As the storm was approaching, my first concern was life safety—getting people out of harm's way. When the phone started to ring, we knew that we were in over our heads, so we started making requests to get helicopters in and to get search-and-rescue teams in. Trained search-and-rescue, swift-water rescue-type personnel were brought in because we didn't have the resources and training to do that kind of work. We had hundreds of rescues all around, in Rocky Mount, Pinetops, Conetoe, Mildred, Speed, and Crisp.

At one point we had sixty-five hundred people in shelters in the county— that's equal to half the population of Tarboro. Feeding, clothing, and taking care of those people for sixteen days—it was unprecedented. Normally, when we open up a shelter for a hurricane, like say Fran, Dennis, or Bonnie, we'd open up the shelter the night before the hurricane was to hit, and then the

A local resident and boat owner navigates the streets of Tarboro during the flood. (Photo by Patrick Schneider; courtesy of the *Charlotte Observer*)

next day when it passed through we'd send people back home. Then we'd close our emergency shelter operations down, and close our EOC. But Hurricane Floyd was a whole different animal. It taught us a lot about coordination, about disaster response and recovery, and we are still recovering as we speak.

And we were used to just evacuating facilities. I never thought that we would have to evacuate an entire town. But Floyd was just a tremendous burden on our local resources. After a few days the Red Cross came in and really assisted us, as well as state emergency management, the Salvation Army, the Mennonites, and all the other church organizations and faith-based organizations. We could not have done it without outside help.

Getting information out was critical. Communications are so important during disasters. With Floyd the rumors were just rampant. Rumor control was one of the biggest challenges that we faced. Our communications equipment flooded and we lost communications with our fire, rescue, law enforcement and EMS personnel there for a while. So we had to communicate the best we could through makeshift towers and cell phones.

About thirty percent of the county was underwater during Floyd. With all the rain from Hurricane Dennis, the river was already at the flood stage when Floyd came through. The flood maps in our county are outdated, which we have known for a period of time. New flood maps are now being drawn by North Carolina Emergency Management and FEMA. We are hoping to hear something any day now and want to get those maps in our hands.

In our current hazard mediation plan we are now required to limit the amount of construction in the hundred-year floodplain. With our hazard mediation buyout program we have bought a lot of flooded properties that were within the hundred-year floodplain. Approximately a hundred fifty properties in the buyout program are in Edgecombe County. So far, we have bought about a hundred properties and demolished about seventy-five of them. The town of Tarboro has a hazard mitigation grant, as well as the city of Rocky Mount. So if you add it all up, there are five-hundred-plus homes that are going to be bought and destroyed and taken out of the hundred- or two-hundred-year floodplain.

In Princeville, the town voted to rebuild the dike. It was built back to its original specifications. The dike is at thirty-six feet, but the water rose up to forty-three feet in Floyd, so it went seven feet over the dike. So the only way to stop another flood like Floyd would be to increase the height of the dike another six or seven feet. It is designed to protect the town, and the town is not in a floodplain because of it. We are maintaining that dike.

There were some odd sights around the county, especially dogs, cattle, and horses on top of barns, and on top of houses.

The churches have done a tremendous job of coming in and stepping up to the plate to provide manpower and resources to help these families rebuild. The state has been there too, with its crisis housing program, community development block grant programs, and unemployment insurance. FEMA's disaster recovery programs have been tremendous. And the military—I just can't tell you how impressed I was with the military as a whole. I am a major in the U.S. Army Reserve, and it was great to see my fellow soldiers and airmen come in and do such a tremendous job. Especially the Coast Guard, the Air Force, the Army, as well as the Marines. We had a battalion-sized military outfit stationed right here in Edgecombe County. It all really made me feel proud to be a member of the armed services.

And we couldn't have done it without the school system. We utilized all of their facilities for our sheltering operations. It was a real coming together of all the county's resources. The key players that operated with me were social services director Hobert Freeman, health director Jim Bayliss, Sheriff James Knight, and former county manager Joe Durham. We were the command group in the EOC, and it was the war room. But all the other people in the field were like the grunts—I'm a major but I can't get anything done if my privates and sergeants don't get it done for me.

Hurricane Floyd was a life-transforming event. Throughout my career I've worked with fire, EMS, rescue, law enforcement, and military. Floyd gave me the opportunity to bring all of those disciplines together and see how well those different disciplines can work in a disaster situation. It gave me a real good appreciation for the community, and for our neighbors. There were lots of instances where neighbors were out there rescuing neighbors. We put a call out to people across the county for boats, and we had hundreds of responses —from pontoon boats all the way down to john boats and canoes. The business community also stepped up to the plate. They provided all types of resources, manpower, and volunteers to help us in every way that they could. It really was the entire community, this entire county working together, and that was the most rewarding thing that I got out of it.

Bob Williams wrote extensively about Hurricane Floyd as a senior reporter for the *Raleigh News and Observer*. As a journalist he brought a unique perspective to the disaster and, along with his fellow reporters, provided award-winning coverage of the event. He has since left his post at the N&O but still has vivid memories of the hurricane and its aftermath. He was interviewed by telephone in July 2002.

Bob Williams

I had been at the *News and Observer* for years and started covering the weather by chance really. I was covering N.C. State University, and since the Weather Service office is over there, they decided they'd just make me the weather expert. That happened in April of '96. In July of '96 Bertha came, and that September Fran hit. As you know, we hadn't had a hurricane of consequence for twenty-some years. All of a sudden, it was "the" story. Those storms taught us how the heck to cover hurricanes again, because nobody in the newsroom had really been through that whole experience. Our hurricane plan had been just send a bunch of people to the coast and see if it hits.

I remember in the intervening years, Bonnie had us all scared to death. You'll recall that it was supposedly huge and mean, and it was gonna rewrite the books. But somehow it turned out to be no big deal—it was more of a shingle-snatcher, as I like to call it, than anything else.

But then Floyd. Floyd felt different to me from the beginning. All of a sudden, ten minutes before every hour you're tuning in the Weather Channel. And it seemed almost from the beginning, this feeling that we're gonna have to deal with this one in a way that we haven't had to deal with the others. I started camping out at the office because we were really watching it closely. When it was headed up toward Florida, I think the thing that hit me at that point, and we wrote this, was it was as powerful as Andrew and the size of Texas. Most of us had never seen anything like that, except maybe churning out in the middle of the Atlantic somewhere.

So we prepared for the worst. We dispatched reporters, quite literally from Georgetown, South Carolina, all the way up to Corolla along the coast, in the usual spots. I stayed in Raleigh, what they call anchoring. After the storm comes ashore, then I get out in the field. By the time it got off South Carolina, I found myself saying to all our reporters down at the coast, get someplace safe. This didn't feel like a storm you needed to be out there rumbling around in, even if you're a hardened journalist trying to tell the story. This one felt different. It was a feeling of there was nowhere to run, nowhere to hide. Unless you're planning to drive to Omaha, you know, you're gonna get some part of it.

So Floyd came ashore and our reporters got out fairly quickly. Oak Island was torn up pretty bad, but it almost seemed like, you know, here we did it again—we dodged a bullet. It wasn't as bad as everyone thought it would be. The day after, the sun came out, it was cool, and it was gorgeous. I rarely have seen the sky so blue as it was the day after. I remember walking out that day and getting some lunch, and saying man it's just really nice here.

Well, the guys at the Weather Service continued to tell us that the rivers are going to come up, and we're talking five-hundred-year floods here. The next morning was maybe the oddest morning I've ever spent in a newsroom. All of a sudden, scanners started crackling away, and we started getting reports from the field in a way that I'd never heard of. At first it was totally unbelievable. The rivers had come up so fast and so far, and the whole eastern part of the state was cut up into a bunch of little islands. And our reporters were dealing with it in just the same way as the people there.

One of my reporters, Jay Price, called me up on the cell phone and said, "It's going nuts out here. But as a journalist, I gotta tell you, this is a really target-rich environment." There were so many stories that day that we could barely tell them. The challenge was to get it all down and get it out. It was almost like we knew we had to record it for posterity. It's kind of a rare feeling in the newspaper business. You know, you write stuff down, and you cover a lot of process and things like that, but this was historic. And we all felt that. And there was no fatigue. We were all running on adrenaline. But that's what you get into this business to do. And I think there was also a sense of pride all throughout the newsroom, because we had made the warnings this time, and hopefully kept those fifty-two deaths from being a whole lot more. Even though I still can't bring myself to believe that fifty-two people died.

And the shots that were coming in, they almost seemed surreal. Those pigs on top of that pig barn. It just didn't seem real. I think another striking picture, that really has stayed with me until this day, was that rock quarry near Wilson that looked like Niagara Falls.

The stew and that smell still defies description. I mean at one point it smelled like raw sewage, but it also smelled like a gas station, and like a just-plowed field—all rolled together. I think another thing that really struck me was you couldn't get anywhere. I mean you couldn't get from Greenville to Wilson. It's like, as they say in Maine, you can't get there from here. It was a real challenge —repositioning the reporters on the ground. We didn't have the resources to be flying around in helicopters. Helicopters were being put to a lot of other good uses at that time, instead of flying reporters around.

Another thing that struck me was I'd never seen Jim Hunt as visibly shaken as he was the day after the storm. I've seen that man in lots of situations; I mean he doesn't get shaken. He always seems on his game. But when he was away from everyone, he seemed like he was close to tears most of the time. And I think it honestly hit him that his state would never be the same. And you know it hit all of us that way.

It also struck me that Floyd hit the people hardest that could least afford and least handle it. And that's something I've always come back to with this disaster, was that it was almost diabolical in that way. You've got these folks that for years have lived on the river bottomlands. It was cheap land. And there's always been a reason that land was cheap. They didn't have much to begin with, and what they did have was taken away from them. I think that was the cruelty of the storm.

I think the government did its best, at all levels, to try and help. But I think an awful lot of people fell through the cracks and had to put their lives back together on their own. And you know that's a noble thing, when you witness that. I think we witnessed that by the thousands in Floyd. I was more struck by the people that didn't have their hands out than the folks who did. Folks were coming in from all over the country to nail boards together for people they'd never met. And that wasn't a story that happened once or twice, it was a story that happened tens of thousands of times.

I remember going into Duplin County, to Burgaw, a few days after the storm had hit. I found this house where there was this old couple, and she was bedridden and couldn't leave, and they had to ride out the storm. The trees had just chased them from one room to another as they fell on the house during the storm. And as I'm talking to these folks doing this story, they're filming a movie out in the town square. The Wilmington film studios had already gotten up and running, and right down the street from the Red Cross canteen was the canteen for this movie set. I guess life goes on, but wow. It was jarring, it really was.

I spent a lot of time in those places, and you find yourself looking at the waterlines 'cause they're visible everywhere. They kind of allow you to reconstruct what it might have been like. I did that a lot in Rocky Mount when I was spending time there. And that was jolting, too, to figure this really rotten, gross water that high in a town like Rocky Mount. It was pretty amazing.

The Baptist Men, the Mennonites, I mean whoever it was, they just descended on these towns, and they rebuilt them—without being called in the least. They just showed up—and quickly. And it was almost that informal in a lot of ways. They would show up in a town, a bunch of guys and a pickup truck, and say, "Where do you need us, and what can we do?" And they'd be banging away—all with a smile on their faces. They knew they were doing noble work, and all of the crap that divides people, and the stupidity of people's differences, that was all gone. There was no place for it there. That was striking, too. Folks that wouldn't even probably talk to each other on the street at another time in their life, were suddenly breaking big-time sweat for each other. And that was fun and heartening to see.

At the same time, I was down there when the caskets started floating up, and that is as gut-wrenching a scene as I ever want to see.

I felt honored that I was able to sit in the position that I did during Floyd. We were a finalist for the Pulitzer for breaking news that following year. We lost out narrowly to the *Denver Post*, which won for the its coverage of the Columbine shootings. And for a paper our size, you know, that was quite an honor. For us, there was no other story. And there was no sense in acting like there was. It seemed odd when we did try to get back to normal. You would be amazed how a young reporter whose job is to cover City Hall rises to the occasion in something like this. And I hesitate to use the word, but there were little acts of heroism all through the newsroom and all through the coverage. Folks that just thought nothing of doing the best work of their lives.

I'm always amazed at how quickly we do, one way or another, get our lives back. With Fran, I saw it firsthand with my neighbors there in Raleigh. It happened much quicker than anyone thought. It's happened the same with Floyd. Human beings, when faced with something like that, have a remarkable ability to somehow marshal their resources and get going again at a time when it looks absolutely hopeless. You cry, and then you firm your resolve and just fix it. I would credit the people, and the government of North Carolina, for their efforts to do that. It's been pretty remarkable. It wasn't always perfect, but the people that needed help usually got it. And people opened up their hearts. If there's a lesson to be learned, I guess it's that your neighbors will be there when you really need them.

Steve Harned

Steve Harned is the meteorologist in charge at the Raleigh Forecast Office of the National Weather Service. With support from the National Hurricane Center in Miami and the River Forecast Center in Atlanta, it was the local NWS offices that were responsible for issuing watches and warnings for Floyd in North Carolina. Steve's insights as a meteorologist offer another intriguing perspective on the legacy of Hurricane Floyd. He was interviewed in his Raleigh office in June 2002.

It was a deep tropical eastern Atlantic storm, so we were watching it for a couple of weeks before it got to the coast. And it became very obvious when it got east of the Leeward Islands that this could potentially be a major storm. And of course, when it was over the Bahamas it was just a monster, both in size and in strength. So as it drew closer, I became more and more concerned. In fact, on Tuesday, just two days before it came inland, as I was watching it unfold, I was for the first time in my professional career really frightened about the potential for what this storm could do and the threat it was presenting to my family and community. Because if it moved inland like it was forecast to do, as a category four moving at a fairly high rate of speed, then we would have something like a Hazel or a Hugo right over the middle part of the state, which was really quite frightening.

I've been through hurricanes before. Hurricane Fran in 1996, of course, and in 1983 I was head of the Houston and Galveston National Weather Service offices and was on Galveston Island when Hurricane Alicia made a direct landfall. But neither of those experiences scared me as much as Floyd did when it was two days out.

Things shifted as Floyd got nearer land. As new model data became available, the initial forecast was skirting the eastern coast of Florida and then coming inland across Georgia and parts of South Carolina and central North Carolina. But as time went on, it was obvious the storm was going to curve more towards the east, as it did, so that was a very good thing. Also, the day before landfall, as it was moving up east of Georgia and South Carolina, we were extremely fortunate that the south side of the storm began ingesting some cooler, drier air from the west. It dropped from a category four to a category two. We saw that occurring, and we were just rooting it on. And then, the track was across the coast east of here.

All National Weather Service offices along the coast and the first tier inland are on what's known as a hurricane hotline. It's an open line where any of us can get in touch with the Hurricane Center immediately, and vice versa. The Hurricane Center conducts conference calls with the affected offices about an hour before the issuance of the advisories. So we are in constant contact with the Hurricane Center and are able to provide our local input.

For us, Floyd was different from other hurricanes in the amount and location of the heavy rainfall. When Floyd finally did make landfall down around Cape Fear, it was a category-two storm. You know any hurricane is a significant event, but it was not a major hurricane. There was quite a bit of storm surge and coastal flooding, but then again, it was not extraordinary. But the heavy rain fell to the left of the track of the hurricane. Many forecasters subscribe to the position that all bad things happen along and just to the right of the track of the hurricane. But this showed that when it comes to heavy rains, that's not necessarily the case. The rainfall, both where it fell and the amount, was the most unique characteristic of this storm.

Floyd was an extremely effective rain producer. I first noticed that about two days before it came at us, before we were really under any influence of the storm. We were just starting to see the first wisp of the extreme edge of circulation of the hurricane and had some developing thunderstorms up over Albemarle Sound in the Elizabeth City area. Those storms exploded and produced a tremendous amount of rain in a very localized area. And it was directly related to some type of interaction with the very outer fringes of the hurricane. That caught my eye—wow! This storm could be just a powerful rainmaker. Clearly it was, and when it later interacted with an old frontal boundary, it just became an extremely efficient rainmaker. It was almost a perfect machine to make rain.

You may remember that up through August of '99 the entire state was in a deep drought. Tropical Storm Dennis came in and dropped five to ten inches of rain over the eastern third of the state, and what it basically did was filled up all the creeks and rivers. Dennis didn't cause a lot of flooding, but it brought all the rivers up to or very close to flood stage. So it just primed the pump. And when the rains of Floyd came across just ten days later, there was no place for them to go. Also, what was just phenomenal about Floyd was you had entire counties receiving a foot to a foot and a half of rain. Think about that, just where does it go? Over all parking lots, all fields, all houses. You had a foot to a foot and a half of rainfall when the rivers were already full. That's why we had such longlasting flooding, far away from the rivers and well away from areas that normally flood during heavy rain situations.

Floyd certainly was a five-hundred-year flood in certain areas. There was no question about it, especially in parts of the Tar Basin. A hundred-year event means that there is about a one percent chance of that occurring in any given year. A five-hundred-year event means there's a two-tenths of one percent chance of it happening in a given year. Now some people said, "Well, we had two hundred-year events within three years." Well, yeah, you could, because the same chance comes around every year. But if you average it out over a long period of time, basically, and there's a one percent chance every year, then you'll see it about once every hundred years.

We did an excellent job with forecasting. The National Weather Service is responsible for putting out river stage forecasts. Of course when we go into flood, we put that out. We work very closely with the River Forecast Center in Atlanta. It's a Weather Service office which has primary responsibility for river forecasting in the entire Southeast. They have the river models, and they work very closely with our office to factor in local effects and then produce the river forecast.

Well, one or two days before Floyd came in, we all agreed this was going to be a phenomenal event. On Wednesday morning and early afternoon, we decided that they should put hundred-year rainfall amounts into their models, which translates to seven to eight inches of rain. From that we got record-breaking flood forecasts at several points along the Tar and the Neuse. We put that out Wednesday afternoon, before the rains had begun. We coordinated very closely with emergency managers and local government officials, and for two or three days before the storm, we were harping flooding, flooding, flooding. It's catastrophic, get ready. Looking at what was happening in eastern North Carolina that Wednesday afternoon, we knew that shops were closing, businesses were shutting down, and people were buttoning up. So we had some excellent forecasts. But no one could have imagined the magnitude of the flooding that did occur. A foot to a foot and a half of rain over entire counties was almost beyond comprehension. Clearly, we were not surprised that we had flooding—but the severity of it was just unimaginable.

Over eastern North Carolina, a hundred-year rainfall event is defined as anywhere between 7 and 8 inches of rain in a twelve-hour period, or 8 to 9 inches of rain in a twenty-four-hour period. During Floyd, Kinston had a twelve-hour rainfall of 7.9 inches, and they had a twenty-four-hour total of 10.4 inches. So that way exceeded the hundred-year level for both twelve and twenty-four, especially the twenty-four. Now Rocky Mount had a twelve-hour Floyd rainfall of 12.5 inches, and their twenty-four-hour was 14.7 inches, so that was far above the hundred-year event. There were several other hundred-year rainfall records, but these are two pretty dramatic ones.

With Floyd, many people were killed by putting themselves into the danger, mostly by trying to drive through or across flooded roadways. It's just kind of a human instinct to think, "I need to get through, and the water doesn't look too deep. I was able to go through this morning, I'll just see if I can nose myself on through." But all it takes is a foot or two of water on the roadway to float a car. Then all of a sudden, people are in trouble. They think, "I'll just drive my car across the way," and they get swept away.

All in all, I think people definitely did respond to the warnings, and even though we had a tremendous loss of life, it really could have been so much worse. I think the public's response was adequate, especially considering the magnitude of the situation.

Janice Bailey   When Hurricane Floyd struck eastern North Carolina, you could say that Janice Bailey was at the wrong place at the right time. A retired nurse and Red Cross volunteer from Maryland, Janice was just visiting with family in Kinston when floodwaters forced her to evacuate her niece's home. But rather than return to Maryland, she ended up staying for months to volunteer her time and help her family. She was interviewed by telephone in December 2002.

My sister and I had been planning to visit her daughter in North Carolina all that summer. She lives in Kinston. I had just retired after working twenty-seven years in nursing. We drove down right after Labor Day and had planned on staying there for two weeks. Well, things didn't go like we had planned. We ended up staying four months.

We were watching the news when Floyd was going into Florida, and then it turned. We were all really nervous, because we could see that it was coming our way. My niece lived in a section that had been flooded before, but we weren't really thinking about that at the time. We were more worried about really strong winds blowing this big tree on her house. It was a really big tree, and some of the limbs were already touching the roof. But it didn't. In the end, it was the rain that got us.

It rained more than I've ever seen in my life. And it started raining a long time before the storm even got there. They said on the news that some areas were in a flood watch, so we helped my niece pack up some things just in case. But we never really thought it would be so bad that we'd have to leave. We could see that the water had filled all the ditches near the house, but it was raining so hard you didn't want to go outside to look.

My niece's boyfriend had to work late that night, and he ended up trying to drive through some flooded streets. After he told us how high the water was on his truck door, we couldn't believe he had made it back. He said there was a police car that was flooded out. Now you know if the police lose a car to the flooding, you know it's bad.

During the height of the storm, there were a bunch of people who had to be rescued from trailer parks down the road. We heard this story about this one elderly man who was in a wheelchair in his house, and the water came inside. The firemen had to pick him up and carry him in his wheelchair above the water. There were a lot of folks rescued like that.

We were in a bit of a panic at our house because we knew the water was getting bad. I didn't want to leave in my car, because I was just afraid to drive on those roads. So we ended up leaving in my niece's boyfriend's truck. At first we went to some friends' house a couple of blocks away, but they were leaving, too. I had worked with the Red Cross in the past, mostly with their blood program, and I knew they would have a shelter set up to take us in. We ended up going to the shelter at the community college. We stayed there for a while, but then eventually went out to live in a trailer away from town that my niece knew about.

Her house was flooded pretty bad. It got worse as the days went by, because the water was still rising. I think it was almost a week later before the river reached its peak. I had a bunch of my clothes in the trunk of my car, and when I finally went back to look at them they were all ruined. At first, my car looked okay. But you could see this line of mud on the side. The inside was damp, but my ashtray was just full of water. So I knew I wasn't going anywhere anytime soon.

I decided that I was meant to stay there and help people. God didn't want me to go home. So that's what I did. I went to work.

I helped out down at a local church for a while, distributing clothes to people that needed them. We had these big vans of clothes and supplies that people had collected from all over. One man who was there got a jacket out of a box, and there was a note pinned to the collar. It said something like, "God bless you. Look in pocket." In the pocket was an envelope with two folded-up twenty-dollar bills. That poor old man started laughing and crying at the same time.

Another story I remember was about a woman who was a neighbor of my niece. She wasn't there when the flood came, so she couldn't get anything out of her house. The water came up inside and floated her stuff all around and out in the yard. When she got home a couple of weeks later, her wedding portrait was stuck in some bushes in her yard. She got it back, and it was okay.

We went a long time without any showers or anything. We had food and water and got some good meals at the church feeding station. I even met some people that were there from near where I live. I was amazed at how many people came in to Kinston from other places to help out. They had left work, traveled hundreds of miles, and were giving their time to help others. It was really heartwarming to see that. That's part of why I stayed and worked. Even though I hadn't planned on doing this, it was just the right thing to do.

As the weeks went by, the floodwaters were gone, but there was still a lot to do. My niece's house was just a mess, and we spent a lot of time cleaning it up. It needed work, too, 'cause the water had gotten into the wiring in one area. The mud and the smell was something I'll never forget. We heard that the city's sewage plant had backed up, and maybe that was part of the problem. I think I went through about three pair of shoes before I finally went and got me some boots to work in. We cleaned her house, and then we kept on working on other houses on her street. We'd work at the church during the mornings and work on the houses in the afternoons. This went on for weeks. Finally, the city came in and did an inspection after the work was done.

The one thing God put here to scare me is snakes. I don't even want to look at a picture of one. Well, this man came by the church one day and told us this story we couldn't believe. Out in his trailer park, the flooding came up real fast during the storm. I think it was dark. He grabbed a few clothes and things and put his bag on his little porch, and went back inside to grab a few more things. While he was in there a snake crawled inside his bag, but he didn't know it. When they came to rescue him with a boat, he got in the boat along with some other people, and they went away. Well, the snake crawled out into the bottom of that boat, and those people screamed and nearly jumped out of that boat. Fortunately, I think it was a game warden driving the boat, so he got it out of there. But can you imagine? I know I'd be over the side pretty quick.

My niece is moved back in now. She's doing okay, but her son has asthma. She thinks the flood has something to do with it. I know that breathing around that moldy water has got to be bad. But she's back in her house, and she got lots of help.

I never worked so hard in all my life. It was all hard work, but I'm glad I stayed to do it. My insurance paid for my car, and I got a new one. We went home right after Christmas, 'cause my sister didn't want to go until she knew her daughter was going to be all right. It was my first real disaster. Even though it wasn't my home that was flooded, I still felt like I was a victim of the flood. Maybe I was a victim, but I guess I was also part of the help. I've even thought about going out with the Red Cross to help in other disasters. Maybe that's what God has intended for me to do.

Bo Fussell is deputy chief of the Wallace Volunteer Fire Department. As floodwaters surged from nearby Rockfish Creek, Bo and his crew rescued almost two hundred patients from a local nursing home that was rapidly filling with water. That was only one of several dramatic events that tested the Wallace VFD in the aftermath of Floyd. He was interviewed in his downtown fire station in August 2002.

Bo Fussell

Leading up to Floyd, we had several meetings here to talk about the storm. We had meetings to review plans and discuss what we were going to do. About every twenty-four hours for the next two days, all of our officers met with the head officers of the town, the rescue squads, and police departments, so that we were well prepared and ready.

So in the last twenty-four hours before it came in, we called a meeting and brought in crews that averaged about twelve men and kept them at the station, ready for any call that would come in. Right before Floyd really got strong, we got a house fire on [Highway] 41 and the wind was real tough. I did not make the fire, because I was in Topsail Beach evacuating my parents. They had forty-two inches of water inside their house after the flood. They lost all the stuff they had in the downstairs part.

The storm started coming in, and we did a few trees down across highways. Power lines were down, and we went to check those out. Then we all just bunked down and waited it out. We were called out twice that night for evacuations from flooded areas. In town there were some cars that had drowned out, and we carried the people to the elementary school, which was our shelter here in Wallace.

Sometime after daybreak that morning, we got a call that there was a plate glass broken out at one of our members' buildings uptown. While we were there, he said he wanted to go by and check on his mom to make sure she was okay. She's in a rest home here, the Brian Center, which is down on Railroad Street about a half-mile out of town. So he and I went down there in my pickup. When we got there, we walked in the building, and there was four-and-a-half inches of water on the floor in the rest home. It was rising from Rockfish Creek. He went on to the room to check on his mother, and I started questioning the lady in charge. She said she could not get a-hold of someone in the main office to approve an evacuation. They were in Arizona, or Missouri, or somewhere, and could not be reached by phone. At that time we ordered an evacuation. They had no choice.

So I called back to the chief, and he dispatched several firemen to the scene. We took what employees' cars could be driven at that point and put patients that could walk in those cars. We had firemen drive their cars out, because I knew if the employees ever got out, we wouldn't get them back. So then some firemen started coming in with some vehicles. The water was rising fast—maybe three or four inches a minute there for a while. I mean it was really coming in quick. And we ended up evacuating, in an hour, close to two hundred people. After we evacuated the first hundred that were able to move, then we were down to those confined to beds or whatever. By that time we were in knee-deep water inside the rest home. Everything was floating around in the building. The power was out, because the main power line into Wallace was down on that side of town.

We called the National Guard, and they couldn't get us anything at that time. Some local residents were listening to all of this on their scanners, and soon we had people bring in dump trucks and flatbed trailers. We were actually putting people in hospital beds up on dump trucks, beds on flatbeds, and wheelchairs locked down, with people just holding them there in place. We brought them into town to the local gym. It took probably three hours to evacuate them all.

They said they didn't have permission to evacuate. And I don't think they knew what to do with them if they evacuated them. The National Guard finally did get us two vehicles, but they were Humvees so we were limited with what we could carry out. Mostly the evacuation was done by citizens of Wallace, putting them in dump trucks and flatbed trailers. By the time we got the last one out of there, we were in waist-deep water inside the building. We have seen the water come up in that area a little bit before, but it had never been anything close to that. By the time we got out of there, it got up I know to about forty-two inches.

Once the patients were out, the last truck out took all the employees and firemen. Some of the patients had relatives come get them from the Brian Center, some stayed there at the gym all night, and some that were in critical condition were bused to other rest homes. The fire department ended up feeding them that night because when we left there they didn't have anything except the clothes they had on. And that's it.

A lot of them had not woke up yet because it was so early. They didn't start panicking until we started moving them. Some were older people who couldn't move, and their beds were just about floating. They were really hysterical. It was a sad time for those people, and you couldn't do very much for them except just carry them out. Local residents brought blankets and whatever they could to lay them on the floor. It was just a sad time.

If he had not wanted to go see his mama, I don't know how long it would have been before they would have called. As it was, we got them out just in time.

At two o'clock, we got a call from our neighbor department at Northeast that they were having flooding and needed a boat and some personnel. So myself and two other firemen left here with a boat and went to Northeast, which is at Hanchy's Store. We backed the boat in at Hanchy's Store Creek bridge. I parked the truck up about a hundred feet from the bridge. At that time there was probably two feet of water over the bridge. We went down the road and started alerting people. By that time, Northeast had about six boats in the water. They had a local trailer park that was flooding fast, and we worked all day. At five o'clock, we brought out my last load.

I looked for my truck, but they had moved it to River Landing, which is about six or seven miles away. The water had gone from two foot on the bridge to above my waist when I was standing on the railing of the bridge. So that means it rose another five feet from two o'clock in the morning to five o'clock in the afternoon.

By lunch, we probably had twenty boats in the water. Wallace, Northeast, and Rose Hill actually had firemen in boats working that area. I understand there were approximately six hundred people evacuated by boats. There was another rest home out there that was evacuated by dump trucks. It flooded on them, too. We went to some lower homes that were further down the road. When we woke them up, you could hear their feet hit the water, and then you could hear everything they were saying. They were startled. Some of them were still asleep, and the water came up so quiet they didn't know.

When we left from there Friday afternoon late, some of the houses had twelve to twenty-four inches of water in them, and some in lower places had thirty to thirty-six. We had so much floating debris. You had fire ant beds just floating on the top of the water. You couldn't see them, and they were just eating everybody up. And there was just snakes everywhere. They were trying to crawl into the boats and everything.

We went back the next morning at daybreak. At that point, there were houses where all you could see were the rooftops. There were some trailers that you couldn't even see. You couldn't see bridges; you couldn't see mailboxes or fences. Cars were underwater and we were hitting them with boat propellers. Most of the people on that Saturday were up on the rooftops, but some of them refused to leave. We had several that refused to come out even though the water was up to their rooftops. They were determined they weren't going to leave. You got to know 'em out there to appreciate 'em.

We worked probably until lunch on Saturday. At lunch, emergency management regrouped us, and we went into mostly recovery. We painted every house with paint that had been checked thoroughly, showing no one was in that house. I know we pulled two hundred out of the rest home here. In the vicinity of Wallace we probably evacuated three hundred roughly, and probably at Northeast, six hundred or better. There were so many boats, including private boats, there was no way to track them all.

For most of these people, they couldn't understand what was going on. They had lived there all their lives—and I'm talking old people, eighty, ninety years old—and they said they'd never seen so much water. It was just unreal. For some of them, it was the first time they'd ever been in a boat. They were scared, they were skeptical, and they were upset. There were several that had to go to hospitals. I don't know if they were heart attacks, but it was from stress anyway. It was just hard to believe that this was happening.

The day that we went back marking homes, everything was above the waterline. There were dogs, cats, snakes, turkeys; anything that was still alive, you saw it sitting on rooftops and in trees. All kinds of animals were sharing the tops of houses.

On Saturday afternoon after we got back in, the local funeral home called. They had gone to pick up a body, but before they could get back here with it, the roads into town had flooded and they could not get the hearse back here with the body. So we actually took our boat down the airstrip here in Wallace. We went and picked up the funeral director and the body and brought them back to the funeral home.

Most of the civilians that had boats out were sightseeing. It was a problem for security, but also for those homes that were maybe a little higher, these boats were making wakes and the water was rolling into the homes. And that was presenting a problem for a lot of the homeowners.

Working together was great. I mean nobody flared up, and when you went in somebody else's district, they were welcome to see you. Any help that we brought, they were thankful for. The homeowners out there were real thankful that we came in and helped them out and did what we could. It really went well. The citizens, the outside organizations coming in, they all worked great. And the local citizens of Wallace really helped out, too.

Bobby Joyner is the former director of emergency services for Pitt County, a position he held for almost thirty years. During the flood, while more than a third of his county was underwater, Bobby worked around the clock at the Emergency Operations Center. Though his own home was flooded with three feet of water, it was nine days before he could

Bobby Joyner

break away from his duties to see it for himself. He was interviewed in his Greenville office in July 2002.

During the flooding we operated the EOC around the clock for about fourteen days. We originally opened four shelters. During the height of the storm, the wind blew a ventilator off the top of Conley High School. We had water get in there, so we had to physically move all those people. Then we had to open up an additional shelter north of the river to house people over there. North Pitt High School did not have electricity, and the sewer system was backing up. So we had to move those people, too. We actually opened up another shelter in Stokes also.

We figured that about thirty-five percent of the county was underwater at one time or another. The county was cut completely in half. You couldn't get from one side to the other without a helicopter. For about seven days, everything we did was with helicopters. During the height of the rescue operations, we don't know how many helicopters we had up here. We had the Coast Guard and the Marine Corps picking up people and taking them to high ground as fast as they could move them. We don't know how many we rescued. It was happening so fast that we had no idea. Once we got all the people that we knew of, we then used Forestry Service and National Guard helicopters. Every day we kept two up here constantly flying, delivering supplies and carrying people back and forth across the river.

One of the other problems we were having was that nobody could get to Greenville from Raleigh. The roads were blocked. We had the Highway Patrol out scouting. They would find a road open and we'd start bringing stuff in from that way, and the next thing we knew that road would be blocked. Then we'd have to look for another route. It was frustrating.

I had three feet of water in my house in Farmville. It all but floated off the foundation. But I never saw my house for nine days after the water came in. I was too busy with the county and just couldn't get over there. On that Sunday the water began to recede and my wife went home. She had been over here helping me in the EOC and she couldn't get home. She got there and the firemen helped move everything out somewhere to store it.

When the water started coming in, my dog was in the backyard. My daughter, who lived two doors down from me, said, "Daddy, the water's coming up the driveway, what do we need to do?" And I said, "Go put the dog in the garage and she'll be all right." She called me back a little later and said the water's

Harry Sydney of the Greenville-Pitt Ministers/Churches Alliance passes down medical supplies to be loaded onto a National Guard truck in Greenville. (Photo by Jessica Mann; courtesy of the *Winston-Salem Journal*)

already up to the garage, and I said put her in the house and she'll be all right. And they called me back and said the water's already in the house. When they actually got to the dog she was swimming in water. But she was all right. My house was one of the ones the federal government purchased.

At the EOC, we were going full blast, people were calling, and I said there's no way in the world there could be as much water in Pitt County as what we're hearing about. So the National Guard helicopters were sent out, and I went up. As soon as we got up above the treetops, all you could see was water. I said, "Good gracious, I can see why everybody's screaming and hollering now."

The EOC was on West Fifth Street, in the county office building. We're on good high ground here and didn't have problems. But another problem we were faced with was that Greenville Utilities had a flooded electrical substation. They supply electricity to a big portion of Pitt County. They were trying to sandbag it to keep it from flooding, but finally it just got too high, and they lost it along with the water treatment plant. Malcolm and I were talking probably every two or three hours on the phone, trying to get him help, and he was trying to keep me advised of what was going on and what his needs were. It was a constant tug-of-war there for a while.

One of the fatalities that we had was a young man, who like everybody else thought he could cross the water in a vehicle. And when he got in the water, his vehicle started floating and he got out, but the water was running so strong that it just caught him and washed him over and he couldn't get away.

I guess the most miraculous story that I know of was told to me months after the storm when I met with a group of people that were deaf. A girl told me a story about how she was in a trailer and was told to leave, but she didn't. Well, late that afternoon water started coming in the trailer, and she got up on top of the stove and had two cats with her. And the water continued to rise. Somehow she got out of the trailer, got up on the roof and spent the first night on top of the trailer. The next day she said she could see the helicopters, but the trailer was back in the trees. She said, "I've got to get off of this trailer, and water's already covering the top of it." She somehow got from that trailer to the next trailer and spent the night on top of it. The next day the helicopters finally saw her and came and picked her up. A lot of that kind of thing went on that we don't even know about.

We were concerned because people were calling, saying, "We're running out of food and we're running out of water." That's what we were fighting here to keep afloat. Keep the hospital in supply so they could keep running. At one time we were about to run out of gasoline and had to have gasoline escorted into the county by the Highway Patrol so we could have fuel to keep our emergency vehicles running.

We had people from, gosh, everywhere come in here to help rebuild. They would come in and work a week, or two weeks. Churches, Habitat groups, and just ordinary citizens. We even had a delegation from Washington, D.C. Congressional staffers came in and worked one weekend trying to help rebuild homes.

I think it was seven days that county government was shut down. And anytime you've got something like that happen, you know people begin to wonder. Schools are closed, they can't travel, and psychologically it does play a lot on people's minds. And once we got back to where we could cross the county and move around, the people that were flooded were still stuck in shelters. People were scared. They didn't know what they were gonna do. A lot of people did not have any flood insurance on their house. I didn't have any on mine. That July I had made my last house payment. I had been in that house for thirty years. So I thought, hey, I'm home free now. Then this happens, and you've got to start all over again.

A lot of people have the wrong understanding about what FEMA can do.

They think that the federal government's gonna come in with a pot of money and say, "Here, here's x number of dollars for you, and here's x number of dollars for that person." But it doesn't happen that way. You have certain forms that you have to fill out and certain procedures you have to go through, and it was very frustrating to the people who don't know those procedures. My application went through but somehow got lost. Finally they found it up there. It was entered into the computer wrong. And people were calling me with this same story. I know that the federal government and the state were doing everything they could, but things didn't always go just right. We had a lot of people that were frustrated and didn't want to bother with it. I talked to some personally that said "I'm not gonna do it." I pleaded with them and they were able to come in and get this stuff straight and finally got assistance.

My wife called the eight hundred number and registered our claim, and they sent us a Small Business application. I told her, "I don't want a loan." But I found out two or three days later that you've got to fill that application out before you can be eligible for anything else. A lot of other people were the same way. If they didn't know these things they got frustrated.

I know a lady personally that had a flooded trailer, and she got to the point that she said, "I'm through with it. I'm not gonna do another thing." She said, "I'll go buy a piece of plywood every month, if that's what it takes, and build my trailer back myself. I'm just tired of working with the system." Most of the time you can talk people through this, but this lady had just given up. She didn't try to get any help. And a lot of people look at it as a matter of pride.

There are some out there that fell through the cracks, and then there's others that rode the system and got some things they did not need. But you're gonna have that. I mean there's no way you can stop that from happening. But I think as a whole, the system works, and a lot of the people that needed help real bad got help. And yeah, we're finding one or two now that did not get all the help they needed.

During this whole thing, I made calls to the National Weather Service to find out what we should expect. And they would say that at four o'clock this afternoon the river's gonna be here, and at eight o'clock in the morning the river's gonna be here. We'd start planning for that, and like two hours later they'd call me back and say, "Hey, that's changed drastically. It's gonna be much higher than that." I mean it was just changing so fast. They were trying to predict it, and they were, but it was outrunning them.

I couldn't give you just one hero story. I think everybody in this county, and in eastern North Carolina, just fell in and went to work. They didn't ask any questions. If you wanted something done, you picked up the phone and asked them about it, and they would do it. Nobody turned us down. Everybody just said, "What do you want, and how long do you want it? We'll be there."

I know I'm fortunate to have worked with the people I worked with. We've got employees that we actually had to run home to get some rest. Or go upstairs and lay down somewhere and sleep an hour or two. And they just didn't want to do it. They wanted to stay here and work as long as they could. I remember we got to a point where we were numb. We had four or five lines ringing, and you'd just have to get up and walk around the building to get some fresh air and clear your mind. Everybody was that way. They wanted to do everything they could.

Jewel Kilpatrick   Jewel Kilpatrick was mayor of Seven Springs when Floyd struck in 1999. The flood devastated this small community, though high water had filled its streets before. All but four of the town's homes were flooded with several feet of water, including Kilpatrick's. She was interviewed in her home in August 2002.

Two or three days before the water started coming in, we were called to the emergency management office. They told us that it would be three feet deeper than it had been in the previous floods with Hurricane Fran. So we knew we were in trouble, because the last flood we had was pretty bad. Floyd would be at least three feet higher.

I came home, and our fire department went around and told people that they needed to start making plans because a flood was coming. They went from house to house moving people that wanted to be moved out. All the residents in Seven Springs had a chance to move out, if they so desired. We had one man that had lived here sixty or seventy years, and he said, "I've lived here all my life, and it won't bother me this time." And I said, "Now I'm telling you, you need to move your stuff because it's gonna get three feet deeper." "Naaahhh," he said. Well, he lost most of his stuff. Some folks were set in their ways and just didn't want to leave. They're the ones that really got hit hard.

Down here we had a lot of chicken farms, and the people would let you store your belongings in that. Now I had a great big cattle truck that I stored my stuff in for the three months that I was out of town, before I moved back.

But most of the people had friends and relatives that would let them store their belongings out in the country away from the flood.

We had somewhere around two hundred people living in Seven Springs at the time of the flood. All but four houses were flooded. The majority of the people down here are elderly and have lived here most of their lives. I have lived in my home for fifty years, and I had over three feet of water in my house. One house had a little over four feet, but the majority of them had about three feet of water.

We had to not only move our stuff out, but we had to evacuate the town. It was about two weeks before the water came down so we could get back in. Let me tell you, we had the National Guard down here, and they were absolutely wonderful people. They stayed their tour, and when it was time for them to go, we begged, and they begged their commander to let them stay. They were just absolutely great. They were fine, fine young men. They stayed about two weeks. They really were our heroes.

There was one person that was the greatest guy—his name was Doug Casey. He was the captain of the volunteer fire department. That man stayed in Seven Springs twenty-four/seven for about two weeks. He was there to make sure that everything went smooth. The man he was working for said if he didn't go back to work he was going to lose his job. Well, this town came first. He lost his job because he chose to stay and see that Seven Springs was taken care of. He was always here. He took charge, made sure that there were no burglaries, and that everything went smooth. He took care of the Highway Patrol and made sure that donations were given out in an orderly manner. He was like the town hero.

It was terrible when folks came back to their homes. What made it so bad was these people were elderly, they were on a fixed income, and they came back to find their houses completely destroyed. Let me tell you the most heart-touching thing that I witnessed during the flood. I was down helping with the traffic, and here comes this great big truck piled high with special belongings, furniture, and pictures. I looked inside the truck and here was this little old lady that was about eighty-five years old. I thought there she is, she spent a whole lifetime accumulating all this stuff, and she's got it all piled in this one truck. And she's having to leave home. That was terrible. It was just terrible to see. You know when you work all your life and then a flood comes and you lose everything, it's just terrible.

These people were hit hard financially. They were elderly, they'd lived here all their lives, they never got flooded because it never came that high, and buying insurance was just a waste of money. You just didn't do it. So the majority of the people did not have flood insurance.

After the flood, just about every state in the United States responded to Seven Springs. We had groups of church people that came in and rebuilt homes for these people, spending their own money. We had a lot of people send in money, too. Of course, FEMA was here, and lots of people brought in furniture, food, and clothes. I guess it was the Volunteer Fire Insurance Services, through the fire department, that came down and gave Seven Springs enough money that we could have a Christmas party that year for all the senior citizens. Everybody got a blanket, food, turkeys, ham, and stuff for Christmas dinner, and there was enough money given so that everybody went and shopped for the children. Santa Claus came to see all the children in Seven Springs that year. It was just great.

I had a great big freezer in a building out in my yard. I didn't even think about the flood in my barn, but I had two men go down and check on my freezer. When they got there, the freezer was floating. They unplugged it, floated it out of my barn, down my yard, went down the street floating the freezer, and had a trailer parked down there. They floated it up on the trailer, drove off to a little house out in the country, plugged it in, and it worked. And it's still working. It's back in my barn again now and it's still working, full of food. I called GE and told them I wanted to give them something they could use for a commercial. They laughed, but they wouldn't use it.

I appeared on TV one time, I forget which channel it was, and it went all over—even outside the United States. They interviewed me about my home, where I had lived for fifty years, and about how I had promised my daddy I would never, never sell it. I was going to have to lose my home after fifty years. A lot of people saw that on television, and it just really touched them. They responded like you wouldn't believe. There was one school in Mississippi where the children had seen it and raised about fifteen hundred dollars to give to our library to buy books. There was one man out in the Midwest that sent fifty thousand dollars to the fund that the fire department started for us. Every family got some money from that fund.

It was all really sort of heartwrenching. You never know how nice people can be. You sort of think, well, people are so hardhearted now that they don't care. Well, this gave you a better outlook on people. There are people who care. Everybody was just absolutely so nice to us. They gave and gave and gave.

We didn't have any fatalities or anything, but we are still reeling from the flood. A lot of people that had their homes fixed real quick are sick, and have been sick since the flood, because of the mold and mildew in the homes. They were just a little too hasty in redoing these houses, and now we've got people who are sick from it. They think it's coming from this mold and mildew. We just have eighty or ninety people that live in Seven Springs now. We've lost six homes, and we've got four more homes that are about to be demolished through the FEMA buyout. And we've got two or three more that Governor Easley has decided to put on hold right now. We're not sure how many we're gonna end up losing. Our tax base is just about zero, and it's getting less and less as people move out. So we're still reeling from the flood. It's not over yet.

Everybody down here is elderly, and they're tired; they've been struggling for three years to get back. Some of these people that have rebuilt are having to move out again now. They're having to sell out because of the mold and the mildew. So I don't know when we'll ever, ever get back to normal again. Seems like there's something that comes up all the time.

This has been some tough five years that I've been mayor. But listen, this town has been destroyed once before by a flood, it's been destroyed twice by fire, and it's always come back. I just don't believe that we're gonna go under this time, either. I know I'm not. I'm gonna be here forever. I told somebody I may drown, but I'm gonna be in Seven Springs 'til I die.

First Sergeant Ed Maness is a twenty-two-year veteran of the North Carolina Highway Patrol. As manager of the Highway Patrol's Video and Computer Training Group, Maness often takes to the skies to record the aftermath of events like hurricanes. He was unaware, however, that his assignment following Floyd would lead to a daring rescue attempt and an award for heroism. He was interviewed in his Raleigh office in July 2002.

Ed Maness

The history of all of this actually started back with Fran. Hurricane Fran, you remember, hit the coast of North Carolina in 1996. It was so devastating, it destroyed just miles and miles of coastline, houses went into the sea, and it was a terrible, terrible situation. Of course, people were evacuated out of their houses onto the mainland. So we found that as soon as the hurricane was

State troopers Terry Carlyle and Ed Maness (*left*) struggle to save the driver of a submerged minivan off I-40 near Wallace. Passing motorist Matt Wilde (*right*) was first on the scene and attempted to dive underwater to break the vehicle's window. (Photo by Christobal Pez; courtesy of the *Raleigh News and Observer*)

over, we had this massive rush of people going back to the beach to check it out. It was pretty hard for our guys to set up a gate and say, "Hey, you can't go back to your house yet. Because not only is it not safe, but we're a little concerned about looters and other things." People got real irritated, especially when they live in Asheville and had a summer home down there. So Everett

Horton, who was our colonel at that time, came up with the idea to go down and film the coastline. Literally take our 'copter and film what these houses look like, and then bring it back to central locations and show it to people— like a town meeting type thing. And so that's where we got the idea of going down and doing this type of video.

So we did that during Fran, and we had our first showing at our headquarters here in Raleigh. And that day we had more than two thousand people that came. They would sit there and watch the coastline, and you'd hear them applaud when they saw their house. Or you had people that were crying because their house was gone. It worked out so well that we had to do additional shows at the fairgrounds. We had people come [from] as far away as Pennsylvania to find out if their house was there. It really was a successful program. Eventually a company came in and reproduced the video and distributed it through Blockbuster.

When Floyd was heading our way, we started getting calls from some state departments, and a call from the federal people, saying, "Hey, look, are you going to go out and shoot footage if we have any big damage?" And of course, we said, "Yeah, we'll be glad to." We usually wait until the storm is over, but we try to get into it as quick as we can.

So the storm hit that night, or early morning hours, and the water started coming in and just continually got worse. That afternoon, Colonel Holden gave me a call and said, "If we can get a 'copter, and one of our guys can get out, I want to start looking at the roads." By then, we were getting reports of massive flooding on the interstate sections. I was packed and ready to go with the camera equipment and everything. Terry Carlyle was our pilot. The colonel said we need to go check traffic, particularly on I-40, down near the Pender County area where this rescue eventually happened.

So we left that afternoon about two o'clock or so. Terry was flying, the colonel was sitting up front, and I was in the back with the camera equipment. Early on, we started seeing damage. A lot of these hog lagoons, you could see where they had come up to the top, and started to spill over, and things like that. And as we continued down I-40, we started noticing that there were patches of water here and there. We felt sorry for the DOT. They were working hectically trying to get these areas blocked as much as they could with barricades. But there were so many areas it was tough. They literally ran out of barricades. They were trying to do anything they could to try and keep people from going through these water areas.

So as we got down I-40, heading east, what really caught our attention was, Terry and the colonel said, "I can't believe it. These people are literally trying to drive through this water." And you could see this water was up on their doors and up to their windows. And they kept driving through it. Our reaction, of course, was, "Man, we've got to get that barricaded off, 'cause somebody's gonna get hurt." Well no longer had that been said when Terry said, "Uh-oh. We got a problem." He had noticed that there was a van coming through, and all of a sudden this van just literally floated off the side, onto the shoulder of the road. Well, if you know anything about I-40 down through there, you know there are embankments that go down maybe six or seven feet. They're like gullies or whatever. And this van had floated down into one of these gullies. Well, when you add about five or six feet of water to what's on the highway, then you've got about a twelve-foot-deep embankment of water. And we watched this van float right in it.

So the first thing Terry said was, "Well, we need to land to see if we can help this guy." Other citizens had gotten out of their cars and run, but they couldn't do anything. So Terry landed as close as he could to the water. The colonel called for assistance. Terry and I jumped out of the 'copter and ran into the water toward the van. We were still on the road, but we were running through knee- to hip-deep water. Terry and I felt like it was just one of those things you do. It was the right thing to do to try to help. And that's what we get paid for.

We had noticed when we got there that there was a young man that was literally standing on top of the van. The van had already sunk, submerged under the water, and he was kind of hanging on to a tree. He was trying to keep himself from being pushed away into the water. I think it was Mr. Wilde, the young man that was there. He had made an attempt to help this guy. He was definitely trying to do what was right also. But we could see that he had gotten to the point where he was having problems.

I saw a power truck that just happened to come by about that time, and I grabbed a rope from it and put it on Terry. Terry had been in the Coast Guard. So he had some experience with swimming and stuff like that. I had done the same thing. I was on the swim team when I was in high school, and I was a pretty strong swimmer. Plus the adrenaline was pumping. You know how that is—when the adrenaline is pumping, you do things sometimes that you just don't think you can do. And you know that seconds count. With my background in EMS, I knew that if we could get the guy out, that there's always a chance that we could save him with CPR.

So Terry went over first and I stayed to secure the line. As he got there and began to try to give assistance to Mr. Wilde, I noticed that Wilde was just a little bit frantic. I guess I got worried that he might take Terry under or something. We had a bunch of people there, so I told them, "You hold the end of this, and I'm going across." Terry had already made a couple of dives, and the current was terrible. He had gone down to the van, and actually tried to break the window. He thought he had broken it out. He was using something to beat against it and had made several attempts to do that, when all of sudden he said, "I think there's an opening there. Either the window's down on the side, or it's broken, or something."

It was a terrible current. The water was just polluted, and there was all kinds of debris, and water coming out of these lagoons, it was bad. There were snakes that had come by. It was just bringing everything to the top.

So the first thing Terry did was got Mr. Wilde secured, and everything was fine with him. He had made a couple attempts at the van, and then it was my turn. I made a couple of dives to get into the van, to try to get the man out. The bad thing about it was that nobody knew how many people were in the van. We didn't know whether it was a man with his wife sitting there in the passenger side with three kids in the back, or just the one man. And all I could think was, "Oh, golly, we've got a whole family in this thing." You know, the worst things pop up in your mind.

So I made a couple of attempts, and I could feel the guy's arm. I could get his arm, but I could not get in there to the seatbelt, 'cause seatbelts are always on the far side. And I couldn't get the door open because of the force of the water. We had tried to do that and couldn't. The bad thing was I kept losing my grip and started drifting away because of the current. The current was just so strong. So we must have worked, Terry and I both, for probably thirty minutes or so. But it seemed like hours. We literally almost exhausted ourselves.

By that time the colonel had really become concerned about us. We were about beat — Terry and I both were. We were also concerned about Mr. Wilde. Because here he is holding on to this tree, and he's been out here longer than we have. He's got a rope secured and he's okay. So the colonel yelled to us to come on out of the water. We didn't have the equipment. By then, the van driver had been under thirty minutes or so. With great hesitancy, we got out. Terry and I both were, I know, thinking the same thing. I can't believe we're this close.

And the thing that haunts me about this is that if I hadn't felt his arm, I wouldn't have felt so bad about this. But I felt his arm. And when you feel a guy's arm, you feel like, "Okay, I've got some control of this situation. I can get this guy out." They do it on *Baywatch* and all these programs on TV all the time. They just pull the guy out, do CPR, and boom—we can pull this guy back to life. And man, it's just a happy conclusion. But it's not that way in reality. It's not that way at all. It was really tough for me, and I know it was tough for Terry.

So we got Mr. Wilde back over by rope with the help of some bystanders on the side of the road. He was a young guy anyway, and he was in good shape. And then Terry and I gradually came back.

It's just an empty feeling now. I guess it's like these sports guys who play a ballgame. You get to fourth down, time's running out, and you lose the Super Bowl. You just don't feel like you completed the project. You don't feel like you finished the game. It was a downer, I'm telling you.

So that's what happened. Terry and I had decided that it was probably about twelve to fourteen feet of water that we were in. Even the rescue guys, when they got there, would not go into it. They had their boats, and they had their equipment, but the divers didn't want to go into it because the current was so dangerous.

The next morning, we had a lot of calls from people who wanted to assist in any way they could. A sheriff's department out of South Carolina volunteered to come in and assist us in trying to get the van up. So we all met back around lunchtime the following day. The water was even deeper then. It had calmed, but it had spread more. From the point where we had landed our helicopter, it had probably spread another fifty yards. That evening, probably around six o'clock, they finally got a hookup on the van and brought it out of the water. I know it was around six o'clock, because all of the news stations were there doing live shots.

That day, after we came out of the water and sort of got ourselves together, we couldn't believe it, but people were still driving back and forth through this water. The colonel said, "We've got to stop this." We had a little island between these two areas of water. People had gotten to the island part and had gotten scared. Now they were surrounded by water. So I snagged a dump truck from one of the DOT guys that came by, and we literally loaded people in it. They left their cars there, and we loaded people on this dump truck and drove through the water to the high ground on the interstate. We secured a school bus from nearby and transferred them to a place where they could get lodging. And when we came back the next day, their cars were all completely submerged. I mean it was that bad. We probably transported about fifty people off that little island.

It was funny, 'cause they didn't want to leave their cars. We had to convince them: "Hey, listen, it's either your car or you. Now make your decision. We can fix your car, but I'm not leaving you here." So we loaded people—little old grandmothers, entire families—we literally lifted them up into the back of a dump truck to get them out of there.

People don't understand that twelve inches is enough water to float a full-size car. Literally take it off the road. When you add a current that's like a beach current, then you're just asking for trouble. And I think that's the main thing that people did not understand. We saw it so many times. People who thought they could get through an area, and when they got in the water they started to slip and slide, and they got scared, and when they got scared they lost it, and when they lost it, they lost their lives.

From this situation with Terry and myself grew the idea of swift-water rescue training. Just about a month ago, we had our first swift-water rescue school, where we didn't just train the Highway Patrol, but we also trained DOT, DMV, and emergency management people. And now, these guys have a fifty-foot rope with a buoy that they keep in their cars. Not all troopers, but just the team. We've started this training and would eventually like to have every car equipped and everybody trained.

I can't say enough about the DOT. These are guys that drove dump trucks into deep water to assist us and actually put themselves in harm's way. Yeah, they're heroes. Everybody in this thing is a hero. When I sit back and think, the real heroes are the people that are still living in trailers, that don't have homes. It's ruined their lives. They've lost their houses, and they've lost their whole life. Those are the real heroes in this thing. I'm not a hero. I get paid to serve the citizens of North Carolina. As Terry would probably tell you, we were doing what we are supposed to do.

[Authors' note: The van driver was Paul Buco of Wilmington. He was one of fifty-two fatalities recorded in North Carolina following Floyd. Terry Carlyle and Ed Maness were both recipients of the Governor's Award for Heroism.]

Annice Narcise

Annice Narcise is a longtime resident of Oak Island who has seen her share of hurricanes. Floyd was particularly tough on Narcise. It destroyed her newly renovated business and placed serious stresses on her health. But in the aftermath of the storm, she offers a refreshing perspective on what it takes to live at the edge of the sea. She was interviewed by telephone in July 2002.

I've been coming to the island since 1963. I went through Diana, Fran, Bonnie, and Floyd. The restaurant, Whale of a Time, was an old arcade building that I had completely renovated. It's in the old Yaupon Beach. We had just opened up in the middle part of August. I had completely renovated the building, built the restaurant, and redid the game room. It's kind of an Art Deco place. It's all stainless steel and copper, kind of an ultramodern place. We serve full-course meals and sandwiches. We have a bar and an outdoor deck that's a hundred and twenty feet long. And we have a Tiki bar out there. I restuccoed and everything. We had a restaurant on the ocean side of it, the game room was in the back, and the kitchen was in the middle. There was a putt-putt adjacent to it, and I owned that as well. I also have a motel down here, but we didn't have any damage at the motel.

When the storm came in, or the eye hit, the water came up and all these boulders broke through the front windows. There were also these big metal railroad ties or something that went through one of the windows. We had about a foot of water inside. But when I got there, it was not water, it was all muck. We had about a foot of this garbage, sand, and muck. The sand and the boulders also covered the putt-putt.

In the 1970s, these boulders were permitted by the state to reinforce our dunes along the beach where erosion was happening. When the water got up during Floyd, the boulders just washed in. They were all along the property line, actually, between the pier and us. And it moved all of them. The water was so high that it raised the boulders up and they washed through the windows and broke the windows. They were mostly big slabs of concrete and debris that had been put out there over the years to protect us from erosion. The tide was up, so that made all the concrete and debris float up, I guess.

It ruined all the equipment, the freezers and everything. We had water in everything, up a foot off the floor. All the barstools got slammed around and everything, moved by the water. All of the equipment was pushed to the rear of the building. Even in the game room, the equipment in there was all washed

into a big pile. You know, I'd say it was a hundred and fifty thousand [dollars] easily.

I stayed on the island during the storm. I wasn't too surprised at the extent of the damage. Actually, I thought it would be worse. I'm lucky to have a building. And I think what saved it was that it did break the glass, and the pressure didn't build up on the outside of the building. After the storm, we used a Bobcat to scrape everything out. And then we refurbished again. We had to replace everything that was damaged and redo it again. We had to repair and get new condensers and compressors for the equipment. I did not have flood insurance.

Well, you know, you just go with the flow. I've never been one to dwell on the negative. If it happens, you just move forward, clean up, and go on. I think maybe I'm one of the few that looked at it that way. I say let's move ahead. It don't pay to look back.

It took a couple months to build it back again. What was so bad was they wanted to take out the electric meter. They did take it out, and I made them put it back. We never did lose our power. The electric company came around, and the city asked them to take out all the meters. I insisted they not take ours out. So that kind of helped me move faster in getting the repairs done. Within a couple of months, we were able to open back up again. I'm a mover. Like I said, I didn't cry over spilt milk. You just move forward, you know?

At first, a lot of the damaged houses down here were condemned. But a lot of them hung in there and didn't accept it. Then eventually they were able to repair. Supposedly, if it's damaged more than fifty percent, it's condemned. But who's to judge fifty percent of the value, you know? The city was adamant about condemning them, but when some people started fighting them, then they had to let loose.

Once I rebuilt everything, I still didn't get flood insurance. Flood insurance was just so outrageous that I just felt like I'd take my chances. They wanted a hundred and twenty thousand a year just for flood insurance. You take your risk. If you figure you let it go by four years, you've got your money right there.

As I said, I don't dwell on the negative. I'm on radiation and chemo. I was diagnosed with cancer after Floyd. And I had a heart attack during this, too. I had just finished the renovations that summer, had the heart attack in August, and then got the hurricane in September. But I discharged myself from the hospital in three days and went back to work.

These are the risks you take when you're on the ocean. We're fortunate they don't happen every year. You knew you were subject to it, so don't go to the ocean and cry and worry. It's part of the environment. You know about these risks when you go there. When you get hit with them, it don't pay to feel sorry for yourself. What does it gain you? You have no business on the ocean if you're not ready for these things. And that goes for anyone, whether it's a house or a business. It's part of the risk. So it shouldn't surprise anyone when it happens.

Charlotte Webb

Charlotte Webb played a key role in helping flood victims rebuild their lives—especially in the area near her Tarboro home. As the Hurricane Floyd program manager for Habitat for Humanity, she helped coordinate countless volunteers and helped many displaced families find new places to live. She was interviewed in Pine Knoll Shores in July 2002.

This job has turned out to be so cool. I get to do good things, and I believe in Habitat's mission. I believe that everyone should have a house to live in, a safe and decent house. When I first started there in Tarboro, they had built two-and-a-half houses in three years. It was pretty much a hobby. I came on board

In Princeville, homes floated up off their foundations and came to rest in odd places. (Photo by David Weaver; courtesy of the *Rocky Mount Telegram*)

and then made a commitment to build twelve houses in response to the hurricane. Twelve in one year then was a big deal. Sometime during the summer, my boss recognized there were several affiliates that had flooding to their actual Habitat houses. We came up with a plan. I became the Hurricane Floyd program manager.

I began working with fourteen affiliates that had flood damage. The state had a program called repair and replacement. If your house was repairable, it would be repaired. If it was not, the state would provide a grant, up to seventy-five thousand dollars, to replace your house. But you had to be a homeowner within the low-income guidelines. They were pretty much the same income standards that Habitat has. Except what we would do is, we would build two houses for the cost of one. We would build one replacement house, and then with the additional money, build a second one. With our volunteer labor, we could build a second Habitat house for someone who was displaced. We were able to help a lot of people that, for whatever reason, were kinda left out in the cold. So that's pretty much what I've been working on in the past two years.

North Carolina goes back and forth between first and second position along with Michigan for having the most Habitat affiliates. Of the fourteen affiliates in North Carolina, seven had flooding to their own houses. So the first goal immediately after the flood was to repair those houses, and each affiliate did that at no cost to the homeowner. They took that burden upon themselves.

I remember right after the flood, sometime that Friday or Saturday I guess, there was only one grocery store in town that was open. The store owners lived across the street from my parents, so I had known them a long time. While we were in the store, the power went out. Everybody has carts of groceries, and the power's not coming back on. So we ran back to the house, grabbed some calculators, and I ended up working at the grocery store all afternoon, checking people out and helping them get their stuff. The National Guard came in and got baby supplies, 'cause they didn't have any. We would write down whatever they were getting and check them out. We stayed there until it got dark.

I remember at first there was a good smell 'cause everybody was grilling out. By that time the river had really come up into all the streets in Tarboro. There was a retirement facility right by the river, and they had to evacuate down there.

I live close to the high school. We had helicopters that were coming and going, flying really low. It was like a MASH unit. You know, you see all those episodes of *M*A*S*H* where they're taking cover. When it really happens to you, and your window shakes, and you see the high school parking lot full, and the football field full, and people living out of the backs of cars, it's just heartbreaking. I never thought that I would have lived to see that.

Little by little, it started getting better. You learned how to take a shower without running water. You learn the things that you take for granted. Flushing a toilet. Brushing your teeth. Some people say they would rather have water than power, and that's true. I can live without power a lot better than I can without water.

That first summer after the flood, I knew if we were gonna build twelve houses, we'd have to have volunteers. We can't do it all with just a few retired people, and I don't mean that negatively. So we started recruiting volunteers. It wasn't a very difficult task, because everybody was so compassionate. "We want to come down, we want to help flood victims, whatever we can do." It was just making sure that we had somebody who could supervise and work with the volunteers on the site. We had a lot of groups we hadn't planned on. We had a group whose job got canceled in Rocky Mount, and I told them to come on down—not realizing there were sixty-five of them. And when you have sixty-five high school kids working on a house and they don't know what they're doing, with three volunteers who really aren't ready for that pace, it's a task. But we got it done.

I remember this one group, they wanted to see some of the flooded areas. At that time, there were still a lot of buildings there, and you could see the flood lines on the walls. You could walk in them and see all the mud. We went in an old apartment, and to walk in and to see the mud, and to see the clothes still laid out on the bed—I mean everybody was just crying. They kept telling me, "We saw it on TV, but we didn't realize it was this bad." It was just like it was when the people left. The clothes were still there, their trophies were on the mantel—I think it had a very big impact on those kids. You know you've got mud six feet on a wall, and I guess they didn't realize the devastation that water really causes. And I think a lot of people didn't. I know I didn't.

These groups were amazing. They just put everything they have into it. For a lot of them, this is their summer vacation. This is the third year that St. Andrews Church has been down. They get down here and have a schedule laid out and plan to take Wednesday or Thursday off. By the time Wednesday gets here, they don't want to take their day off. They want to keep working. They are so happy with what they're doing. They get to meet the homeowners. They listened to the stories of what the homeowners were going through. The homeowners came out and worked with them, and they didn't want to stop. They wanted to get as much of that house done before they leave as possible.

Emotions are running high all the time. For example, they ran into somebody in WalMart—a lady with five children and no air conditioning—and they took their own personal money and bought fans to put in the lady's house. They're so giving. And it's nice to see that in young people. You don't see that every day. We've had a lot of groups come down like that.

We've had a lot of Mennonites from the Pennsylvania area, and Ohio, Virginia, West Virginia, and this group from Dover, Delaware, and some from California. We've had local groups from Durham, Raleigh, and Charlotte. UNC med students have come down and spent their week of community time helping Habitat. I mean, we've had a lot of North Carolina people come in. And there's probably a lot that I don't know where they've come from.

We did a big project in Princeville, and that was when I moved from Tarboro Habitat into this job. FEMA came over and wanted to know why that particular area didn't have a project. They didn't have a reason. But a lot of people knew that the bridge that separates Tarboro from Princeville separates a lot more than just the water. It separates the people, and it's always been that way for as long as I can remember. Habitat doesn't accept government money to build houses. But by this point, Lowe's had come into the picture and wanted to donate a million dollars to Princeville. The town manager wanted part of that to go to Habitat. We finally got an arrangement together to get started.

The town bought a five-acre tract of land, and we were going to do twelve houses in twelve days. That was the intent. But the date kept getting pushed back. There were a lot of groups that stuck by us, though. The Mennonites and the Methodists were working in Princeville, and we all pulled together and got our foundations in. The Mennonites came in the day after Christmas and got our houses framed. In two-and-a-half days, they framed twelve houses and had trusses on ten of them. The Department of Corrections had prefabbed the wall panels, so that sped things up a lot. Westminster Presbyterian Church in Durham has a group called the Geezers, and they came in and helped get our floor system in. They work a lot with Durham Habitat. So many different groups had to pull together. The Mennonites were especially amazing to me because I thought these men all knew each other. That was just my perception. I came to find out some were from Pennsylvania, some were from Ohio, or wherever. But they just came together, looked at the house plans, and went to work. So now I know how their true barn-raising works. I mean, they don't need to know each other. That was pretty cool.

So we did it. Within twelve days we had all of the houses dried in, and siding on a majority of them. I was pleased with that. And then twelve families moved in at the beginning of May. Lowe's donated all the materials and sort of went above and beyond what you would see with a normal Habitat house. We had nice little street lamps at every house. They just gave and gave and gave to the homeowners. When we did our dedication, they came out with this huge basket of tools that they would need around the house, like screwdrivers, hammers, pliers, and hundred-dollar gift cards to Lowe's.

Even though Floyd was a bad thing, it's done a lot of good. It's brought a lot of people together that you wouldn't have seen come together. There are volunteer groups that keep coming. They know it's going to take five or ten years, and they still keep coming. Lowe's didn't have to do what they did. But they did. The churches that come in and give money don't have to. St. Andrews youth group gave the Goldsboro affiliate fifteen hundred dollars as a donation, and they didn't have to. They could have gone to camp where they could have just had fun and played the whole week. But instead they work hard. The state didn't have to provide the programs that they set up. But they did. I mean, it lets you know how much people care.

Habitat builds partnerships with communities, families, churches, businesses, or whatever. The homeowners are my favorite part of Habitat. I have an extended family now, especially with the project in Princeville. They will come up and visit me. My mom and I always do a lot of baking around Christmas, and this past Christmas we baked twelve extra of everything. We made these plates and we went over there and were glad they were in their homes. They were so excited. One of the ladies came up to me and hugged me and began telling me about her girls unwrapping their presents under the tree. I asked what her girls had gotten her for Christmas, and she said, "I don't know and it really doesn't matter. This is my Christmas present—my house. It's mine, and you helped me get it. And this is the best present I could ever have." And I just stood right there in her living room and cried.

J. C. Heath is a marvel of country wisdom, honesty, and courage. After water flooded his Snow Hill home into the second floor, the seventy-two-year-old patiently took his house apart, cleaned it, and put it back together. Most of the work he did himself. He was interviewed at the Greene County Administrative Building in August 2002.

J. C. Heath

I've lived in Greene County off and on all my life. My home is one mile northwest of Snow Hill.

I built my house up as high as I thought the water would ever be. And according to what old folks had told me about the water levels, it was about level with that I guess. When the water begun to come up, I saw I was in trouble. So I got me some help, and I got some cement blocks and I blocked up everything in the house. Three foot probably, about. The refrigerator, the stove, washing machine, the piano—everything I could raise, I raised up. And anything I couldn't raise up that I could tote upstairs, I carried upstairs. About dinnertime, the water was already in the house about two feet deep. I had blocked my stuff up, and I came back and blocked it again. I'd add a block, and thought it won't never get that high. So it kept rising, and about middle of the evening, I guess, I told my wife to just leave and go on over to my daughter's house. I'd stay the night and come over the next day and get her.

After she left, I took a ladder and put it up over against the house. I tied up

Greene County farmer Bobby Nimmo helped rescue many flood victims on Beaman–Old Creek Road in Snow Hill. He also used a boat to get the payroll to his migrant employees so they could buy groceries in Farmville. (Photo by Donna Hardy; courtesy of the *Kinston Free Press*)

my boy's boat to the end of the house. The boat stayed at my house all the time, an aluminum boat about twelve foot. The water kept rising, and I kept waiting for it to quit. I stayed there until about nine-thirty or ten o'clock, I reckon. I saw it wasn't gonna quit rising, so I decided I would leave. I went upstairs, come down the ladder, got in the boat, and paddled over to my higher ground.

I put the car on the hill, 'cause I knowed it wouldn't never get up there. And I told my wife, just leave the car and I'll come back and get that tomorrow. About ten o'clock that night, and the water was still rising, and I went ahead and left. The water was about four foot deep in the house.

I put my car on the hill and made arrangements to come back and get it. Well, when I come back the next day, the water was up to the dash. It wouldn't crank, it wouldn't do nothing but sit there. I had carried the truck out when I went, naturally, but when I come back I couldn't even get in there to it. So my son-in-law had a boat, and we had to put the boat in over on the highway to get back in the house. The only way back into the house was through the upstairs window. The water was up in the second floor before it was all over with.

We hauled out what we could. We hauled three or four boatloads of furniture across that water, and put it in his house and a barn. I went back to get something out of the house, and I run the boat up on the back porch. I reached over to hold on to something on the wall to balance myself and pull my boat over to the porch, when it pulled off the wall and I fell out of the boat. I just got wet from here down, my head didn't go down, I just come up quick. I reckon I'm the only fellow you've ever seen that fell out of a boat on his back porch.

I think it was probably about two weeks before I could get back in the house to do anything. In fact there was water in the house for two weeks.

So it got redone and I moved it up the hill. At that level it was probably ten feet higher than it was before. I moved it I reckon about seventy-five or a hundred feet. I done most of the work myself. I got house movers to move the house over, and he just jacked it up and left it. I had to tear out all the downstairs floors and walls, but the upstairs floor I didn't take out. My daughter and her husband helped a little bit, and my boy helped me, but they had to work and I done what I could myself. I lost a refrigerator, a washing machine, a dryer, and a piano.

I didn't have any flood insurance. FEMA offered to buy it but I told them it wasn't for sale. I didn't like the offer. And what they told me was if they bought it, and I took a place that they bought, that I would have to stay in it five years. Ain't nobody gonna lock me up for five years and say you got to stay there unless it was a jailhouse. I just don't like some payment that someone's trying to force on you. I'd rather have nothing than to start over.

Now a group of people offered to build me a house. It wouldn't cost me a cent. I believe they call themselves Interfaith Ministries. It wouldn't have cost me nothing, just move in. But I built mine back. I fixed mine back. The people were really nice about it, but I guess that's just not my way of doing. And these were people from Pennsylvania. They kept coming down and telling me that they'd fix the house and all I had to do was just get the stuff and they'd fix it. I said, "No, go help somebody else. I can work on mine right now, but some people need help. Go help them."

I tore out the floors and the walls, and I put right near forty gallons of Clorox in it. I sprayed the walls with a power-washer with Clorox feeding into it, and I had a hand sprayer that I just sprayed straight Clorox on the walls. I went over the whole bottom part of the house. It changed the looks of the walls some, but it didn't hurt anything. I left the floors out and the windows and doors out for a good while so they would dry. After they got dried out, I put Clorox on them and still left them sitting for a while. I wasn't gonna fix it 'til I was satisfied it was all right. Some of the electrical upstairs I didn't have to redo, but everything downstairs had to be redone. I just moved back in it between Thanksgiving and Christmas of this past year.

It probably cost me thirty to forty thousand, but another house would have cost me twice that. But I've still got an old house. It's a good solid house and it ain't going nowhere. The house actually tried to float, but the chimney is so heavy that it couldn't. It cracked the foundation where it was floating up off of it. But the chimney's so heavy it couldn't go nowhere.

The highest water around here that anybody had ever knowed anything about was around 1927, I think. My daddy lived in this neighborhood most of his life, and he said he had never seen the water no higher than the floor of my house. It's been up close to my house level probably a couple of times, but that was before the house was built. My daddy was born in 1892. Of course, he was dead when this flood come, but he hadn't never seen the water no higher than what he showed me before.

There's lots of reasons this thing happened. There's too many big parking lots and highways. Everybody's paving and putting concrete on everything, and building houses, and the water's got nowhere to go but to run off. These roads right out here ain't got enough bridge space for the water to get out. Them bridges out there ought to be four times as long as they are. And I think Raleigh turned us too much water. The Neuse River couldn't drain out, and Contentnea Creek couldn't drain out, and it just backed right up. It comes from up around Wilson.

The water was about eight feet deep in the house. I was the lowest house on that road. My neighbor across the road had sixteen inches in her house. There was three houses across the street that had about three feet in them. They fixed them back and lived in them about a year and then give them up. I think the government promised them something. They tore them down and moved them out.

A lot of other folks around here had about the same problems I did. Some of them left in the middle of the night. The woman that's across the road from me, she left in the middle of the night. There was about a ten-thousand-gallon tank that floated through her yard and ended up in a ditch and got hung up in some bushes.

FEMA bought me a little old trailer, about as long as this room, and I told them to come get it. I said I can't live in that thing. I just can't live in nothing that little. I went over to my daughter's house and stayed about two or three weeks. Then I lived over here in Snow Hill in an upstairs apartment that belonged to my sister's husband. I stayed there until I got me a trailer set up out there. I went and bought me a trailer, fixed it up, and set it up out there so I could work on my house when I wanted to.

I bought everything except some SB board. The Interfaith Ministries said they had some in a warehouse, and if I could go get it, I could have it. They were good people. They offered a lot more than I took. They're still around, because I see in the paper every once in a while that they're doing something. The insurance company replaced my car 'cause I had just bought it.

This whole thing's affected my wife more than it has me, because for me it's over. I mean it's over as far as I'm concerned. I don't know if she'll ever completely get over it. It ain't bothering her all that much, but she thinks about it more than I do.

Most of the photos and personal things I had moved upstairs. I had an old clock that was sitting on the mantel and I forgot to move it upstairs. When I come back it had fell all to pieces. It was put together with glue, and was probably eighty years old or more. That glue come apart and it just fell right down to the bottom. And the piano fell all to pieces. You couldn't even pick up the piano to move it, it just fell all apart. The piano was sitting up on those blocks, and as heavy as it was, how did it fall over? Only thing I can figure is the refrigerator floated by and knocked it off.

When I got back out of the boat and looked through my windows, you could see my refrigerator floating around in my living room. It had done come out of the kitchen and through the dining room and was in the living room. I don't know if it knocked that piano off or not.

That water was a stinking mess. I don't know what all was in it. At Wilson and Stantonsburg, the sewer systems all backed up and that came through. All the farm chemicals between here and Wilson came through. There's trees that have died around my house. I don't know what that mess was, but it's killed some of the trees.

When we have a disaster like this, for some people I think it does them a little good. It makes them realize things they didn't realize before. They realize that everybody gets in a bind once in a while. But the people that tried come out all right.

A strange thing happened, though. I had a watch. My daddy's watch. It was laying on the mantelpiece, and I had set a lamp over it. An old kerosene lamp. When that water rose, I forgot it. I told my wife it will never make it. But I went back and got it, picked it up and wound it up, and it never missed a beat. It was underwater in an air bubble under that lamp. I wouldn't never believe it, but not one drop of water got in that watch. And if I tell you anything, you can count on it.

David Cummiskey   Gunnery Sergeant David Cummiskey is a rescue swimmer for the U.S. Marine Corps based at Cherry Point. He's trained to save lives at sea by descending from a hovering PEDRO helicopter. But inland airborne rescue efforts during Hurricane Floyd presented unique challenges to rescuers like Cummiskey. He was interviewed in Pine Knoll Shores in August 2002.

I've been in the Marine Corps seventeen years and a rescue swimmer on PEDRO since 1995. I've had fifty-four lifesaving missions since I started swimming. I'm the Marine Corps evaluator and model manager for search and rescue. I inspect all the Marine Corps units and their rescue swimmers.

I've heard a lot of different things about what PEDRO stands for. I've always heard that it was the international call sign for a search-and-rescue helicopter. Friend. That's my answer when people ask, anyway. Some use ANGEL, others use PEDRO. We have three choppers that fly out of Cherry Point. One's usually in maintenance, one's standing ready for duty, and one is for backup.

As Floyd was approaching, there were a lot of conversations about flying the aircraft away from Cherry Point due to the force of the winds. We weren't sure if the hangars would be able to take it. But finally the decision was made to stay.

On the sixteenth, the first crew launched around noon. A crew of five went

Marine rescue helicopter PEDRO airlifts a desperate trucker from the cab of his rig after floodwaters covered both lanes of I-95 in Nash County. (Photo by Chuck Liddy; courtesy of the *Raleigh News and Observer*)

out—two pilots, a crew chief, a rescue swimmer, and a corpsman. They were out for about ten-and-a-half hours and were just nonstop picking people up. Communications were not good in these areas we were going to, and all the power was out. Everything was completely underwater. There were command and control centers at Greenville, Tarboro, and Roanoke Rapids. We would stop at these to get updated information.

We carried a state trooper with us the first night that I went out. He had a lot of information. We had communications with the command centers, and they would dispatch us where we were needed. We would have people on a rooftop over here, or people in a church over there, or reports of a man screaming and nobody knows for sure where he is.

My crew came in at eleven o'clock that night as the first crew was coming back in. We heard stories of their rescues, and they were really impressive. The magnitude of the flood was impressive, too. At Cherry Point we were like an island. We couldn't see what was really going on at Tarboro, or Conetoe, or Vanceboro, or some of the other areas. So we went out, flying with a new crew of five, with night-vision goggles. We flew on to the command center on Highway 64.

The first one we came to was a family of four on top of a mobile home, where the water was at the rooftop. This was up near Tarboro. I was lowered down by the rescue hoist and put a mother and daughter in the basket together. They went up, followed by the father and daughter. There was a whole trailer park, and it seemed like there was a family of four on top of every trailer. So we just went all through the park and brought them all up. People were trying to bring their possessions with them. We took what we could, but when somebody tried to grab a computer, we told them maybe that's not what's important here. We picked up about sixteen people and flew them back to the command center.

We kept getting calls over the radio that a voice had been heard from someone in distress. We went over there and flew around and around. We had the night sun on at this time, which is a thirty-million-candlepower light that pretty much turns nighttime into daytime. We were wearing our night-vision goggles, too, but we're not seeing anything. So I said, "Land me, and the trooper and I will walk up to the overpass where they say people hear him. I'll take a radio and call you in to where we think the voice is coming from."

As I understand it, when he tried to cross the overpass, his car got washed away. They saw him get out of the car, and that was the last they saw of him.

He was a young man, maybe twenty-six years old. We went up there, and you could hear somebody. We tried hollering back, kept zeroing in on him, and finally we found him. I called in the night sun on him. They marked him with their GPS, came back and picked me up, and we went back for him. There were high treetops and a narrow area that used to be a road. It was now a raging river, just like rapids. Our pilot got between the treelines as best he could so the rotors wouldn't hit the trees. Then the crew chief lowered me down, and I saw this guy just holding on to a tree. I asked him if he could let go and come on out here, and he said he wouldn't let go. It was probably a good call on his part not to let go, 'cause the water was moving pretty fast. I grabbed a tree branch and started walking myself over to him. I stayed attached to my line, in case something happened they could pull me up.

I got really close to him and the branch breaks. The next thing you know, I'm about fifty yards down the river. So I'm waving my light, and the crew chief immediately pulled me back up to the helicopter. He said, "Well, what are we going to try now?" I said, "Let me catch my breath, and this time I'll try to swim, instead of trying to climb to him on a branch." He dropped me as close as he could, and I just swam to him against the current and got a-hold of him. I put the horse collar around him. He had no problem letting go of the tree then. We pulled him up and took him immediately to the command center because he had hypothermic conditions. He'd been in that water for eight hours.

At that time, we were probably in about a seventy-foot hover. When we train, we usually do it at fifty foot. We could go closer in a freshwater environment, but in a saltwater environment you don't want to hover too low for too long, 'cause you'll get salt water in your engines. But the trees were the problem here, and that's why he couldn't just get me over there. The cable would have gotten wrapped up in the trees.

He was thanking everybody and shaking their hands. We got blankets over him to warm him up. He was mighty glad to be on board. We didn't really have time to exchange names or anything, but he was obviously thankful. We dropped him off, and the trooper took him to get some first aid.

Then we went off to a report of somebody waving a lit rag out the window of a house, signaling for help. When we got there, there's this guy on the second story with a t-shirt on fire and he's waving it. We hovered over the house, I got down on the roof, staying connected, and I just kind of slid down and asked him, "Hey, what's going on here?" He said there were twelve people in the house—elderly people and children. The water was already above the first floor, and halfway up the steps. So everybody's upstairs. So I was like, "Wow, what are we going to do?"

We decided it would be best if I went down and came through the first floor, where you could still breathe if you held your head up. I'll bring them out the front door and put as many people as I can in a basket. It's more controlled. It's just a safer way to get them out of the house. Some of these elderly people were still on the first floor, in the kitchen in the back in chest-deep water. Some were on the steps, and I just swam them out the front door. We were just basically treading water. It was maybe three in the morning by that time. And some way and somehow, we got twenty-six people on that helicopter. It was probably more than we're supposed to have, but we got them all on there.

We always set a fuel limit, and it got to the point where we had to head back for fuel. We had to go to the Rocky Mount airport. Once you topped off the fuel, you had about three hours until you needed to get gas again. After we got fuel, we went back to get two men that we had to leave behind. We had to leave them because we were low on fuel, and we were just packed. So it was just one after another, picking people up and getting them out of there.

Loading these elderly people in these baskets and lifting them up, they were just petrified. I think they were just in shock for the most part. And that goes for everybody. Everything was just destroyed. You'd see everything floating by you.

The first day was just constantly people in distress. Fear of drowning. Homes destroyed. The second night people were saying, "We're going to stay; we're going to wait it out." And we're trying to explain to them that we might not have a chance to come back and this is your opportunity to leave. Well, some would come with us, and some wouldn't.

During Floyd, in three days, we probably took on board a hundred eighty people in my helicopter. All the PEDRO crews got three hundred ninety-nine people. And that's not counting the animals that were brought on board. There was a ferret, dogs, cats, birds—there were some peculiar animals. We had three nights of missions, and the water was rising the whole time. By the second day the rain had stopped for the most part, but the water was still cresting.

Sometimes as we're heading back, you look down and still see people that need to get out, and that's the hardest part. It's an awful feeling to fly over and know that you can only put so many people on.

There were lots of hazards. When we were hoisting from the housetops, we were only like ten feet above them, and there were obstacles like telephone poles and electric wires. Since the power's out, there's no frame of reference on the ground—just flashlights that people may have had or fires they may have started. But those were few and far between.

Most all of the people rescued were on roofs. There were some who came out of trees or off of cars, but mine were mostly roofs. There was the trucker who was lifted from his rig up in Rocky Mount. We also had one of our aircraft whose hoist failed while they were out on a mission. So what they did was they rigged up some ropes and rappeled their corpsman down so he could hook up to them. Then they lifted them up in a hover and did what we call a short haul to a dry area.

There were a lot of babies. Normally I'd just put two in the basket, a mother and a baby, or a father and a baby. We tried not to send children up alone. It's just not comfortable to be lifted up in the air to a helicopter, especially in the middle of the night. And the chopper is really loud, and we don't have enough hearing protection for everyone. So they're flying, they're scared, they're cold, they're wet, the helicopter's loud—but many were just thanking the Lord that they're alive. And they knew they were going to be taken care of.

We got a letter from a mother and a son in Greenville, and they were so touched by what the rescue swimmers did for them that the son joined the Navy to become a rescue swimmer. We thought maybe we should tell him that we're Marines, but it doesn't matter. We go to the same school. But that was pretty impressive, and quite a compliment to us.

Those three days kind of blend together. The third day was mostly delivering supplies. We took a guy in a wheelchair, and that was kind of interesting. That was by Conetoe. The first flights were in Tarboro, Princeville, and the Rocky Mount area. Greenville was completely underwater. There were dead animals and the likes everywhere. Pigs, cows, snakes in the water—you had to just kind of block that out. We had a real bird's-eye view on the whole thing.

About half the people we pulled up were people that we were called to. The rest were people that we just saw and went in to get. I mean we'd get a call, and then we'd see so many others. You just couldn't help it. You had to get them. They would wave a flashlight or start a fire. People don't realize how just a spark can be seen with those night-vision goggles. We could find them better at night than during the day if they had a light. We had people getting picked up with nothing but Bic lighters.

We were recognized very well for what we did. I've been in the spotlight because of it, but if it wasn't for my crew chief being able to put me right where I need to be, and the pilots who keep that helicopter in a perfect hover, then it wouldn't happen. It's a team. It's everybody. None of us could have rescued one person without the whole team.

We had twenty-six of our air crewmen recognized with the Air Medal for their heroic actions during Floyd. And four of us received the Navy Marine Corps Medal, which is the highest award you can receive for heroism in peacetime.

This is the greatest job in the world. I love it. I actually look forward to going to work. All my swimmers do. They want to go out. They don't want anybody to ever be put in harm's way, but if somebody is, they want to be the one that's on when it happens. It's very rewarding work.

Ken Mullen   Ken Mullen is chief of the Rocky Mount Fire Department. He and his crews had prepared for Hurricane Floyd, but they could never have anticipated the dramatic flooding that swept their city or the overwhelming number of calls for help they received. With great creativity and courage, the city's firefighters rescued countless people trapped by the flood. Chief Mullen was interviewed at his Rocky Mount headquarters in June 2002.

I've lived here in Rocky Mount all my life, and I've been with the fire department twenty-eight years. I was promoted in September 1998, so at the time of the hurricane I had been chief for about a year. We had no idea it was going to be like it was. We had developed an emergency response plan for our city, with what each department would be responsible to do. We felt real good about how well we were prepared. But we'd never seen anything like this before.

Fran was pretty much a wind event. We had some rain, and then we had flooding here three days later. Our water actually comes from the Louisburg area, so it was about three days before we actually experienced any flooding. With Floyd, we were expecting some wind and then some flooding a few days later. We hadn't really had a lot of storm damage here from hurricanes since about Hazel.

We had people begin to call us around ten o'clock that night. We had everybody set up to come in at midnight. But our people, being the dedicated group

that they are, started coming in at eight and nine o'clock. That really turned out to be great, because we started running calls around ten o'clock or ten-thirty. We were going in places where we'd never seen any water before. I've been here all my life, and I've never seen flooding in some places where we were getting calls.

I think people began to get lulled into a sense that, "Well, I've never seen any water here before, so it can't get any higher." We had some flatbottom boats, but soon we knew that they were not going to be sufficient for our needs. We began to call our people that had experience with boats and outboard motors. They brought their boats in, and we dispatched them out with an engine company to go in these areas and get people out of trees, off of roofs, out of the second floor of their homes, or anywhere they could get.

We had one call of a lady hanging on a bridge over the river on Nashville Road. We also had calls from a subdivision called Westhaven. Those people

Chief Ken Mullen and the Rocky Mount Fire Department. (Photo by Jay Barnes)

said they had neighbors hanging in trees, some trapped on the second floor, and some going into the attics of their homes because the water was rising so fast. So we concentrated on that area first, and then went to the lady that was hanging on the bridge. We had an apartment complex called Riverside Apartments that was built back in the late forties, so everybody in town's familiar with it. We had some flooding up in that area before, but none ever got to the apartments. We began to get calls from people who swung their feet off their beds and landed in knee-deep water. That's how quick the water was rising, and again, in places we'd never seen it before.

We had guys that were very experienced in operating outboard motors telling us they were running sixty-horse motors wide open, and it was all they could do to stay against the current to get to somebody.

It was a very trying and difficult time. Our people were facing all kinds of problems that they'd never seen before. They were able to adapt and use what equipment they had. There were some really interesting stories of how they thought things out and used the equipment on the trucks and devised ways of getting to people that we'd never trained for. This was all occurring within a two- to three-hour time period. We were trying to move from one part of the city to another, but we were basically cut off. We had trucks leave stations, and when they left, they didn't go back. It was like a day and a half later before they went back to that station. The city was actually divided into about five different sections by old flooded creeks and by the river.

That morning, we had five or six feet of water in the river on our gauges. That night, if I'm not mistaken, we got to a height of thirty-one feet at our dam. And our dam is at least twenty-five feet, so it was six feet above the gates of the dam. There was just no way to anticipate that kind of water.

When we lost power, we lost our ability to talk to our citizens. We could get 911 calls, but what I'm talking about is getting information out to them. We lost our ability to communicate with them on cable TV, and rumors were flying rampant the next day. It was very difficult.

The police sometimes do what's called "stacking" calls. For example, a bank robbery is going to get priority over a stolen flowerpot. In the fire service we don't "stack" calls. If you make a call for the fire service, we go right now. During Floyd, we placed two of our employees in the dispatch center, which is something we don't normally do. We wanted to put some people in there who could make decisions and dispatch us into areas where we needed to go. That night, they came in and got me out of the EOC and said, "We need you to see something, 'cause we don't know what to do." When I walked in they told me they had eighty-seven calls stacked. And we had every piece of equipment in the city out on a call. These were eighty-seven people that needed rescue of some sort. They were having to put them in some kind of order and figure out where to go next. Do you go to the guy who's standing on top of his car and the water's rising, or do you go to the mother with three kids who has water in the first floor of her home? Those were the kinds of things we were faced with that we hadn't been faced with before.

We never stalled a truck out. We did have guys that said they could feel their truck moving with the current a little bit. We actually had a house fire in one of the flooded areas. We filled boats with hoses and breathing equipment and our guys kind of walked the stuff in. We put the fire out, but before they did, the water had risen around the truck to the point that it was about to float. Our guys actually pushed the truck back out until the wheels hooked up with the road again, then they backed it on out. All kinds of improvising took place in these incidents.

There was one group of guys that were in a vehicle, and it stalled on them. They got out and started to swim through the water. They got to a stand of trees and grabbed them and held on. They were just hanging there, when all of a sudden a Carolina fishing boat comes floating by. They grab it, get in the boat, and tie themselves to the tree. They were there probably eighteen to twenty hours before anybody ever saw them. I believe they were rescued by helicopter. Most of our stuff was done by boat. We used backhoes, front-end loaders, pontoon boats, anything we could get our hands on.

We've got nine people here in the fire department that lost their homes. And those guys continued to stay here and work. They'd go home and make sure their families were out, and then they'd come back, knowing that they were losing everything they had. We had guys out operating front-end loaders trying to get some people who were on top of cars, and everybody just pitched in. I do classify our people as heroes in public safety, but I think you've got to also look at what ordinary citizens and other city employees did. We obviously couldn't have done it by ourselves. Everybody pulled together. It was a time when you didn't see any turf battles. Our secretaries came in and worked our phone banks, and they didn't know anything about public safety. You should have heard some of their phone conversations with those people. A lot of people just wanted somebody to talk to. You heard a lot of "I'm scared to death here." I think I'd have to call them all heroes.

We only had three fatalities. But that's three too many. They were all people trying to drive through flooded areas. Two occurred on bridges. The other was a gentleman who had a house down in a rock quarry. His home was actually dug into the side of an old quarry. His family got out, but when he went back to try to get his vehicle, the creek overflowed into the quarry, washed the road out, and washed him right into the quarry.

One story that sticks in my head was this little old lady, about seventy-some years old, that was going to swim out. The guys were in a boat and saw her coming by and thought they recognized what it was—they thought it was a dog. So they reached down and grabbed her by the hair on her head and started pulling her up. She yelled something like, "Let me go, boy! I'm gonna swim out of here! Worry about those other people, I'm all right." She would duck under the water, swim about ten yards, come up for air, then she'd duck under again and swim some more. I guess she made it out just fine.

Hazel Sorrell   Hazel Sorrell is one of North Carolina's living treasures. This eighty-six-year-old mother of eight is founder of the Benson Children's Home and has been voted North Carolina Mother of the Year and Retired Educator of the Year. But perhaps her greatest challenge came when she moved to Wilson and established an interfaith group to help families cope with Hurricane Floyd. She was interviewed in her Atlantic Beach vacation home in August 2002.

My family moved to North Carolina when I was quite small. We moved around, but I graduated from high school in Coats. I was married, had eight children, and moved to Benson. I had Benson's first kindergarten and then taught public school for thirty-six years. I started the Benson Area Ministry after my husband passed away. We called it BAM. It's still operating today, providing food, clothes, light bills, rent, or whatever's needed.

I moved to the Wilson area in 1998, just before Floyd. Not long after I got settled there, it hit us. Diane and I went to help the area that was flooded. We were dragging stuff out of people's houses. They were just in shock, in tears. It came across Ward Boulevard and flooded that whole area around Toisnot Lake. We went to McDonald's and got a bunch of hamburgers and drinks and took them down to feed the people who were working. At our place, we looked out our back door, and the water was up to the concrete. The flood was at our door. It was level with the doorknob on a building out back.

Hazel Sorrell and her Wilson Interfaith worked hard to meet the needs of flooded families in Wilson County. Along with her daughter and codirector Diane Hardison, Hazel helped organize the group and oversee the reconstruction of dozens of homes. (Photo by Jay Barnes)

I was very interested in the families that had all the losses. The associate pastor at the First Methodist Church left the church to work for the city. He was coordinating the ministries of all the churches in the area. So I jokingly told him, "If you need any help, I'm available." Well, he called one day and invited me to a board meeting. So I went to the meeting, and they elected me executive director on the spot. They wanted to see if I could get us organized, up and running. This was the Wilson Interfaith Recovery Committee.

This was in January after the flood. I got us organized as an interfaith. We had to get a board that represented all the different churches, had to get incorporated, get our 501(c)3, and all that stuff. I found us an office, got it painted, and by May we were open. I started with the Salvation Army referring people to me, and I would find out what their needs were. Just meeting the needs of food, clothing, light bills, and rent, or whatever the need was. Some people had lost their stoves and refrigerators. Maybe they had a place to stay but didn't have anything to put in it. I worked with the Salvation Army that way to help families who had lost things, and then we hired a construction manager.

The Salvation Army had two hundred thousand dollars that was there for Hurricane Floyd, and we contracted with the Church of the Brethren. Now that church is not known very well down in this area. They're from Maryland, Pennsylvania, and up in the Great Lakes area. A different team came every week, and they sent a manager that stayed a month. He looked after the different teams they sent in. He knew them and he knew their ways.

These families were in the city of Wilson and in the county. They were the ones that fell through the cracks. They didn't get any help from FEMA, they didn't get help from the state, nobody helped them. They were ones that didn't qualify one way or another. Some of them didn't realize they had damage until it was too late to apply. Some of them applied and got very little. Some of them got nothing.

Anna Knight was one of the first ones that came to us. She said she looked out and saw her neighbors flooded, but she wasn't flooded so she didn't do anything. Water was under her house, but it wasn't up in her house. Then her little girl got ill with a fungus that came on her knee. She brought some of the child's toys down to the office. They were just eaten up with mold and mildew. The water had gotten up in the insulation and the heating and air-conditioning system, and they had used it right on. They were all sick. So we got her house fixed on Fourth of July weekend.

Sixty-three homes have been reconstructed, and that doesn't count the ones that we have given furniture or appliances. Six of those homes were total rebuilds from the foundation up. Beyond that, there's just hundreds that we have helped out in other ways. We worked a great deal with the elderly. Nobody just seemed to care whether they got any help or not.

One thing I worked to do was to get both black and white churches on the board, as well as county and city. I made a real effort to get them all working together. I went to the black ministerial meetings, and to the white ones, and tried to bridge a gap there. That was one of the great things that came out of it for me, was to see them working together on a daily basis.

We had one man that came to us and pulled a FEMA check out of his pocket for a hundred sixty-eight dollars. His house was sitting beside Contentnea Creek and was completely flooded. I don't understand why he only got a check for a hundred sixty-eight dollars. We had to do his roof, his floors, his walls, his bathroom—everything was just flooded out. We helped those folks who had fallen through the cracks and just didn't get help from anywhere.

Another one that we helped was Nellie Ruth Taylor of Elm City. Her mobile home was damaged by the wind and the rain. It sat there and rained in her home for two years before anything was done. She had rags stuffed along the side of her floors. A possum tried to get in one night—I can't imagine—it was awful. We put a new trailer in for her, and now she's a happy soul.

There was also Sheila Pierce. She lived right beside a creek, and it came up and flooded her house. When they tore into it, they found that termites had gotten in there and started working on it. And there was a bed of moccasins under the house, too. It was something. We called Terminix. It was a brick house, but it had all this damage inside. It was a mess. We had to redo the whole thing.

Also, this work put about a hundred fifty thousand dollars back in the local economy, with roofers, electrical, and carpeting work through vendors in the area. Some would really be touched by what they saw and would turn around and make a donation.

A lot of people didn't apply for aid in time. And some of them had heard through the grapevine that if you applied, and they found out that you weren't really damaged like you thought you were, they'd take your house. You know there were all these stories that were getting around. They heard all kind of tales, and they were afraid to apply. And that's sad to me, because there was help there for those that did qualify for it.

We got a check the other day from the Church of the Brethren for five thousand dollars, as they were closing out their Hurricane Floyd fund. With it was a letter. They said they had never felt so welcomed, and they cherished the bonds of friendship they now had in our community. We still have homes to do, but our construction manager is just doing what he can part-time. Our organization is still intact, and still working, three years after Floyd. We are still working five hours a week. We answer phone calls and get grants.

This work just makes you feel like you're here for a purpose. When you're eighty-six years old and still here and able to help somebody, it makes you feel like that's what He left you here for. To help those that can't help themselves. How fortunate we are, 'cause these things could have easily happened to us.

It was a real eye-opening experience. It's been hard work, but it's been enjoyable, because we're helping people, and you can just see how much they appreciate what you're doing. And that just makes it all worthwhile. We hope to continue helping people that need it. I just wish Bill Gates would discover us!

Delia Perkins   No North Carolina community was more devastated by Hurricane Floyd than the town of Princeville. With her town completely evacuated and her offices under more than twenty feet of water, Mayor Delia Perkins was faced with the challenge of bringing Princeville back from disaster. It was especially difficult for Delia, since floodwaters reached the ceiling in her own home. She was interviewed in her temporary office in Princeville in June 2002.

Princeville was founded by freed slaves that came over from across the river. It was founded in 1865, but incorporated in 1885. It is the oldest city chartered by blacks in America.

I've been involved in politics in Princeville for about fifteen years, and I've been the mayor for a little over four years. We'd had a lot of problems in the town leading up to Floyd, and we had just started to come out of a bad situation. The town was just beginning to move forward when along came September 16 and Hurricane Floyd.

The problems started, I guess, on a Wednesday. We had back-to-back storms and a lot of rain. We did have some low-lying flooding on that Wednesday, but not a lot. We had to move some citizens out from a few areas. That Thursday it continued to rain, but we did not think it was going to be anything major. Water backed up because of some old sewer pipes and drainpipes that were stopped up. That Thursday night they saw that the river was rising quite fast, and it got to the point that we decided to get citizens together to sandbag the opening where the railroad goes through the dike. It's a little bit lower than the dike. The dike, from the bottom up, is thirty-seven feet.

Everything we thought was going pretty well, but the water kept rising. I talked with the National Weather Service, and their news was not good. They said that they thought the water would come about six feet over the dike. Maybe. In the meantime, we had twenty-one hundred people in the town that we needed to decide what to do about. We weren't sure how much water would come over the dike, or even if it would come over the dike. So I spoke with two other commissioners and told them what the Weather Service had said. I told them I thought we needed to evacuate just for the night, to make sure that everyone would be okay, and they agreed. We asked the people to stop sandbagging and to just go home, get their families, and evacuate the town. That's pretty much what happened all Thursday night. We thought they'd go home the next day.

Mayor Delia Perkins of Princeville sits on the steps of the old Princeville town hall in July 2002. During the flood that submerged her town, only the roof of the building was above the water. (Photo by Jay Barnes)

Former Red Cross president Bernadine Healy and the Reverend Jesse Jackson console Pinetops resident Martha Johnson in front of the Princeville town hall two weeks after the storm. During his tour of eastern North Carolina, Jackson called for a top-to-bottom reconstruction because the area's economy was lagging even before Floyd arrived. (Photo by Stephan Savoia; courtesy of Associated Press)

There were some people that decided they didn't want to leave. Many were in the lower part of Princeville, mostly what we call Southern Terrace. We had all the fire trucks out, all the police cars out, and everybody was trying to get people to move. By that time they had opened up shelters. The water started rising so fast that they decided to open up two schools. They opened up Tarboro High and Martin Middle School, and most of the elderly went to the shelters. There were other citizens that went to family members' houses, but the majority of people decided to wait it out in their cars in the parking lot at the mall.

We still did not have any idea that it was going to be anything other than a lot of rain that probably would build up and then go away the next day. I stayed at the mall all night. That Friday morning I asked the police department to come over and check to see how things were, and then we could decide what we were going to do. One of our police officers went into the police department and heard a load roaring sound—that was the sound of water coming over the dike. It didn't come over the dike until that Friday. He got out and called us, but by the time I got down to the river bridge, the water had just started rushing and consumed the town.

It was like a war zone. By that time they had called in the Coast Guard, the Marines, and the Army. They had helicopters and boats to go and get people. Some people woke up, decided to come back home, and went down in Southern Terrace and got trapped. The water just came in so fast. They had to rescue all of those people. We didn't lose anyone, and we were lucky, because the whole town was just consumed with water. Right here where we are sitting there was about twenty-some feet of water.

Edgecombe emergency management stepped in to oversee things. They worked with different agencies to find cots, blankets, medicines, and food. The Red Cross came in and helped find a way to get food and water. They started to truck water in because Tarboro's system had shut down. I remember seeing down on Elizabeth Street, people were going down to the edge of the flood to get water to take back to flush the toilet.

We knew we had a drainage problem already, and that was the reason the water was not moving. It stayed everywhere. Even when the water started to go down, we had to wait because a lot of the caskets came up out of the cemeteries. So we could not let anyone come back over here until we could get those caskets. It was already traumatic, what had happened. Then not knowing if maybe that was your mother or your father in that casket, made it really tough. This town was shut down for quite a long time.

It was about ten days before the water receded out of the town. Once they were able, they went in to check the houses with scuba gear to see if there were any bodies in them. Then they had to remove the caskets. Some of the caskets were still floating, and they were trying to keep them from floating away. There were problems with snakes, too. Once the water started to go down, it looked like a scene out of a Halloween mystery. Everything was covered with mud, and the trees looked dead. Some trees had been uprooted and had fallen over the streets and hit the light lines.

All the residents had lost everything. But I think a majority of the citizens, though they were upset, most of them were able to still keep some sort of sanity. It was heartbreaking to think about people that had been living in these houses for quite a long time. To think that your house was gone, your furniture was gone, all of your pictures, everything was gone. If you didn't just have a really strong will, it was something that could make you or break you. It was a fine thread that kept some people from going completely over the edge. I think that their faith in God, and the spirit of the volunteers that came in, were two things that helped people cope.

The police chief here at that time was Rodney Cognell. He was on a boat and had rescued a young lady and her child from their home. Somehow before they got back to land, the young lady panicked and turned the boat over, and the baby went down in the water. Rodney went down to get the baby, had the baby in his arm and was trying to get back up, when the mother caught him around the neck and held him down. He had on a lifejacket, but she was holding him down. He had to break the mother loose from him so he could get back up with the baby. He said that was one of the worst things that had ever happened to him. Miraculously, the baby came out of it all right.

There were people down in Southern Terrace that had to be picked up by helicopters. A lot of the people that went back in after the first night went home and went to sleep. When they woke up, the water had come up around the house. They had nowhere to go, except to wait until someone would come back to pick them up.

It was God's grace that no one lost their lives. We lost some animals, but there were no human fatalities here. We had one little cat that stayed with the fire department, and no one knows where he had been or how he survived. We also had some dogs that had been tied up, but their chains slipped, and they had been able to swim and get on top of houses.

The biggest heroes we had in Princeville were those citizens, those neighbors, those friends, that came from all around the country. Those that couldn't come sent donations; those that could come came to help clean out the houses. We had the Methodists, the Mennonites, the Baptist Men, and some I'm not sure who. We worked with Habitat for Humanity, and we built twelve houses in a little section over off of Otis Avenue. We had Lowe's, that was a true blessing to the town. Lowe's gave the town a million-dollar donation that helped us with the Habitat houses and a lot of other things too. We've just had lots and lots of people from all over the country. Citizens came down from Atlanta, Georgia, Mississippi, and Washington, D.C. The true heroes were all the people that came to the town's rescue after the flood. We were talking last week, and there were about twenty-six thousand volunteers that had been through here that we could count. But there were lots and lots of people that came into town and walked along the streets and just did things for people.

It makes me feel great to know that there are so many people willing to help us out. It puts a new perspective on life. We've had surgeons, lawyers, judges, and doctors who've come in just to clean mud out of houses. We've sobbed together, we've cried together, and we've had people who've came back to help over and over again. I've been invited to go out and talk about the history of the town, all the trials and all the struggles that we've gone through since the flood, and it's been a humbling experience.

When FEMA came in, they said we can do either/or: we can rebuild the dike or we can purchase the homes, but we can't do both. So it was something the municipality had to make the decision on. We had a lot of controversy, because we had a lot of people who felt like they just wanted to sell out and move. But the majority of people wanted to stay. And after I found out what FEMA had to offer, I saw that it would not put anybody back into another house for what they would receive. Running away, to me, was like you don't believe in yourself, you don't believe in God. So we had a council meeting, and three of the council members voted not to go with the buyout, and two people voted to go with it. So the dike was rebuilt. The Corps of Engineers will inspect it to make sure that it stays intact, and everything's like it's supposed to be.

The different government agencies have been very nice to the town. It took us a while to understand FEMA, and for FEMA to understand us, but once we got that understanding we've not had problems. In fact, we've got good relationships with the state and federal agencies. It's been two-and-a-half years since Floyd, and we're well ahead of where we thought we would be.

Our whole council lives here in Princeville, and they lost everything they had. Even though I had lost everything, I had my health, my family was fine, and the next thing I needed to do was to be about the town's business. So a lot of things that a part-time mayor would not have to do or would not even worry about doing, I had to step up to the plate. It was do or die, and somebody had to get up and do it. It was frustrating. A lot of people who I've known for quite a long time did not see eye to eye with some of the things that we were doing. I had to adjust, take the punches, and then move on. It was hard.

When I finally went back to my house, everything was gone. It was hard at first to go back in and see thirty years of everything destroyed, but they're material things. Material things can be replaced. I've been able to pick up some pictures from my family members, my sister, my brothers, that I can have copied. But it takes a toll on you to think, here I am, my husband's retired, I've got everything paid for, the furniture's paid for, there're just a few things left to pay for, and then you're home free. And then one day something comes along and takes everything away.

Sometimes you don't know why things happen. I'm a firm believer in that sometimes God lets things happen in order to get your attention and refocus your life. And I think Floyd was something that should have refocused a lot of people's lives.

Chris Hackney

Staff Sergeant Chris Hackney was on assignment with the Army National Guard when he came upon a mother and son trapped in a sinking SUV in Duplin County. Along with others in his convoy, Hackney helped bring the pair to safety. He was clearly in the right place at the right time. Along with Sergeant Charles Smith and Private First Class Forrest Kyle Strickland, he was presented with the Governor's Award for Heroism for his efforts. He was interviewed in a Hardee's restaurant in Pittsboro in July 2002.

At the time of the floods, I had been in the Guard right at ten years. But this was actually my first deployment. I had volunteered for some stuff, but I had never been actually deployed. I was in Clinton, which is the headquarters of the Thirtieth Heavy Separate Brigade. It's a mechanized infantry. We were taking a convoy from Clinton to an airfield in Kinston. It was a logistical field the state had set up. That's where all your supplies, water, and stuff flew in and landed at the airport, and then were lifted out by Chinooks or trucks. Anything that went to Tarboro, Princeville, or anywhere like that, of course there was no way to drive in so they had to fly it in with Chinooks. But for everywhere else they used trucks. A lot of it went out in Humvees, you know, in small loads.

We had gotten a convoy together and were on Highway 117, headed to Kinston. It's a four-lane road that runs somewhere outside of Clinton up toward Kinston. Somewhere in the middle there is a low-lying area called Goshen Swamp. I guess that's where everything in that area drains. Of course, with the hurricane and the flooding that we had, the water was up extremely high.

When we first pulled up on it there was a lot of traffic backed up, because most of your civilian vehicles were not able to pass through it. We moved around them to get closer to see if we could even get through it. I was driving somewhere in the middle of the convoy. As I looked ahead, I noticed that one of the lead vehicles had actually pulled out into the water and the guys had gotten out. I noticed a large crowd down by the bank, and a lot of people were

standing down by the water. At first I thought they were just looking at the water, because everybody was just in awe of what was going on. Nobody had ever seen this type of flooding before.

Once I saw those guys getting out, I realized there was something going on. I saw there was a Toyota 4Runner out in the water. There's a median in the middle, and the front end was nose down in the median. It was probably eight or nine feet deep. The back end was kind of bobbing around up top. Inside the vehicle there was a lady and her son who couldn't have been more than six or seven. She was standing on the back of the front seat with her son just trying to stay above water. It was power everything, so when it went in the water the windows shorted out. I don't know whether she or her son could swim, or whether she wasn't comfortable swimming with her son in her arms. So basically, they were staying there.

The National Guard used large trucks to transport food, water, and people through flooded areas across eastern North Carolina. (Photo by Donna Werner; courtesy of the *Kinston Free Press*)

Our guys, Sergeant Smith and PFC Strickland, had moved on into the water. I went in behind them. By the time I got there, they had already gotten the little boy out. The water was about chest deep, but it was kind of weird. The water on the surface didn't really look like it was moving. But a few inches down, it was moving pretty good, which made it hard to walk. It was a really strong current underneath. It was weird.

You had to sort of swim to get over top of that rough current just to get there. It was up to my neck as we got out to the vehicle. Strickland had already gotten the boy out. The window was halfway down, but the lady wasn't strong enough to open the door with the current going by. So we were able to get the door open. Strickland carried the boy back to his vehicle, then I helped Sergeant Smith get the lady. She wasn't a hundred forty pounds—let's just say that. She was a heavier woman. Smith actually carried her out. I held her the first few feet, but once he started going with her, he had her. He's a bit taller than I am, and he's thicker than I am. He's a strong boy. She kind of held onto his back, and once I got him moving in that direction, I got into the Humvee. They had pulled theirs in to sort of block the current, but with six feet of water, they went as far as they could go. The water was still coming up during this time. After we left, the floods either engulfed the 4Runner or washed it on down, because it was gone shortly thereafter.

From the time we got to them until we got them back to shore, the whole thing was probably about fifteen or twenty minutes. The people watching gave us a standing ovation, I guess you'd say. Once we got the lady back to shore, all she was concerned about was her 4Runner. She wanted us to pull it out. We told her that's not part of the mission, to save 4Runners. We're supposed to be going to Kinston. So at that point the EMS got there and kind of handled that situation, and we just got back in line. Once we got everything lined up, we had to cross the median and go through the Goshen Swamp on the southbound side, on the wrong side of the road.

We went on to Kinston, and to be honest, we didn't think too much more about it. Then we got a call from our headquarters. Evidently, one of the members in the convoy had said something to somebody, and they wanted a written report of what happened. So I wrote up a report, and I really didn't think that much about it. Then we all got a Meritorious Service Ribbon from the Guard, which is a pretty nice award in itself. I was tickled. I guess we were just in the right place at the right time.

Then I got a letter in the mail from the governor's office. I opened that letter and it said, "You have been selected for the Governor's Award for Bravery and Heroism." I thought, well, maybe they must give away a thousand of these things, you know, and they just send you a letter. But as I read on down, it said there are thirty recipients this year, and it really was a much bigger deal. I guess it was my fifteen minutes of fame. They had a big ceremony at the Trinity Methodist Church in Raleigh. All the news folks were there, and of course the governor, and we had a big dinner thing down at the bottom beforehand. It was a very nice event. I mean it was an honor, but it was just totally unexpected. Still to this day I don't know who put us in for it.

I learned a lot in this flood, and I saw a lot, and I hope I never see anything like it again. At one point, I was with some guys with a rescue squad in a bass boat, and I think the depth finder was reading twelve to fifteen feet. And this was going right down the highway. There were stranded people and animals. We saw dogs that were chained up in the backyard that people just left, and the dogs were floating around still on a chain. We saw a lot of livestock like hogs and stuff up on top of houses. Sometimes they were dead floating, and sometimes they were standing on top of houses, just kind of waiting.

I guess fire ants are bad around that area. You'd see big piles of stuff floating on the water that you thought was just a log. When you'd get to it you'd see fire ants stacked up on top of one another, floating in the water. As long as you left them alone, you were all right. But if you took a stick or anything and just touched them with it, they would just—Woosh!—because they were trying to get out of the water too. You had to drop that stick fast, or you'd be covered with them. Lots of snakes, too.

We train for war, but this was like a different kind of war. It's different kinds of weapons. You learn it's a war against time, and then supplies. Instead of throwing rounds down around your people, you're trying to throw food and water down around your people. And get it there as fast as you can. And get people out of situations they need to get out of.

I can remember flying into Tarboro on a helicopter with a load of water, shampoo, and food and that kind of stuff. I mean you could see people behind the school, cheering us in the stands, like we were in a football game or something. It was really an eye-opening experience. You realize what you take for granted when you've got folks cheering for bottled water and shampoo. It kind of brings you back to where you really are in the whole scheme of things. You know what you're dependent on, and what you've got to have.

Steve Burress

Steve Burress is chief of the Pinetops Fire Department and the Pinetops Rescue Squad. As flooding from Hurricane Floyd swept into several nearby communities, Burress and his crews launched a massive rescue effort in the early morning hours of the flood, ultimately saving hundreds of lives. In places like Dodge City, rescuers used chainsaws to cut holes through roofs to evacuate residents from submerged homes. Burress was interviewed in his Pinetops hardware store in July 2002.

I've lived in Pinetops almost all my life. The Pinetops Fire Department, the Pinetops Rescue Squad, and the South Edgecombe Fire Department were the three main departments that were involved initially in the rescue operation in the days following the flood.

The first calls that we received came in that Wednesday night, or really early Thursday morning. I was called by Edgecombe central communications somewhere after midnight and was told that we had some families down on Bynum Farm Road that needed to be taken out. They wanted to know if we could do it but also said that the National Guard was coming there with one of the big trucks they had. So they were going to get them. Later on, around three A.M., I was called again. We were told that three families needed to come out. I told them we would get somebody there as soon as we could.

We went down to the area, and of course the floodwaters were coming up. The water was a quarter-mile back from the entrance to Dodge City, which was the lowest area. And to be honest with you, we just were not aware of the magnitude of what was taking place. This area—Fillmore subdivision, Bynum Park, and Dodge City—these areas had seen some level of flooding before. The water began to rise and the people were just not anticipating the magnitude of it. They'd never experienced anything like this.

When we went in that Thursday morning, we went down there thinking we had about three families that needed to get out. When it was all said and done, we brought somewhere in the neighborhood of three hundred people out. We had houses that had probably as many as fifteen, eighteen, or twenty in a house. Because as the water rose, these people would go to the next nearest house. Of course some of them couldn't get out to do that.

When we first went down, all we had was a twelve- or fourteen-foot flatbottom boat and a larger fiberglass boat. Well, they had been doing some logging in the area and had a log skidder out there. One of the boys on the squad is a tractor-trailer driver, and he's familiar with that type of equipment. So he went and got that log truck. We were gonna take that to pull our boat down there, get these people out, and come on back. You know, a simple operation. Well, it weren't meant to be that way. The first thing that happened was the water was so bad that it washed the logger right off in a ditch. At that point it was probably three to four foot deep, and the current was pretty strong.

Then we had to come up with another plan. Word spread throughout the community, and everybody started coming with their boats. It was really heartwarming, because you always hear people talk about friend helping friend and neighbor helping neighbor, but there's no doubt in my mind that enemies helped enemies down there that day. As many people as there were there helping and working, all of them couldn't have been friends.

It wasn't a black-white thing that day. There weren't no black, there weren't no white—everybody just got in there and helped. We probably had about fifteen boats. These were whites that came out to help, and we were rescuing a black section. Everybody came out and done everything in the world they could. This was probably one of the most dangerous situations we've ever had. I related several, several times to it being our Oklahoma City bombing. We're just a small department. We've got three ambulances and a crash truck, and praise the Lord has blessed us with good equipment. But still we're not equipped, and never could be equipped, to bring out that amount of people. The back of my Expedition was my command center.

Another thing was we were isolated. The roads to Greenville were blocked. Anybody that got in and out of Pinetops that day and part of the next day came in by helicopter.

We started working our way in to the flooded areas. We had boats, we had Jetskis, we had a pontoon boat that you could put fifteen people on, but it was all a very dangerous operation. We had LP gas tanks breaking loose, and the current was terrible. On Friday, we had what we thought was six missing, in reality we had seven missing. We found one in a house that was on the outer perimeter that nobody had told us about.

Each house we went to, our people were hootin' and hollerin' and bangin', and nobody would come to the door. They got people out through windows. We had to take chainsaws in and cut holes in the tops of houses. We had to cut through the shingles on the roof. Then we got them to crawl out the holes and get in the boat. We got some out of gable ends where they knocked the gables out, 'cause people had escaped to their attics. This was in the Dodge City area, and that's how deep the water was.

The chainsaw thing came about when we became aware that we had people that were up in attics. We were checking each house, yelling for them, and you could hear them inside. They would knock on the roofs or whatever, they banged on the houses, and heard somebody banging back. Of course you're in a boat up to the end of the house now, so you can hear them hollering out the gable ends. People were scared to death. They were literally scared to death, and rightly so.

There were adults and children, and we just did get out of there before we had to deliver one baby. But we did get a helicopter and get her out before then. We were bringing them out and carrying them down to Carver Elementary School, which was a shelter. This was still on Thursday.

We had two unaccounted for. One got out on the Tarboro side. The other one that was missing was a man that drowned in his house, and we got him out. I don't know why, because there was no reason for him to drown, unless he had a seizure. The water wasn't but about three feet high in his house.

One of our boys went in this house, opens this door, and there's a man on the bed. You know how when you get a mattress it still has a plastic bag on it? Well, he had never taken the plastic bag off the bed, and the mattress had floated all the way to the top of the house with the man still on it. As the water went down the next day, three, four, five feet, the mattress came right on back down again. He never got off the mattress and he was still alive. There's no doubt the water had carried him all the way to the ceiling. We got him out, put him on the helicopter, and evac'd him on out.

In one of the houses, I think they found a hog on a bed.

The situation with the Mayo family started in the wee hours of Thursday morning. Ben Mayo was loading people in his boat to get them out. I don't know if this was his first load or what, but he had about a dozen, or somewhere in that neighborhood, in his boat. Well, in the process of trying to come out, the boat capsized. I was not aware of this until late Thursday afternoon, after I had gotten back to the command post. Somebody started telling me about a boat capsized with six people missing. Two of the ladies that we had taken out—the two ladies that were in the trees at the far end—they were on the boat. There were about five or six that got out okay.

Ben, his wife, his daughter, his two grandchildren, and one more little girl, I believe, are the ones that actually drowned. Once we found this out, well, this presents a whole new ballgame. We're finishing up the rescue operation, and now it looks like we're going into a recovery. Ben, he was a hard worker. He worked at one of the plants down here, and he's one that didn't sit still long.

So Friday we went back and had to start dragging for the drowning victims. At that time some of the rescue dogs that search for cadavers underwater happened to make their way here. They said they had heard there had been a drowning down here and were told that they were needed. They were a Godsend to us. They found every body, every drowning victim. Just like your bloodhounds can catch a scent, these dogs found them all. On Saturday and Sunday, we found two one day and three the next. And on Tuesday morning we finally found the last little girl. They were the North Carolina Search and Rescue Dog Association out of Clyde, North Carolina.

The people that we got out of the trees were two ladies that were in the boat that capsized. As the current washed them down, they were able to grasp hold of some limbs and pull themselves up in the trees. I think they wrote an article about it in the newspaper. They were just about at the point of giving up, out there all night. They had been there since three o'clock in the morning, and when we finally got to them it was twelve hours later. They spent twelve hours in the trees. In hindsight, we feel like we should have known to go in there to start with. But you know, it's hard to ride by people that are on their roofs and not pick them up.

Ben had tried to get out in his truck to start with. When we were back and forth in and out of there the first day, he had an F-150 extended-cab pickup sitting right in the middle of the street. Several boats hit the top of it with the propellers of their motors. The next day when we went in there, the water was down enough that you could see the cab part of the truck. So it went down at least four or five feet.

Sometime later they had a program at school. The communities—Dodge City, Bynum Park, and Fillmore—presented the squad with a little plaque, thanking us for what we had done. So many people that you would see on the street were always thanking us for what we had done, and it meant a lot. It was a very emotional situation for all of us. It just makes you feel good inside when you see your community come together. It was by the grace of God that we went in there and came out with everybody we went in with, plus about three hundred more.

Buster Leverette and Cynthia Burnett

Dr. Cynthia Burnett and her husband, Buster Leverette, operate Burnett Veterinary Hospital in Burgaw. In the aftermath of Hurricane Floyd, they worked around the clock, often risking their own lives to rescue hundreds of dogs, cats, horses, cows, and other animals from flooded homes in the Pender County area. Their veterinary hospital later became a hub for animal rescue operations. They were interviewed together in their Burgaw offices in June 2002.

Buster: Normally, when hurricanes are named, our clients start calling to make reservations for their animals. The structure of our building is pretty sound, and it's made it through every one of them so far. As it gets closer and closer, we get more and more phone calls from people wanting to board their animals, because most veterinary hospitals won't board during hurricanes. We stay here during storms to take care of the animals. It just so happens that with Floyd we had about seventy-five boarding animals. We were really packed. Luckily we had just added on sixteen hundred square feet of space, because if we didn't have that, we would not have had the capacity for the three hundred fifty-three animals that actually came through here. Those were just the rescue animals, not the boarding animals.

As the hurricane came in, it stalled, and we realized there was a whole lot more rain involved. People were really scared. At our house the ground was dry, but as water started pouring in from other areas, people were shocked to see the water rise that fast and come into their dwellings. Electricity was out, they had nowhere to go, and if they didn't escape the day before, they were stuck. Our house didn't flood, but there were several others around there that did.

Cynthia: Saturday morning after the flood, an equine veterinarian friend from down in Wilmington called and said that one of her clients had horses that were in a flooded area in Pender County. The water was rising, and she was going to try to pull them out. She had a horse sling coming from Southern Pines, and there was a rescue helicopter coming from someplace else. They were going to meet and airlift these horses out. Actually, it was three horses and a mule. She asked me if I wanted to come watch, because she thought it might be interesting. She said she might need more drugs to sedate these horses. Her supply was down in Wilmington, and she asked me if I'd bring some extra drugs just in case.

So we went down there. The helicopter was going to be late because it was rescuing some people, and obviously, people take precedence over horses.

Then we got word that the helicopter wasn't coming because there were just too many people in need. Daylight was quickly leaving us. We decided we needed to make some decisions. Well, we decided to go in and try to rescue them by boat. So we borrowed a couple of john boats and it was basically dusk by the time we got there. We walked the horses into chest-deep water, but as soon as they got in deeper water and their feet left the ground, they would get scared and try to run back. There were two large horses and two smaller horses, so we decided to take the two smaller ones out first.

Buster: This wasn't something we'd ever tried before. I'd take one of the horses and slowly introduce it to deeper and deeper water. But when it got to a point where it started to float, it panicked. And when horses panic, they have a tendency to run. If you have a horse that gets scared and wants to run away, you can turn them in circles to calm down. So in the water we basically swam in twelve or fifteen circles, in probably a fifteen-to-twenty-foot radius. All of a sudden it started swimming toward deep water, so I just went with it. We swam and we swam, and I was just holding on to that horse. I had no lifejacket on, which was crazy. But we kept swimming, and the next thing you know we had gone almost a mile. I was grabbing limbs and stuff, trying to keep myself up, and then the horse got tired, gave up, and went completely underwater. The horse was probably close to seven feet tall. It had just completely given up, but I was pulling its head above the water. They caught up with us in the boat, and I was screaming to them to get over here. I put the horse's head up over the front of the boat, and we moved along for about ten minutes. Then that horse got its second wind, and it decided it was going to try to climb into the boat. For thirty minutes I had to fight to keep that horse from getting in the boat.

Cynthia: Yeah, that was special.

Buster: By this time it was pitch dark. The horse was completely exhausted, and it just collapsed about the time we got into knee-deep water. We got it up, got it out of there, and went back for the second horse. The water was still rising the whole time.

We went back for the second horse and slightly sedated him. I just held his head beside the boat and we had no problem carrying him on out. Some people had called for the EMS, and the next thing we know there's about ten huge fire trucks and EMS vehicles with those great big floodlights on them. When

Buster Leverette (*left*) organized volunteers to rescue hundreds of stranded animals in southeastern North Carolina following Hurricane Floyd. His wife, Dr. Cynthia Burnette, used her veterinary hospital in Burgaw as an emergency shelter for more than 350 animals. (Photo courtesy of Cynthia Burnett)

we came around the corner with that last horse, there was about five hundred people there, cheering and hollering. The lights were so bright it looked like daylight. They ran into the water cheering and helped us in. We were exhausted. We just hoped that those two other horses would manage through the night, 'cause they were already shivering. Hypothermia was very much a concern.

We went back in there first thing the next morning, and sure enough the water was deeper so that just their heads were sticking out of the water. And these were bigger horses than the first two. The water was probably six feet in the yard, and they were expecting it to rise two more feet. This time they were sedated, and we had straps under their bellies, but we still had to keep their heads above water.

On the way out, we could see all these houses and trailers that had water waist high inside them. We saw this one porch that had started to float, and on it was this old dog. It was decrepit looking, just barking for all she was worth. I mean just begging for somebody to come and get her. And there was a piece of two-by-twelve, about three feet long, floating through the water with two chickens on it. On the way back I told Cindy, "I want to go back for that dog and those chickens." I just felt uncomfortable leaving that dog out there. I or-

An anxious crew of dogs looks for high ground after being rescued from the sunken neighborhoods of Princeville following Hurricane Floyd. (Photo by Dave Saville; courtesy of FEMA)

ganized three or four people to jump in the boat. I didn't even think about carriers, or collars, or leashes, or none of that stuff; we just jumped back in the boat and headed back out to that little community. As soon as we got the boat near that porch, I mean he just jumped right in the boat. He was just so happy, wagging its tail.

Off in the distance you could hear barking and cats meowing. And you could see little Chihuahuas scratching on the windows. There was a little trailer park community down in there, and there were animals all over. I just couldn't leave them down in there. So I got a chicken, and then we started searching house by house. This was off of Stagg Park Road in Burgaw.

Cynthia: When he came back with that first boat full of animals, people were standing by the edge saying, "Oh, let me tell you where my house is! Can you please go get mine?"

Buster: They were drawing me maps on paper towels. I had one person draw me a map to their house on a shirt with a magic marker. They said, "You go this way, then you go that way, and there's a big tree over there. Please go and get him."

Cynthia: We came back here to get all our extra kennel carriers. He would go out and find the animals, people were standing on the shore waiting for them, and we'd give them to them. If there was nobody standing on the shore waiting for them, then we'd put them in the carriers and bring them back here. He would bring back chickens and things that nobody would claim, and we would just find someplace for them.

Buster: We saw cats on top of houses, cats in trees, and we actually climbed up there and got them. We saw a few snakes. This probably hurt me as badly as anything I saw: There were some pit bulls that some people had chained with big logging chains to axles of cars, and they were biting tree limbs to stay above the water. When I got to them, you could hear them flopping in the water and just "errrrr errrrrrrrr" because it wouldn't let go of that limb. I realized this great big chain was tight under the water. So I dove under and felt this chain hooked to a car axle. I lifted it up and put it in the boat along with the dog. When I got back, I got some bolt cutters and we cut them chains. I probably found eight or ten of them dogs with logging chains.

I also found a German shepherd that had been chained to a tree, and it had figured out a way to get up on this deck. But he had only his ears and nose sticking out of the water with the chain pulled just as tight as he could. I mean he almost drowned himself barking to get our attention. By the time we got over there and got him in the boat, we realized there were cats and dogs inside the house. I didn't have any keys to these houses, so I had no option but to kick their doors in or knock their windows out. Every animal that we picked up was happy to be on the boat. They didn't care if they were cats with dogs, dogs with chickens, chickens with goats and pigs. They didn't care—except for this one pit bull. We put him on the boat and he tried to eat a cat. I set him back off on top of the roof of a little barn and said, "You stay there until I have an empty boat."

There was this big sow that I saw sit on this porch for probably two or three days. I couldn't get near it because it was just too aggressive. Finally hypothermia kicked in and it just collapsed and we hogtied it. I had Angela from Channel 3 with me in the boat that day.

Once we felt that we had cleared all the houses in that little area, we started expanding. The news of what we were doing got out, and we got a phone call from the U.S. Humane Society. The guy said, "What do you need?" And I said, "I need some help to get these animals. There's a lot more out there." So the next morning I had six rescue units here wanting to go to work. They had come from Myrtle Beach, Fayetteville, Snead's Ferry, and Columbus County, and they came with full crews with boats, and they were eager to go.

Cynthia: I was still seeing appointments on Monday, when our head receptionist came in and said, "Cindy, NBC *Nightly News* is on the phone." This man said, "I'm calling for Tom Brokaw, and we heard you guys were saving some animals, and we'd like to come down and join you." The next morning, they went out on the boat with him. After that aired that night, PETA, which is the People for the Ethical Treatment of Animals, called the next day and said they were going to have a person down here within twenty-four hours that would stay at least a month, if not two. By Friday we had eight rescue teams. Across the coastal area, we had search-and-rescue guys just showing up ready to go. Buster coordinated them, took them out, and we brought the animals back here to our makeshift shelter. We logged what they were and where he got them from so we could try to reunite them with their owners if we could. We had three hundred fifty-three animals brought in here, but there were more than that rescued off the water.

Through all this rescue effort, the N.C. State College of Veterinary Medicine got involved. They sent a couple of veterinarians down, and there were some other vets from the mountains that came down. There were dogs that were stuck with absolutely nothing to eat except an empty horse food bag. I mean they had eaten cardboard, and string, and all kinds of stuff that had knotted up their intestines. I was doing surgery on them, and a lot were very sick with gastrointestinal problems from drinking the polluted floodwaters. We lost some of them. I'd say that half to three-quarters of the ones brought back here were eventually reunited with their owners. The local news was very instrumental in that, because once or twice a week they would come up here and run a spot on the six o'clock news. People came in and said, "Oh, I saw my dog on the news! We thought she was dead." Little kids would come in and just cry and cry because they were so happy to see their pet.

It took a whole crew just to handle the donations of pet food and supplies. Not just individuals, but companies. They were donating food, blankets, cat toys, bowls, and leashes, and shampoo, and veterinarians from all over the state donated medicine. WalMart donated a tractor-trailer load of dog food, cat food, and cat litter, and it was delivered by the National Guard. What we didn't use for the animals we had rescued, we donated back to the families that were flooded. We became a hub. We had volunteers come from all over to help us clean up and keep them bathed and medicated. This went on for two or three months. We finished everything up right before Christmas.

Buster: One of the most unique rescues happened one of the days I had the NBC news crew with me. The water was eight feet deep over at Holland's Shelter, and across the street this guy called and said he had a horse and some cows on the deck of his house. So we go out there and sure enough—there's this full-size horse, four full-grown cows, and a yearling calf standing in knee-deep water on his porch. Hypothermia was already kicking in; you could see it in their eyes. He was ready to shoot them, but I said let's try something.

So we got his dogs and cats from the barn, and we went across the street to Holland's Shelter and got a cat on the roof. When I climbed up on the roof, I saw this floating dock that was probably sixteen feet wide by twelve feet, with fifty-five-gallon barrels up under it. It was a floating pier on the river, but it had risen over the posts and was held by these ropes. So I went over to it and cut the ropes, floated it over to the house, and jammed it up against the side of the deck. We took an ax and chopped the railings away from the porch and the floating dock. I tied the horse up with lead ropes, grabbed his halter, pointed him in the right direction, and he jumped right on there like he'd done it a hundred times. As soon as he went on, the cows followed. They just jumped right up on there. The problem we had was all that weight. As the cows and the horse would shift their weight, that dock would sink to the left, or sink to the right. So to offset this, we got two people up on there, so as the cows move to one side, we'd move to the other side. Then we took our boat, hooked it up to that floating dock, and started going down Highway 53. We floated that dock down the road a couple miles until we got to land, and they stepped off like there was nothing wrong. People said it looked like we were dancing with them, because they'd step one way and we'd step the other way.

Cynthia: When he started rescuing these animals, I'd ask him, "Well, where'd you find this one?" And he'd tell me, "Well, I found it in this house balancing on a curtain rod on top of a window, and it only had about two inches of air left." Or he'd say, "This one was hunkered down on the top shelf in the back of a closet in the bedroom and I almost missed it." Or, "They were floating on pillows, or on top of the refrigerator, in the kitchen cabinets, or cries from up in the attics." I mean it was just amazing some of the places that he found these animals, and what they were doing just to survive. There was no electricity, and there were several cats that he only found by their screams. If he went into a closet it was dark. I just feel sorry for the ones he missed.

I remember these people who had this horse, and they refused help. They wanted to pull it out themselves, without sedation, and without any type of flotation device for the horse. So they just drug it out with a boat, and the horse was trying to swim the whole time. The horse ran over top of a street sign and severed its leg. The horse was totally exhausted because it swam the whole way out, and its leg was severed so that it can't even walk on it anymore. It was very sad.

The two vets from the state came and asked if I could help with two horses that had been standing in floodwaters for two weeks. The people didn't bother to try to get them out, and the skin had rotted off of their legs. They were totally infected with maggots. Both of those horses ended up dying. Very sad.

Buster: The process of getting animals back to their owners went fairly quickly, but we had a bunch that we just couldn't place. One day this lady called me from a law firm down in Atlanta, Georgia, and said, "I saw you on the news and I've got some stuff for you. Can you come and get it? We've got food and donations, and if you've got any animals you don't have homes for, I've got twenty homes." I was just amazed. All the way from Atlanta, this lady had orchestrated this through her law firm. So a friend of mine, who is a regional activities director for Miller Brewing, got his truck and a big long trailer, paid for the gas and everything, and he and I trucked down there one Thursday. He made some signs that said Hurricane Floyd Animal Rescue Team.

So we pulled into downtown Atlanta and called her up. There must have been two or three hundred people who came out to greet us. They brought us bags of dog food, chains, collars, and checks. The first time down I took mostly cats and dogs; I took ten of each. They said, "Which one of these can I take, which one can I keep?" Then we loaded up that trailer just slam full of donations. People wanted directions to get back here because they wanted to come help on the weekends. When we got back home, they called and wanted to know if we had more animals. I said, "We've got two pot-bellied pigs, a couple of goats, a turkey, and some chickens that nobody's wanted." They said they knew somebody that owns a petting zoo. So I made another trip down, and they had even more stuff for us. It was pretty amazing.

Cynthia: I think I experienced every emotion that I could ever experience, and I'm not usually an emotional person. Fear—because my husband was going out on water every day that the National Guard was telling everybody they couldn't go on. Joy—seeing the pets and the animals that he was saving. Sadness —knowing about the ones that he didn't. Anger—frustration with people who were coming and trying to get food and stuff that weren't even in the flooded areas. Exhaustion—total exhaustion. Getting so little sleep from trying to do everything that you possibly can. I can't think of an emotion that I didn't experience. It was doing something not because you had to, but because you knew you wanted to, and you knew it was the right thing to do.

Buster: The great thing for me was seeing the kids' smiles when they picked up their animals. That's probably the best reward that I could ever receive from anybody. Truthfully. That, and knowing that we helped. And every single time I drive down Highway 53, I look and think, "I remember when the water was up to right there." I drive along and think, "That's where we took that pig off the top of that car." And it'll be with me forever.

Faye Stone

Faye Stone is the deputy executive director of the North Carolina Commission on Volunteerism and Community Service. During Hurricane Floyd, she played a critical role in developing the state's response to the disaster. Working out of Governor Hunt's office, she established a toll-free emergency hotline and helped manage the Governor's Hurricane Floyd Disaster Relief Fund, which ultimately raised millions for victims of the flood. She keeps a purple piggybank on her desk to remind her of Floyd. She was interviewed in her Raleigh office in June 2002.

I work in the Commission on Volunteerism and Community Service in the governor's office. I've been in this office for about five years. During Hurricane Floyd, I became the governor's representative to emergency management and then became a member of the State Emergency Response Team, or SERT. I worked in the logistics section, in donations management.

About ten hours before Hurricane Floyd was scheduled to make landfall in North Carolina, Governor Hunt decided that for the convenience of the citizens in the state, we would create an emergency information hotline. It really blossomed into a real operation. It had never been done in North Carolina before. We knew that Floyd would be a major event once it arrived. I was tasked with putting that emergency information hotline together. I was responsible for getting the equipment, getting the phones, securing a location for it, arranging for staffing, and making sure that the right information was available for the operators on duty.

We started with eight phones in a small conference room one floor above the Emergency Operations Center here in Raleigh. I went down the halls and pulled eight people from the governor's office to serve as operators for that night. We clearly had no idea what we were doing. I happened to think about stopping by the Governor's Office of Hispanic and Latino Affairs. I asked the director if he could provide me with someone who was bilingual. That truly turned out to be a blessing, because I would estimate that at least sixty percent of the calls the night before the storm hit were from Spanish-speaking people. I mean, we had calls lined up on hold waiting for the bilingual operators. We all learned how to tell people to hold for just a moment, because there were just so many people from that population. We were really very lucky that we thought of that ahead of time.

We started off at four o'clock in the afternoon, and Floyd made landfall early the next morning. We made it through that night with just those eight phones, and the next morning we expanded with another ten phones. Four hours later, we added another ten phones. We wound up with something like thirty-eight phones. It was quite a process. We rapidly outgrew the little room we were in. It was quite an experience bringing people in and trying to tell them what to do, especially in the first couple of days, because it was just so hectic. We've come such a long way. Now we have a room on the third floor that's prewired for thirty phones and thirty computers. We had no computers during Floyd. It's amazing that we got through it all.

There were so many different kinds of calls that came in the night before the storm hit. The governor would go on TV and they'd flash this one-eight-hundred number on the bottom of the screen. Every time the governor was on TV for anything or that number was shown, our phones would just ring off the hook. People wanted all kinds of information. We had to stay current on shelter information. We had to know which shelters were operating, which ones were at capacity, which ones could accommodate disabled people, and we had to tell people what they needed to do with their pets. We had to know where feeding sites were. A lot of highway information was given out during that first four or five days. It was very, very difficult for people to understand that they could not travel in that part of the state. A third of the state was underwater. You actually had to be quite forceful with some people and tell them it was extremely dangerous.

Getting up-to-date information for the operators was a difficult process. I would run downstairs to a briefing and come back upstairs and tell them the latest. I would walk in the room and ask everyone to please put their calls on hold. It was the only way to get the information across, and it was vital information. It was a constant thing just updating those downstairs operators.

There were rumors of all different types. It was a challenge staying ahead of them. We received calls about floating caskets, or, "I hear there are floating caskets. Can you tell me where they might be? Am I in any danger?" And we didn't answer any questions we didn't have the right information about. That is something that every phone operator that came in was told. Don't add fuel to the fire for rumors. There were many, many calls on road closings. "Can you tell me if such-and-such a road is closed?" Or, "Can you tell me if there are snakes floating out here?" It was such an overwhelming experience. We had all kinds of phone calls.

It started as emergency information, but after three or four months it was no longer emergency information. And believe it or not, the hotline is still right here, rolled over into my phone. I do get calls on it even now. Not a lot, but maybe one every few weeks. The nature of the calls has changed, and now mainly it's people who've fallen through the cracks in the system. They never applied for FEMA, they never applied for this, they didn't apply for that, but yet they still need money, and I still get those kinds of calls.

There were over three hundred eighty state employees that served as operators at the hotline, and they logged over four thousand hours. Daytime was considered time worked, but if they pulled the night shift they volunteered their time. If it had not been for state employees, I don't think that hotline could have been operational. It would have been very, very difficult to find enough people to volunteer.

In a two-and-a-half-week period in September, from the activation of the hotline until the end of the month, there were 25,400 calls. That's a lot of calls. In October there were 10,372, and the average length of call was fifty-one seconds. By February of 2000, about five months after the storm, we had 463 incoming calls, but they were around four minutes in length. We truly went from being an emergency hotline to an information and assistance hotline. From a hotline to a help desk.

I actually did not man the phones very much. But one night I was at the hotline for seventy-two hours—consecutively. Just making sure that people got the critical information. It was just like a passion. I get teary-eyed talking about it.

Every once in a while, like at two in the morning, I would answer phones. As the waters were rising, this guy called one night. He was from Tennessee. He had been in Wilmington or someplace along the coast, and he needed to get back home. It was something very important. When he called, I told him that it was not a wise thing to do. I strongly discouraged him from doing this. And he said, "Well it's a little too late 'cause I've already tried." He turned around and went back to Wilmington. He tried a second time and the route that he chose was flooded, so he went back again. The third time he tried it, he made it for a distance, crossed a bridge, got to an intersection, started down another road, and that road was flooded. When he turned around and tried to get back to Wilmington, the bridge had washed out of the road. So he was stuck between a road that was flooded and a washed-out bridge. He was calling from his cell phone, and this was the wee hours of the morning. It was very stressful. Emergency management brought in massage therapists. I never knew if this man made it. I asked him to call 911. He didn't give me his name, and I don't know if he was one of the fatalities or not. But I'm assuming that he made it.

Another call that I answered was a man who was calling from inside his home, and he said he was standing in a few feet of water. His backyard was flooded, his dog had drowned, and he was just floating in the water. He didn't know how to get he and his wife out of his house. There was a time period of about five days that was extremely stressful, with stories like that in every other phone call. It was tough. It's very hard to talk about it. It truly is. I'd like to think that what we did helped.

We all knew that the area of the state that had been hit was not one of our more prosperous areas. We knew a lot of the victims were very poor people, and that a lot of them had lost everything. The governor just felt compelled to try to help just any way he could. So he decided to establish the relief fund. This idea came in that first seventy-two hours. I don't think he knew where this was going to go, but he just thought it was something that had to be done for the people.

Governor Hunt was just so wonderful in appealing to people. He was just so genuine. And I think that's because it was so personal to him. He had friends who were flooded and he knew people who were suffering. His home county was flooded. It was extremely personal for him. So he started asking people to help. I remember when the first check came in, and the mail room contacted me and said, "We have an envelope here that says Hurricane Floyd Disaster Relief Fund. What am I supposed to do with it?" It was all I could do to keep from drowning at the hotline. But I said, "Send it up to my office." That was the first check. The next thing I knew it was like three days later and I had seven Xerox paper boxes full of checks that came in that day. A decision had to be made quickly as to what was going to happen with this money that was coming in.

United Way agreed to manage the fund for the governor's office. Jim Morrison, the United Way president, agreed to waive the administrative fees for doing it. Little did Jim know that it was going to grow to more than nineteen million dollars. Over sixty-six thousand donations came in from every state in the nation and from around the world. Money orders from Japan, lots of money from servicemen from around the world, money from Canada, the United Kingdom, Ireland, just so many different countries. None of us knew that it was going to grow to what it became. It became so big, so quick, that they couldn't manage it in the United Way office. So we moved it to the revenue building. It was an overwhelming thing.

We had people that wanted their donation to go to help animals, and others who wanted their money restricted for a certain person that they saw in the newspaper. There was a young girl in a shelter whose picture appeared in several newspapers. It had an article about how she and her family had to leave their home, and they didn't know if they'd be able to go back to the same house. It showed this very darling little African American girl. There were several donations that came in specifically earmarked for that girl and her family. So we had to find that girl.

The purple piggybank is a plastic piggybank that came from the grandparents of a small girl in Pennsylvania. She saw on the news the devastation and the children that had been taken from their homes, and she decided that she wanted to help. So she took her purple piggybank down to a local store and advertised it as a place where children could put their money. So this purple piggybank arrived in Governor Hunt's office with $202.26 in it from the grandparents of this little girl. It had a note inside, saying that she wanted to send it to the kids. Unfortunately, we had to cut a huge hole in the piggybank to get the money out. But we still have the piggy, and it's kind of like a little symbol.

Sometimes when I'm talking to different groups about Hurricane Floyd, I'll use it as a little sign of how people of all ages helped.

Then there was a couple who got married in the Northeast, and I can't remember the state, but they sent a check and a wedding invitation. Here I'm tearing up again. They were getting married, and in lieu of wedding gifts, they had requested that their guests donate to the relief fund. We actually got that, believe it or not, from three or four different couples. Just an overwhelming response. We had a little boy who sent a quarter and two pennies taped to a piece of paper. On the other hand, we had Barnes and Noble booksellers, who gave a little over thirty-eight thousand dollars, restricted to buy books for schools that had lost their libraries. We had many foundations that gave money. Michael Jordan gave a quarter of a million dollars. It was a check from him with a very brief note to the governor. So we had things like that. The Hanes Foundation in Winston-Salem gave a huge amount. There were just so many foundations and trust funds that gave money. Food Lion, Lowe's, and NASCAR were big players. NASCAR drivers put together a huge donated-goods drive, and they brought fifty-one tractor-trailer loads of donated supplies. And every person who donated, whether it was twenty-six cents or two hundred fifty thousand dollars, got a thank you letter. Mr. Tolson came in to try to get corporate support. Norris did a fantastic job. The fund really grew tremendously because of Norris's efforts. There were so many organizations that gave money. Organizations that you wouldn't normally think of, like the Bar Association. I mean people were so generous in helping other people. Just so generous. They're all heroes, every one of them.

One of the heroes was a lady by the name of Judy Cromer. Judy was a volunteer center director in Pender County. She had been on the job about two months, and she became a true hero. She pulled together a volunteer management process in Pender County that was absolutely wonderful. She was so good that the governor asked her to present to a cabinet meeting four or five months after the storm. She pulled together all of the organizations in Pender County that were using volunteers and served as a clearinghouse. Plus, she volunteered an awful lot herself. Many, many, many long hours. She was a hero that you'd never hear about.

All I have done was sit here and cry. But they're happy tears. They're very happy tears. Working in emergency management, especially after the terrorist attacks, a lot of these friendships and business relationships came about because of Hurricane Floyd. They have become very vital to the whole community safety. It goes beyond hurricanes. It just goes beyond that. We're stronger now.

So in addition to doing emergency information, I was doing donations management. It was really a massive task. It was unbelievable. There were so many people that were flying by the seat of their pants in that whole event because it was so huge. But I can tell you it wasn't just me. I would run into Governor Hunt at two or three in the morning in the stairwells of this building. I would run into Richard Moore. There are some people at emergency management that, I mean, we're like blood brothers. It was just something that I hope I'll never have to go through again.

People sometimes ask, "What is the one thing you brought away from Hurricane Floyd?" The one thing that I can see was, I was so exhausted when I finally went home that I fell up the steps going into my apartment, and I have a scar on my leg. That's my Floyd scar.

I'm sorry I teared up.

[Authors' note: The Hurricane Floyd Relief Fund received over 66,000 contributions and raised more than $19 million.]

Al Price   Al Price is district chief of the Rocky Mount Fire Department. Though he was in the city's command center during the early stages of the flood, he eventually got out to assist other firefighters with house-to-house rescues. He described the flood as "simply overwhelming." He was interviewed in his South George Street station in June 2002.

Most of the time I was in our command center, so I was not out on the street. I was kind of an incident commander. My job was to make sure that we had enough equipment and to get the equipment and personnel to the areas when the calls came in. I did that for about twelve hours, until I got completely stir crazy. Then I decided that I would actually get out.

The first call I responded to was a lady who lives about a half-mile behind the station, and her husband was in need of oxygen. As I was going out, I didn't realize what I was getting into. We had a ladder company and a squad company down there operating at the time, and they were actually plucking people out of trees and off of houses with a bass boat. There were trees falling. The wind was still blowing at this time. Trees were actually coming down, and one of them missed the ladder company by about twenty feet or so.

I went back to the command center again, and did it for maybe four or five more hours. After a while, I said, "I've just got to get out again—I can't stand it no more." So I went back out, and by that time it was daylight and things had gotten pretty calm. I linked up with one of our firefighters and went to his house. The water was still rising. As we launched his boat, a gentleman came and told us that his parents lived in a house that was flooded. So we rode down to the gentleman's parents' house. He said, "I think they're in the attic"—and they were. We went around to the back, and the water was up almost to the top of the carport. You had to bend your head down pretty low to go under it to get to the back door. As soon as we get under it, this guy jumps out of the boat and disappears. I thought, "Oh, my God, what am I gonna do? Not only have we got his parents up there, but the guy is gone." Well, the guy finally bobbed back to the top. He swims over there, dives down and goes under the door and goes inside this house. So I jumped in, and we actually had to swim under the water to get inside the house. He went upstairs and got his parents, and we got them out. It was the God-awfullest sight in that kitchen—to see refrigerators and freezers and the kitchen table and chairs, and all this stuff just floating in the top of that room. You only had like maybe two feet of air between the water and the ceiling, and you had to make your way through all of that debris. Which doesn't seem like a whole lot, until you have to move a three-hundred-pound refrigerator out of your way to get through. This was during the day, so at least we had a little bit of light.

We got them back out on dry land and went back knocking on doors, because we realized that there were probably other people down there. We got about four or five houses down, knocked on the door, and you could hear this faint voice in the back. I went over the side, and the water was up to about my shoulders. I tried to push on the door, but it was kind of swollen. So we worked on the door probably fifteen minutes, trying to push it against that water, and we finally got it open. When I went inside the house, there was a little old lady sitting on the middle of her bed, and the bed was floating in the room. She was just kind of floating around that room. And she said, "Oh, my God, I'm so glad to see you! I just thought I was going to die right here." By that time Earl was tying the boat, and he came on in, too. He literally picked her up in his arms and carried her out. I grabbed two or three things that she wanted, and we walked her back out and put her in the boat.

Over in the Westhaven division, they actually picked some people out of trees. The water was really swift because they live close to the river. These were very large homes. The water actually got up so that it was coming into their attics. They had to climb out onto the peak of their roofs, and eventually they had to let that go, and they were physically in pine trees. When the firemen got there, they had to have a boat with a fairly large motor on it because the water was so swift. You couldn't go in there with just a small pontoon boat or something, it wouldn't work. You could get to them, but then the water would sweep you right on past them. Fences were no problem, 'cause we were several feet over the fences in these areas. On Taylor Street, you could look down in the water and actually see the cars as we were riding over them. But over there the water was so deep, the cars were long gone. They were probably twenty feet under the water.

Overwhelmed, I think, would be the first emotion that I felt. It was just so enormous, the magnitude of what was going on. It just overwhelmed me. I've been to major fires that burned out city blocks, but with those you felt like you had control. You were trained extensively to handle those kind of situations. We just weren't trained for this. I just don't think we were ready for anything of this magnitude. I just felt overwhelmed. At the same time, I was just so amazed at some of the stuff our guys were doing. We actually put out the call for all of our companies to come in. It was just way too dangerous to be out there. And not a one would come back. They just stayed out there, and they weren't willing to give up.

Clifton Mills

Clifton Mills is the DOT road maintenance supervisor for Jones County. During the floods that followed Hurricane Floyd, he and his crews worked to clear debris and to block off flooded roads in the area around Trenton. But tragically, he lost an employee and a lifelong friend when maintenance worker James Wilder drowned along Highway 58. Clifton was interviewed in his Trenton office in June 2002.

James Wilder had been employed with us for about five years, but I have known him for thirty years or more. I grew up within a few houses of where he lived and we kind of grew up together. He was a truck driver and a general highway maintenance worker. He mowed grass on the sides of the road and did all kinds of manual labor. He was well liked by the group. He had no problems with anybody. He was always a happy-go-lucky person. I don't think I ever saw him with a frown on his face. He was always happy and carrying on, and he was a real Redskins fan. Several of us in here are Cowboy fans, so that would always give us something to talk about after the long end of a weekend. James had no enemies out here, I could truthfully say that.

That Wednesday night as the storm was hitting, we shut down, came in, and got ready to spend the night and ride the storm out. We had most of our twenty-five employees spend the night, and we had some cots. We knew that once the storm subsided, we were going to have to hit it full force.

We got some rest for a few hours. Early Thursday morning, the wind died down, it started to become light, and we began assessing the reports we had of where trees were down. We were having some general high water that I would call normal. So early that morning, we started sending crews out to clear the roads. James was with a crew leader, Jesse Mercer, in his pickup along with Gerald Grey, another highway maintenance worker. They went out 58 North toward Kinston. I had some reports that there was trees on 58 and we had to get it cleared. There were not that many. After Fran or Bertha, we would have hundreds of trees on the road. Well, this time, I'd estimate we only had fifty or so.

The closer they get to the Lenoir County line, the more water they encounter. They'd already crossed the Trent River bridge. You'd have to picture this wide-open field, and the elevation goes up to the bridge, then it drops back off at the other side. It was getting on about lunchtime. They decided that since there was so much water up there, that they were going to shut down and come back in to the office and kinda regroup.

About 12:30, they were on their way back down 58. They crossed over the bridge onto the Trenton side and came up on a car that was ahead of them. It was Mr. Jack Whaley. The water's over the road, but it's not very deep—about ten inches or so. But as water goes across the road like that, it tends to be higher on the side it's coming from and lower on the side it falls off to, like a water-fall. So Jack bears over to the lefthand side of the road where the water wasn't quite as deep. He gets too close to the shoulder of the road and he gets swept down into it. The water was rushing across the road, and it just swept his car over. It was a vast open field that looked like a lake on both sides of the road, but across the highway it was rushing.

Jesse calls us on the radio saying, "We've got a man that's gone overboard, and he's sitting on top of his car." The car didn't flip over or anything, but it's submerged, and Jack had managed to crawl up on top of his car. When John and I got there, all you could see was him—his car was totally submerged. We told our secretary to call 911.

We drive on up in the Explorer, no problem, and there is Mr. Whaley sitting out there in the water. He was probably in the water almost an hour. So the fire truck comes with the boat. All of us, including James, help them get the boat off the truck, tie a rope to the boat, and then they go out in the water to rescue Mr. Whaley. No real big deal. Got him in, got him in the fire truck, and loaded the boat back up. We noticed that after we got Jack in the fire truck, the water had gotten higher. Jesse's pickup and the fire truck were facing Trenton, so I told Jesse to follow the fire truck, and we'd turn the Explorer around and follow you guys. So they went on.

Well, Jesse had four people in a small pickup, so they decided that James and Gerald Grey would ride in the back of the truck. Well, as they started out, the water raging over the road was hard enough that it started moving Jesse's truck a little bit. The current was trying to push it to the left. For some reason, James must have thought that the truck was gonna go overboard, and he decided to exit the truck out the back. The tailgate was up. Somebody shouted and got my attention, and I looked back over my shoulder, and I saw James come out the back of the truck. He stumbled. And when he stumbled, the current swept him out into the big field over there, in the lake.

He didn't say anything. Gerald was sitting there with him, and he didn't say nothing. He just got up and out of the back of the truck. Somehow or another, his foot caught the tailgate or something, and he stumbled when he got over into the water. If you can picture, the water is still maybe ten inches deep, if it was even that.

When I saw James had jumped out, I immediately started hollering, "Don't fight it, go with it." James had on boots and his wet-weather gear. The way the water was raging, I don't think he could even hear us. I started running down there to him, then had to wade through the water to get out there. The first thing he did was he tried to swim back to where he went over. Well, the water was raging there, and he was trying to fight against that current.

The firemen came back towards him with some life preservers, but they were probably four hundred feet away. I was the first one to get back there to him, but he was way on out there in that field. I could tell he was struggling. I'd guess the water right there was seven or eight foot deep—not real deep, but it was over his head. I was yelling for him to come to me, 'cause if he swam maybe ten feet towards me, he probably would have been able to touch bottom.

So I go down to him, and there was a Marine lance corporal over there. Just as the firemen get there with life preservers, the Marine told me, "Look, I'm an expert swimmer." So the Marine grabs a life preserver, tucks it under his arm, and dives out into the water. James was probably fifty or seventy-five feet out there. About this time, James went down. I remember him turning around in the water, and our eyes met. That's something I'll never forget. Just as our eyes met, he went down, and he didn't never come back up.

The Marine had gone way on out, and now I was worried about his safety. So we ended up having to worry about rescuing the Marine. But they got him back up, and then started the search for James. There were three or four civilians out there with their cars, so we ended up evacuating and leaving their cars parked up on the bridge. We called in the search-and-rescue helicopter PEDRO, as well as some other rescue squads to come and look for James. They looked right on into the night that night. All through this time, the water was continuing to get deeper. I don't think any of us would have been able to get off that bridge if we had stayed much longer.

John immediately called our supervisors. Really tough. I can say that was the worst day of my life. Especially knowing him as well as I did. And losing a worker—losing somebody so close. We're just like a family. And everybody took it pretty hard. Naturally, it was our duty to have to go tell Miss Mattie and the family. I think they were already aware that something was going on. And they were being flooded, too. It didn't flood them out, but it came up under them, and you couldn't drive up to their house. I had to walk up there. A lot of their family was there. And I had to go in and tell them that we had lost James —that we couldn't find him—that he in fact had drowned.

During this time, to add to all this, the water was still rising here. The water got five feet deep in this office. I was the last one to leave here, and it was probably waist deep out in the yard. We moved our operations right on out to the Civic Center, which was a shelter.

The family took it pretty hard. When they found him on Saturday, I went with his oldest son to identify his body. We rode in my pickup. But the family was real understanding of what happened. He was out doing his job in a real time of crisis. None of us realized it could be like this. I had no idea that morning that the water was going to be five foot deep in my office. It was a lot worse than anybody expected. The Trent River was a mile wide. It was just water everywhere.

It's hard for people to realize that ten or twelve inches could carry you away like that. It's a constant force pushing you the way the water wants to go.

During the rescue when we helped Mr. Whaley off of that car, James helped us pull the rope to bring Mr. Whaley back in. I do know that before we even got out there, James was shouting instructions and encouragement to Mr. Whaley so that we didn't lose him. He was definitely involved in his rescue.

They had a big ceremony in Raleigh to honor the employees of DOT. There was a special speech about James, and they told of how he had died in the line of duty trying to assist somebody. All of his family was there at the ceremony. The assistant secretary of transportation came down and spoke at his funeral. A lot of people attended his funeral.

He was a caring and happy-go-lucky person. He was a good employee to supervise. He was always happy at work. That Thursday morning, he was ready to go out and do his job, just like everybody else. No questions asked.

Drew Pearson

Commander Drew Pearson is the operations officer at Coast Guard Air Station Elizabeth City. During Hurricane Floyd, he was a search-and-rescue pilot who flew a C-130 aircraft around eastern North Carolina, coordinating the rescue operations of squadrons of helicopters. He was interviewed by telephone in September 2002.

I'm currently the operations officer here at Coast Guard Air Station Elizabeth City. I've been in the Coast Guard for eighteen years and have about fifty-four hundred hours of flight time—all of it in the C-130 aircraft. I was in Washington, D.C., and then I returned to Elizabeth City in August of '99 as a search-and-rescue pilot. At the time I was a lieutenant commander and had been here a little over a month and a half when Floyd rolled around.

Our relief operations started on the evening of September 16. Prior to that, we had mobilized to move our aircraft away from the path of Hurricane Floyd. We flew three C-130s and one helicopter up to Charleston, West Virginia, to get them out of the path of Floyd. That's a normal routine when a big hurricane is on the way.

As we were leaving, we did a patrol that took us down to the edges of Floyd. We flew a C-130 down the coast and put out radio calls on the hail-and-distress frequencies to alert people who weren't aware of the storm. Then we went to West Virginia, and the storm moved through and dumped all its rain.

By the sixteenth, the storm had passed and the rains had calmed. A decision was made to launch aircraft from Elizabeth City. One plane escorted a helicopter offshore to rescue people from a merchant vessel that was in distress. It had some of its cargo shift, and three or four injured sailors were brought back.

We'd had a long day getting the airplanes back from West Virginia, and right around nine o'clock I retired for the evening. At about nine-fifteen I was awakened by a search-and-rescue alarm, followed by a pipe or announcement. The announcement was to put the ready helicopter on the line, that three hundred people were stranded on their roofs in Tarboro. That was the first time in my eighteen-year career that I'd ever heard of putting the helicopter online for three hundred people inland. The Coast Guard is a maritime organization, responsible for search and rescue at sea. We normally don't respond inland. So that got me up out of the bed.

Our command center in Portsmouth, Virginia, was being inundated with requests for assistance. They were trying to help local authorities in the Tarboro area. They turned to us and said, "What can you get out there to start helping?" Elizabeth City has a complement of three HH-60 Jayhawk helicopters, and we started calling in crews to fly them that evening. We were able to get people in here very quickly.

With three helicopters out searching, we made a decision to put a C-130 in the air to control the aircraft activities down on the surface. That was the aircraft I flew that evening. We also deployed a person to the Emergency Operations Center in Tarboro, so that we could communicate with people on the ground. Then we just started making things happen.

We took off at about ten o'clock that night. We had three helicopters out and the C-130, and there were other military assets that started to come and assist. That evening we started a very focused, urgent SAR effort that lasted the next forty-two hours. The helicopters from Elizabeth City were out finding people stranded on rooftops, in cars, on highways, in trees, and in the rivers. We don't normally operate inland where there are hazards like trees, wires, light poles, cell towers, and things like that. With three helicopters all going after the same people, you could end up with helicopters hitting each other. From a command and control perspective, we were deconflicting the aircraft.

So we broke out a chart and a road map, cordoned off sectors, and worked with the person we'd put on the ground to take reports the emergency operations folks were getting. These were police reports of stranded folks. I'd try to find where the road was on our maps so that we could send a helicopter to go to them. I'm translating a road location into a latitude and longitude so that they can put it into their global positioning system to allow them to get there quickly and recover people. Then they would bring them back and hand them off to the local authorities who could get them the care that they needed.

We finished our round about eight the next morning. We were relieved by another C-130 that came out and had to control additional assets. By the time the next morning rolled around, there were helicopters from the Army, Navy, and Marine Corps. Everything from HH-60s, which is what we fly, to larger helicopters like the CH-46, CH-53, and the CH-47. They were coming from everywhere. When you have over twenty-five aircraft in a relatively small area, they could very easily run into each other. And we do not have a radar to track helicopters below us in the C-130.

I got some rest and came in the next day to fly again. That day we had twenty-seven helicopters out providing rescue support—still pulling people off of roofs, out of homes, and taking them to care centers. Over that forty-two-hour period, with the coordinated effort of the DOD services that came on the second day, we estimated we had assisted or saved over two thousand people. The Coast Guard flew at least three hundred eighteen flight hours and directly assisted or saved over four hundred fifty people. At times they were putting so many people in the aircraft that they just couldn't keep count of them. They would load them on and drop them off, and there was no manifest as to who was picked up. They did quick counts and tried to keep track. It was a very fluid environment.

In the Coast Guard helicopter, the HH-60-J, they were doing about three hours at a time before they needed to get fuel. When they're hovering down low, they burn fuel much quicker than when they're transiting. Some of the helicopters, like the CH-53, can stay out there for eight or nine hours. And they can carry forty people—much larger numbers. So there was a whole mix of aircraft that had different capabilities.

Most of the Navy assets came from the Hampton Roads area. Some came from Fort Bragg and some from Cherry Point. Seven Coast Guard aviation commands provided assets to us from Clearwater, Florida, Detroit, Michigan, Traverse City, Michigan, Atlantic City, New Jersey, Savannah, Georgia, [and] Mobile, Alabama, in addition to Elizabeth City. They flew helicopter missions, brought in additional C-130 crews, and used Falcon jets to move people to and from different locations. It was a very focused, quick-response effort.

The Coast Guard has done some amazing things in the past, like the mass removal of migrants from Cuba and other places. But in response to an inland search-and-rescue mission, I don't think there's anything that this would compare to. This may have been the first time we've undertaken anything like this.

There was a lot of recognition handed out. When President Clinton visited Tarboro as part of the relief effort, they selected people who were involved with the rescue operations to meet with the president. They got a pat on the back from the Commander in Chief, as well as from our four-star admiral, James Loy.

Inland search and rescue is normally an Air Force mission. We took control of this rescue effort on September 16 and held it for forty-two hours. The United States Coast Guard responded to a mission that we are not historically equipped or trained to do. We responded with enough force and enough people to manage an inland SAR for forty-two hours and helped save over two thousand lives. The Air Force took the mission from us on the 18th of September and set up a rescue operations center at Pope Air Force Base. They continued the efforts after we were done with the initial response.

I was lucky enough to be assigned to do the turnover at Pope Air Force Base. We were giving it over to the Air Force. I was flown there in one of the Falcons that came up from Mobile. I got dropped off, and there was a car waiting there for me with an Air Force colonel and his driver. The colonel walked up to me and said, "You Coasties pulled our ass out of the sling in this one. We never could have responded like you did, in such a short period of time. You saved our butts in this one."

If we hadn't been able to do it, I'm not sure how many lives would have been lost, or how much more suffering people would have endured. We made a difference. That's why I joined the Coast Guard eighteen years ago, to make a difference. I can't tell you how many countless cards and letters we received from people in the Tarboro area. They were truly appreciative of what we did in September 1999. Now whenever we have a chance to fly over that area, we look down at it a little differently.

Barbara Stiles

After Hurricane Floyd flooded communities around her Goldsboro home, Barbara Stiles knew that she wanted to help the flood victims in her area. She volunteered for the Red Cross and then became the director of Wayne County Long-Term Recovery, an interfaith organization established to assist families in need. In that role, she saw many examples of how devastating the flood had been and how uplifting the connection was between volunteers and victims. She was interviewed by telephone in September 2002.

I'm a Wayne County transplant. We were stationed here at the air base several times in the past and came back to Wayne County for permanent residency. We had just moved back here and had been here about four months when the flood came.

September rolled around, and we had three storms back to back. Any one of them alone probably would not have done all the damage. But it was all just too much for our area to handle. Part of our county was just totally devastated. We have pictures of one area with just rooftops showing. Seven Springs is in our county, and the whole township was underwater except maybe five homes. So we had quite a bit of devastation, and no one here had ever seen anything like it.

After the flood, I decided to call the Red Cross and see what I could do. Our community was underwater for quite a while and we couldn't get out. I lived in Walnut Creek off of Highway 70, on the way to Seven Springs. We were pretty much locked in. In fact, where we live there were two dams that broke surrounding our community. As they would reroute water, neighbors would call one another and say, "I'm going for milk, do you want anything?" And whoever knew where a road was opening up, they would make a run for it and take orders from all the neighbors.

We had water in the front and back of the house, about two steps from the top. But nothing came in our home. Across the street from us, our neighbors had water with quite extensive damage. They had a sunken living floor that really was sunken. But we were in very good shape compared with a lot of other people.

I went to Red Cross to see what I could do. What they needed was one community person that would accompany incoming volunteers on their routes to see how people were doing. For some reason, they took me down to New Bern and I wasn't familiar with it. But I saw some amazing things down there.

I had been following Hurricane Floyd in the papers, and I figured I could get involved in some other way. An article came out about a long-term recovery committee that they were forming, and I called to see if I could volunteer for that. I had to wait a few weeks for training, so in the meantime, I saw in another article that they were looking for a director. I had past experience in working with a lot of volunteers, but not anything with disasters. So I submitted my application. I went in and was hired on the spot as a full-time director to coordinate volunteer efforts by an interfaith organization, Wayne County Long-Term Recovery. This interfaith was created in October right after Floyd, with the chamber of commerce as the lead agency and with a lot of supervision and guidance from FEMA and the North Carolina Interfaith Disaster Recovery. Carolyn Tyler was our leader from the statewide interfaith. It took a lot of time to get bylaws and all of that together, so it was April before I was hired. But surprisingly, we were one of the first interfaith organizations that was formed.

The committee had a really careful screening process but had some flexibility. We figured we were created to bridge the gaps that existed for those who did not fit the government programs. Our policy was that they had to meet a certain income level, which was just above the FEMA standard.

We worked really closely with our board. We had people from the Department of Social Services, Salvation Army, and people who did a lot of casework. We worked closely with North Carolina Housing Recovery Assistance. We formed a resource committee, and every case that was more than a thousand dollars in expenditures was brought before that committee for checks and balances. We would bring a case together, and perhaps the Salvation Army would say they would pay a thousand dollars, and the Methodists would take another thousand. This was one way to keep them on board and help us stay in existence a lot longer and not spend all our money.

Of the people that we helped, I would say the average person received a thousand dollars' worth of materials for repair and usually an amount of labor to match that, so the average expenditure was about two thousand dollars. We might have spent fourteen thousand on some in extreme situations, and on others we might have spent only two hundred. It just depended on what the needs were. But we would scrutinize anything major very carefully.

One story I remember was a woman who called to say she had lost everything. When we asked her what she meant by everything, she said that when they rescued her, she did not even have time to get her false teeth. So she had to go to the recovery center without her teeth.

Another one I remember was a gentleman that came to us in August 2001, almost two years after the flood. He was a skinny little man, just less than five feet tall. It was a hot August day and he walked in with a sweater and a hat, while the rest of us were dying in almost one-hundred-degree weather. He said that he had some roof damage from the flood. He had seen some people working on his street and wanted to see if they might be able to help him. So two of our caseworkers went out to see what kind of damage he had. They came back in total disbelief. A tree had fallen on his roof and damaged the whole backside of his house. The ceiling in the kitchen had fallen in, and the ceiling was about to fall into the bathroom. Every time he went into the bathroom he was really risking his life. In the kitchen, the whole floor was covered with ceiling debris, including his breakfast on the morning it collapsed about two months before. He said he wanted to make sure he left the evidence in case somebody did not believe him.

After the storm had knocked the tree down, he had gotten his nephew to throw a tarp up there. But he did not realize there was a slow leak going on, so for two years it slowly deteriorated. It got to the point he could not live in the house anymore, so he moved into this little house that we have been calling the gazebo. It looked like a little playhouse that you might have built in your yard for your daughter. It was ten feet square. This small house was situated in his front yard on a very busy highway. So every time a car would go by his house, the headlights would shine in this little house. He was living in there with a cot, a microwave, and a fan. He just did not know what else to do or where to go.

His original house smelled like mildew and needed to be totally redone. The yard was strewn with metal. He was trying to get a few extra dollars by gathering metal which he had for years and years. He was eighty-five years old and you could hardly walk in the yard because of all the metal. So I asked him what he planned to do with all this metal. He said that he had been collecting it for some time now, but he was too old to haul it. I asked him if it would help if we got a dumpster out here and had someone come and pick it up. He just started crying right there. Tears just started welling up in his eyes. We had not even talked about repairing his home yet. He was just so touched that someone would help him. So we had a dumpster there the next week. He was the first one there putting stuff in it.

Soon we had a group of teen volunteers from the Christian Reform World Relief Committee arrive from Canada. This man was so impressed that these teens came all the way from Canada to work on his house. This was about a week after the September 11th disaster in New York, and the teens asked him what he thought about it. He had not heard a word about it since he had been totally cut off from the world. When the teens told us this, that's when we realized that he did not know where to go for assistance. He was in his own little world.

It took about four days for the volunteers to repair the roof and to redo the interior walls by replacing drywall and installing insulation. Once this was completed, the house was painted and the smell was out. Within four days, he was back in his house. It was a good experience for both the gentleman and the teens.

Our organization has helped approximately a hundred forty-five families. One hundred eleven of those were repairs and six were new mobile homes that we purchased. The Salvation Army really came through for us. They purchased five or six of the homes. We bought FEMA trailers and we really got a good price from FEMA.

I have no construction background. I could hang a picture on the wall, and that's about it. But we were able to get the right people involved with the Christian Reform World Relief Committee. They did assessments on more than fourteen hundred homes, and we were the first community they came to help. They actually knocked on doors in the flooded community and left flyers if people were not home. In many cases, people were not home because they were living with relatives. They left our number to call. Approximately eight hundred people responded to those flyers. When a caseworker went out to see what the needs were, they found people with nothing. They had a sofa and that was it. They had been sleeping on it at night and sitting on it during the day. The caseworker told them they were eligible for furniture, and they could get help with repairs on their home, but often their reply was to go help somebody else who really needs it.

We saw so many cases of people who thought they were in much better shape than they actually were. One year after the flood is when a lot of the severe depression set in. Early on they said, "I can do this," but after a year had passed they realized that they were still there and nothing was getting much better. In Wayne County, most people are now pretty well taken care of. Approximately four thousand homes were flooded here.

The flood did not discriminate. There were people that were interviewed that were probably the most well off in our community. Businesses were hurt, like Carolina Turkey and Goldsboro Milling. They lost a hundred-fifty-thousand turkeys, plus one of the vice-presidents had water up to the door. They were dealing with their businesses and their homes, which was stressful.

The economy has not changed much, but individuals will tell you that they have not quite gotten back on their feet. One Hispanic family that we know had their home flooded and did not get back in their home until this January. I just heard recently that they are divorcing, and I am sure that the stress of the flood had a lot to do with it. When they came to us in July last year, they thought they had been discriminated against. But the problem was that there was no communication. No one could find out exactly what they needed. They were not given the right forms because no one knew what they needed to do. So an interpreter was brought in, and they sat down with county representatives and got them in the program. We committed ourselves to about three thousand dollars' worth of furniture once they got their home. Well, by the time they got their home, our organization had dissolved and did not have a penny left. They showed up a month after we had dissolved and had closed the door on all funding. We thought they had been taken care of when we helped them in June by giving them the vouchers and everything. I am sure the stress of this added to their marital problems. The gentleman lost his job, and I'm not sure if he lost his job because of the flood. Now we have a Hispanic woman on her own with six children here in our community, so that has to be tough.

We are near the air base here, and one of the airmen was going through a divorce just before the flood hit. His wife and children had left him. He lived in one of our hardest-hit communities where most of the houses were underwater. The majority of those houses were totally lost, since most were under the water so long. Most of this section was bought out. This airman was staying in a FEMA camper and would not leave. His home had grass growing up around it, and he was apparently very depressed. We had to go to the base to find someone in the family support center to get him to come out.

So we called him and told him, "You've got a team coming in—kids from Cincinnati. They will come and help you clean up the yard and do anything on the inside. They have some good team leaders and are just the thing you need." He said, "Yes, let's see what they can do." We became excited because he was beginning to participate in the program. The teams went out there and cut his grass. The man did not have a lawnmower because it had been stolen. We also saw in the paper that he had been mugged. He had hard luck written all over him from start to finish.

So the team cleaned up his yard. During one lunch break, after they'd been there a couple days, the team leader told the teens that we are each connected to one another. He told them, "As we work on these houses out here we must remind ourselves that we are connected to each of the people that we help. We are learning as much from them as they are learning from us." The leader took a string and tied it around each person and formed a big circle. Afterwards, they cut a length from the same string to make a bracelet for each person, and they tied them on their wrists. He told everyone, "This is to remind you that we are all connected. So as you are working with families, just touch your bracelet to remember that connection."

So when it came time to eat their sandwiches, one of the girls asked if she could make the homeowner a sandwich. She made the sandwich and noticed that she had lost her bracelet. She asked if she could get another one for herself and one for the homeowner. They said sure. She cut two new lengths and explained to the homeowner what it meant. So the kids went back to work in the backyard, and just then a jet from the base flew right over the house. One of the young teenaged boys stated that he was going to fly a jet someday. The airman asked the boy, "Do you like jets?" The boy replied, "Yes I love them!" The airman said, "Well, I work out at the base. Do you want to go see the jets?" The boy said, "Sure," and the airman said, "How about now?" Everybody stopped work, jumped in the van, and rode out to the base. As they walked into the squadron, the people at the receptionist desk asked, "Sergeant, is this your family?" The airman looked at his wrist, held that little piece of twine, and said, "Yes, it is." From then on the airman stayed in touch with us.

Todd Davison   Todd Davison is the Region Four flood insurance and mitigation director for FEMA. His agency played a lead role in both the response and recovery phases of the Floyd disaster. Though FEMA sometimes comes under fire from those who have lost their homes, Todd has his own perspective on FEMA's proper role and the expectations held by disaster victims. He was interviewed in his Atlanta office in August 2002.

I've been with FEMA since 1986. I spent eleven years in our Washington headquarters, dealing with issues related to flood insurance and mitigation programs. Currently, I hold the position of flood insurance and mitigation director here in FEMA Region Four, which covers eight southeastern states including North Carolina. That includes the Gulf Coast and East Coast—the hurricane belt. I've been here in Atlanta for six years now.

In that role, I primarily deal with issues related to the prevention of damage in disasters, both economic and personal. But as everybody in FEMA does, when we have a response under way, most people wear a different hat. So I assume the role of director of the regional operations center. We mobilize a whole series of protocols and operational plans for evacuation, and for prestaging of resources such as ice, water, generators, plastic, emergency medical teams, and the like. You'll remember the disaster mortuary teams that were working on caskets out in Princeville, the helicopter rescue missions for life safety, and the air search-and-rescue teams. Our role in the operation center here in Atlanta is to coordinate and to try to prestage assets and resources and put them where they're needed.

At the time, you'll remember, Floyd was threatening Florida, Georgia, South Carolina, and North Carolina. Obviously, it was a moving target. We were hedging our bets, trying to predict where landfall was coming, and we were having an extremely difficult time doing that. We ended up making some operational decisions about the movement of people, resources, and assets. We missed it a little bit, but generally we got it right. We were able to have a lot of the materials in place. Floyd ended up not being the wind event everybody thought it would be, but it was clearly a heavy, heavy precipitation event that brought about flash flooding.

One of the most important missions during the evening that Floyd hit was swift-water rescue operations—both by boat and by air. That was a combination of local, state, and federal responsibility. But we don't make those decisions from Atlanta; it's basically request-driven. In other words, we're not pushing resources; the locals through the state are pulling them from us. We

Frustrated residents of Old Sparta erected a sign on NC 42 that became a landmark in the months following Hurricane Floyd. (Photo by Jay Barnes)

Flooded residents wait their turn in line at the Salvation Army in Kinston five days after the passage of Floyd. Up to 150 heads of households were allowed to pick up food that day with a referral from Social Services. (Photo by Francisco Kjolseth; courtesy of the *Charlotte Observer*)

Members of the North Carolina National Guard unload bottled water from a helicopter in Greenville. The National Guard played a key role in providing relief to isolated areas. (Photo courtesy of the *Charlotte Observer*)

have a pretty elaborate system of coordination for what the needs are. It was clear in those early morning hours we were getting a lot of requests for helicopter support to airlift people trapped on top of houses, up in trees, sitting on top of trucks on interstates, or wherever people were stranded.

FEMA doesn't coordinate the actual air rescue—that was the Coast Guard if

I remember correctly. But there were helicopters of various ownership in the air at any one time. Fort Bragg, the North Carolina National Guard, the Coast Guard, the Marines out of Cherry Point, and there may have been others, but these were the primary folks. FEMA essentially reimburses these federal agencies for their expenditures during these emergency operations. We have ways to pay the Army, and pay the Coast Guard and the Corps of Engineers, and these other federal agencies. We do this under a pretty well-scripted plan called the Federal Response Plan. In the first wee hours of the morning during Floyd, the life-safety missions were terribly important. And they went on for quite some time. They went on for a good forty-eight hours before we were comfortable that we had plucked everybody out of these trees and off of these rooftops.

One thing the public probably never sees is the prepositioning of things—like water, ice, and generators. Generators are a premium commodity after a hurricane because you'll need them to run critical facilities like hospitals, police stations, fire stations, and shelters. So working with the state in a coordinated way, we prestage a lot of those generators. We know we don't want to keep them here in Atlanta in our warehouse.

So two or three days before the storm, we would obtain large quantities of ice, deliver it to the area we think it's needed, and store it in refrigerated trucks. The amount of supplies we brought into North Carolina was about right. But the problem was getting it there. We had to air-transport it into Kinston because all the roads were flooded. Our operational plan assumes you can drive to these places, and that's not always a correct assumption. So while we did prestage a lot of things, it was difficult after the storm to drive anywhere in the eastern part of the state because of the highway closings.

It was clear Floyd was becoming disorganized immediately before it made landfall. It was kind of a big sloppy storm, and we were somewhat relieved, initially. We were relieved that this wasn't going to materialize into a Hugo-type event. But then twelve hours hence, when it dumped all of that rain on an already saturated landscape, we knew we had some problems, beginning at three o'clock in the morning. We were getting frantic calls. Normally we're focused on wind events and expecting power lines down, trees down, and roofs blown off of houses—kind of like we had with Fran. We just didn't expect the widespread flooding and the immediate evacuation needs. But we adjusted for that probably within several hours—not just FEMA, but the whole emergency management community.

Generally, we highly encourage people living in flood-prone areas to purchase and maintain flood insurance, with the understanding that disaster assistance is not set up to make people whole again. It's not a hundred percent. In fact, it's quite a bit short of that. There are expectations in a postdisaster environment that FEMA can and should come in and take care of everybody's needs in whole. But the way the laws are written, and the way Congress devised the program, it's not intended to do that at all. It is devised to come in immediately and take care of humanitarian needs, and to get people back on their feet again—not necessarily to make them whole again. So there's an issue of personal responsibility and expectations on the front end versus once you get into a postdisaster environment and people are either underinsured or have no insurance at all. There's an immediate expectation emotionally— through the media, through the political environment—that our agency can and should make everybody better off in the situation. Maybe up to the point of taking care of all their needs—to make them whole again. When I say make them whole again, I mean reimburse them for a hundred percent of their losses. Rebuild their houses like they were. Even though they didn't carry insurance.

So the whole flood insurance program was set up as a way to promote personal responsibility. Floyd brought on floodwaters to areas that had never flooded in historical times, and perhaps may never flood again in our lifetimes. So a lot of people that did get water in their houses really had no expectation that they were even at risk. Now some clearly understood that they were in floodplains and either could not afford the insurance or just chose not to buy it. And some areas didn't even have flood maps so they would know. Or the maps were not adequate.

After a disaster of this size, there is tremendous human outpouring. People want to help, politicians want to help, the media is hyperfocused on the situation, which is all good. But there's [an attitude] of expectation. There's not enough, or it's not fast enough. Every single disaster we've been in of this size, there's always that—we're not meeting the expectations. The expectations are too large for any government, in a feasibility sense, to respond to these needs. However, I think we did a reasonable job in helping the locals, and the Red Cross, and everybody else, shelter folks. But there was also tremendous pressure immediately to get folks out of shelters into temporary housing, in these mobile home parks and these travel trailers. The reason we got into that, if you have a hurricane that hits a more populated area, you have a lot of rental resources—you can put people up in apartments, you can put people in hotels

—there are already existing housing resources there to accommodate the people that are displaced. In the case of eastern North Carolina, you really didn't have the infrastructure in place to accommodate the needs. We had to create those. We had to build mobile home parks and travel trailer parks, and that takes some time.

Floyd hit an area with all kinds of different income levels, but generally speaking we would call it a moderate- to low-moderate-income area. A lot of these homes were generational properties for which maybe no mortgage existed, or if there was a mortgage it had been paid off. The title had not transferred in many, many years in some cases, so the requirement to purchase flood insurance wasn't there. If there's no real-estate transaction that's occurred on a building in the last twenty or twenty-five years, there would be nothing that would trigger that requirement. In Florida, maybe ninety percent of the homes in floodplains carry flood insurance, but in North Carolina it was less than twenty percent. So we had flooding on a very uninsured portion of the population.

We had tough decisions to make. Working with the state and local governments, we had to decide whether or not houses could be reoccupied from a health and safety standpoint. With contaminated water that stood in these buildings for seven or ten days, could those properties be cleaned and cleansed and reoccupied by people that were perhaps elderly or young or had respiratory problems? At the same time, there were people that wanted to make longer-term decisions. We did initiate with the state a very aggressive acquisition and buyout program of flood-prone properties.

The buyouts are at preflood fair market value. We're limited by law to not make people better off than they were from a monetary sense. All we can pay for is the preflood fair market value for these properties. So you end up with what we call gap funding. There really isn't enough money to give people the option to go outside the floodplain and buy a like piece of property. Not without some other program providing that assistance. The North Carolina legislature did a tremendous job of providing that alternate funding. I think the state really took on a lot of the responsibility for meeting these unmet housing needs.

In 1996, Fran triggered some of these long-term acquisition programs. Floyd brought about almost a continuum of that. Since Fran, about seven thousand properties in North Carolina have been elevated and/or acquired.

If a homeowner wants to sell his property through the buyout, he can't make that decision alone. The local and state governments don't want to go out and buy properties in a checkerboard fashion. There has to be a necessary level of planning involved in how to acquire these properties from communities in a contiguous sense. For effective acquisition programs, local governments have to demonstrate a lot of leadership in bringing their communities together to say, "How do we want to do this? What's the vision of the future of this community?" It can be very complex. It's not just a simple real-estate transaction. It's a lot more than that.

We do implement our housing programs and our disaster assistance programs in concert with the Small Business Administration. We have some income tests for certain programs, like the individual and family grant program. You have to demonstrate a certain low-income level. In order to get FEMA assistance, you see that SBA will not loan you money—for a collateral reason, or you don't qualify for their loan program. So the first step in the disaster assistance game, at least on an individual level, is going to SBA.

It's difficult, because you have disaster victims of all income levels and education levels. Some people have never engaged in real-estate transactions. Some people get very confused by multiple programs, and some are intimidated, quite frankly, by the whole concept of filling out paperwork and exposing their lives to somebody else. I think that people were discouraged for a lot of different reasons.

But we try to be as clear as we can when we talk about the eligibility issues with SBA. You essentially have to be rejected by SBA before FEMA will entertain your application. And that's the way it should be from an income-testing standpoint. The whole idea is that if you haven't taken out insurance to protect yourself, then you have some level of personal responsibility. And SBA is the next form of assistance past flood insurance for doing that. Take out a loan to recover from the disaster. Now if you can't even qualify for a loan, then FEMA will come in and help with certain humanitarian needs to get you back on your feet.

It's a dynamic between what's the appropriate role of government versus what's the appropriate level of personal responsibility people should take before an event. You can argue those things philosophically in a predisaster environment, but they become very emotional in a postdisaster environment. Because people are hurting and out of their homes.

From the Red Cross, to the Salvation Army, to the Mennonites, the Baptist Builders, all the church groups—there's always a tremendous outpouring in big disasters like Floyd. FEMA helps coordinate that. We work with the Red

Cross in our mass care programs, to try to coordinate those voluntary agencies. We set up something called unmet needs committees, with all of the volunteer groups that come in.

What you saw in Floyd is not uncommon in large disasters where there is a tremendous outpouring of people, traveling great distances at their own expense. I myself went out to Kinston and helped build city-sponsored housing. They had their own Kinston version of a Habitat process going on. When we finally got Sundays off, even federal employees would go out and help do these things. It's fun, and you feel like you're more directly helping in many ways.

What was very effective was the within-state mutual aid. Folks from the Piedmont and the western part of the state were coming over to help the folks in the eastern part of the state. That happened in a variety of different programs, from the city manager of Cary going over to help the city manager of Princeville, or the public works director of Greensboro coming over to help the public works director in Greenville. Engineers going out to help other engineers. All of this was set up when Governor Hunt issued an executive order for mutual aid across the state. It was quite impressive. I had not seen this done, within state, to that degree. One-third of the state was tremendously affected, and two-thirds of the state wasn't, but there was tremendous outpouring of help. In my experience, that was the most extensive mutual-aid coordination that I had ever seen.

It was pretty clear that Floyd was a flood of just gigantic proportions, both in terms of magnitude and breadth. Very intense and widespread. The maps in some cases may have been accurate, but the flooding was of such a magnitude that it exceeded the frequency of our maps, if you will. In other cases, it was pretty obvious that some maps were not as accurate as they needed to be. You have areas that are urbanizing and suburbanizing in the greater Raleigh area and the Neuse watersheds and some of the other watersheds. It's pretty clear that those manmade changes do affect flood hazards. A lot of the flood maps in North Carolina were seventies vintage. In the seventies, engineering practices for hydraulics and hydrology weren't what they are today. We know a lot more about modeling of floodplains now than we did. We just haven't had the money to go back and revise those maps.

It became obvious to the state of North Carolina that if they wanted their maps to be comprehensively updated, they were going to have to pay for a large part of it themselves. And so part of the $836 million was dedicated to revising the state's floodplain maps. That process will take about six years. It really has been a great partnership with a collaboration of agencies, from emergency management, to DENR, to DOT and the like, and federal agencies as well with the Weather Service, the Corps of Engineers, and FEMA. Without question, this puts North Carolina in position of having the best flood maps in the nation. And you have a consistency of data across the state.

I think there is an increasing philosophy on personal responsibility. The money will be increasingly tied to decisions of personal or community responsibility and planning. You're seeing it now. Our hazard-mitigation grant program laws were changed recently so that we will no longer do buyouts, acquisitions, or relocations in communities that don't agree to develop and implement a mitigation prevention plan. What you probably will see increasingly in the future is that while that assistance will be provided, we're trying to insure that we can use that disaster to learn from and change practices and policies. I know we'll never eliminate the vulnerabilities, but we can reduce them.

We're trying to tie the availability of disaster assistance, generally speaking, to performance and accountability of state and local governments. And individuals. While we'll always, I'm certain, provide humanitarian and life-safety kinds of emergency services, decisions of personal responsibility to protect your economic investments are increasingly being leveraged against the availability of those funds. So those communities that plan better, those communities that build prevention programs, are going to fare better in terms of cost shares and the like. We've invoked the same kinds of responsibilities for local governments and public infrastructure, whether it's schools, city hall, fire stations, or whatever it is. If those buildings aren't insured, there's a limit to what will be covered.

That's a trend that's been happening now for several years, and it's probably going to increase in the future. While there's an understanding that we need to provide disaster assistance, the question is, how many times in a row should you provide it? At what point do individuals and governments institute efforts to reduce their vulnerability? It's a general trend that I think we're seeing grow over time. But there will always be a natural level of frustration and unmet expectations. I've never been in a disaster yet when that wasn't the case.

Billy Kornegay

Billy Kornegay is a town commissioner in Grifton. He experienced Hurricane Floyd as a local government official, but also as a victim: his home and his mother's home next door were flooded by almost two feet of water. Three years after the storm, Billy still isn't back in his house. He was interviewed by telephone in September 2002.

It all began in September of '99, and the flood hit us on the 16th during the night. The next day after the storm everything was kind of clear. I thought we'd be all right. But that night, me and my wife went home and prepared to spend the night with my mother, who lives right next to me. We never got a chance to sleep in that house again. My wife would never get a chance to sleep in that home again, because she passed away in May of 2000.

The police came by that afternoon about four o'clock with loudspeakers telling everybody they need to evacuate because high water was coming. And we did. We all got out of our place. We could only get out on one street, because all the other surrounding streets were already covered with water. We went over to Lenoir County to my niece's house, which was a good mile from where we lived. We thought we'd be okay there. After about two hours, about the time we were getting ready to bed down at her house, we had to leave again because the water had crossed the bridges and was starting to surround the Lenoir County side of Grifton. From there, we went to Greenville, about eighteen miles up the road.

By midnight that night, the police, rescue squad, and fire departments were rescuing people and getting them across the high waters, either to Kinston or Greenville. By the next morning, Grifton was surrounded by water, down Main Street, down Water Street, and all around on the Lenoir County side. You could not move from one side to the other except maybe by boat.

I had seen some high water around Grifton back in 1963, if I'm not mistaken. But nothing like this. I had never seen nothing like this before. When it poured down rain, it rained so hard that you could not see to drive. Because at the time I was having to take my wife to chemo. She had just had an operation for cancer in August; she had colon and liver cancer. So I was having to transport her to Greenville for her first treatments of chemo. When I tried to take her on Thursday, Greenville was shut down.

There was water on the roads like mad. Normal life had just come to a halt. There was damage to roads, railroad tracks, homes, and businesses. The town fire, rescue, and police departments had to move. The newspaper was under-

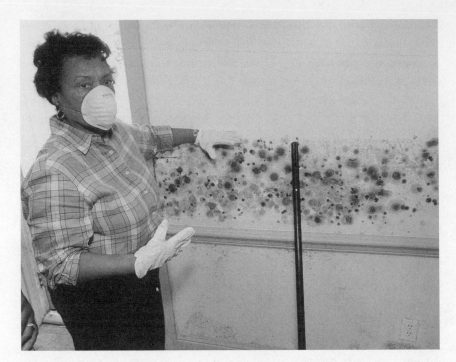

water, and the only supermarket we had was underwater. In some of them, the water went all the way to the roof, and others it was fifteen to eighteen inches from the roof. I went into homes just across in Lenoir County that looked like a washing machine had twisted them around. The furniture was turned over and moved around from one room to another, if it could float in there. It was just a mess. Stuff just piled up and turned over. A lot of homes, like my home, couldn't be reached for about three or four weeks because the water continued to stay there.

I had to leave real quickly. That night when I left, I only got something for overnight. The next morning I told my wife that I was going to go back down there. I came back down to get some clothes, and I was in there less than half an hour. But if I hadn't of left when I did, I wouldn't have gotten out with my car. I had to come back across the park that was in front of our house, and almost got stuck coming back through there. The water was still rising through that time. I got very little out of the house, but I did get us some clothes. After that, there was no more going back for a long time.

It is heartbreaking to lose so many things. While I was in my house that day, I was able to put a lot of pictures and things up high to save them. Now it's three years later, and I'm still not back in my home as of yet. I don't lack much from being back in it, and my mother's still not back in hers. In looking at the walls, I had probably twelve to eighteen inches of water in different areas. My mother's home was a little bit lower than mine, and hers got two foot in some areas.

The Baptist Men are working in my home. They had to completely strip out the walls, the floors, and everything in it. Then it had to sit and dry out, and the ground had to be dry before they could start to put the floors back. They also had to use a disinfectant to wash it down to kill the different bacteria that were in the water. All the electric lines and all the air conditioning was underwater and it had to go. It was stripped down to just the bare outside walls.

After three years, I'm still not back in. They're still working. During this three years, I was lucky enough to rent a home less than a half-mile from my home. It was big enough for my mother, my wife, my sister, and myself.

I did have some flood insurance. But the flood insurance, with what I owed on my home, took that. It took that to pay off. And I didn't qualify with FEMA to get a grant to redo my home. I was able to borrow some money, but I didn't qualify. I was caught in-between those that got grants and those that could afford to do it themselves.

My mother is eighty-some years old. I had to fill out all kinds of paperwork to try to get her grant. I had to first fill out paperwork for a loan, and I'm asking, "Why do I have to fill out paperwork for a loan, knowing that she's eighty-some years old? She ain't going to be able to work nowhere." But that process had to go on in order to qualify for the grant. These are the same kind of comments that I've heard, too. I fought this a lot through the town board meetings and through the newspaper, to let them know that these people are old, and they've been working all of their lives. They're seventy-five and eighty years old, and they didn't need to go through all this type of paperwork to get their houses fixed. We know they won't ever hold another job down. There were so many people that didn't have children around here, or didn't have children at all, that didn't even know how to fill out the paperwork. And I'm sure there's a lot of paperwork that got thrown in the trash.

There's people right now that still need help. But without that paperwork, they couldn't get it. It was a double whammy. We had people who couldn't get back to their homes, who were having to stay at the schools, sleeping on the floor. Some were at churches and different places. They were just everywhere. It went on for months.

We had Richard Moore to come down and visit Grifton. I think that we was one of the first that got the trailers for the flood victims. Governor Hunt came down, too, because he saw how slow things were moving and he tried to speed things up. We had Senator John Edwards and Eva Clayton and a bunch that came down, because we were the worst-flooded area here in eastern North Carolina, aside from maybe Princeville.

With the buyouts here in Grifton, there's quite a few folks that are not really satisfied. They didn't think that they were treated fairly. I haven't heard from that many that thought they were satisfied. Not everybody has participated a hundred percent. Some have taken their money and bought other homes in Grifton. We've got the Field of Dreams that's got about fifty-some new homes that's been built, and the flood victims had the first choice of buying them. Some have bought trailer homes and put them in different locations of town.

During the evacuations, there were some people that really didn't want to leave their homes. And as some were going across the Highway 11 Contentnea Creek bridge, they said the water was almost pulling them into the river. They said they had their steering wheels cut all the way to the left and the back end was slipping toward the creek. There were just some fierce moments.

There was one guy who was down toward the creek in a trailer, and he said when he woke up to get off the bed, he was stepping in water. It came up around his waist in the trailer, and he didn't even know it because he was sleeping. He somehow got on an old tire, and that's how he got out of the trailer park safely.

There were some cars in people's yards that once the water came up, it just flipped the car right bottoms-up and set it on some stumps. But thank God that everybody got out safely. There weren't anybody that got drowned within this area. And that's almost a miracle with everything happening at night like it did.

These kind of events turned the average citizen into a hero. Everybody pitched in, and there were people coming from all over everywhere to help. The helicopters were coming in with food and bunches of clothes, and different families were volunteering, giving to us all. It was really amazing how quickly the town pulled together. People from all races and walks of life worked together in ways they hadn't before. I heard one or two people say they went to school together and were classmates, but they hadn't really spoken to one another in years.

And bless my Lord, they were at the same shelter, sleeping on the floor right against each other. It just brought people together who thought maybe they were mad with each other, but they didn't know what they were upset about. It just brought blacks and whites and Hispanics and everybody together.

We had about five or six churches to get flooded out, and the black churches were offered to have services in the white churches. They would give them two Sundays a month, and keep two Sundays a month. And vice versa. Some had services together. It just got to where everybody worked together as a family town. There were really some positive things that came out of it.

We had lots and lots of heroes. One was Marian McLawhorn. She's our state representative in Raleigh, and with her being up there, she was able to connect with a lot of people to get the ball rolling for us. She was everywhere she was needed. She was here when the first helicopter came in with the food and stuff. Other heroes were just coming out of the woodwork.

It makes me feel really good to see the work and the effort that the Baptist Men have done in rebuilding my home. I've got a bunch of new friends. They work their regular jobs, then they come down here. A lot are retired, some have been builders, and some are not retired. A bunch of schoolkids from the colleges came down and cleaned houses. It's just amazing what they have done, and what they're still doing.

Grifton is coming back, and I believe it's going to be better than ever. It's coming back. There's lots of people that had moved out of the area that have now moved back. And they seem to be happy.

Ronnie Rich is a lieutenant and twenty-eight-year veteran with the Wallace Volunteer Fire Department. Though his heat and air business was flooded with waist-deep water after Floyd, his first priority was to help rescue a young boy who escaped out the back window of a sinking pickup truck. Ronnie was interviewed at the Wallace fire station in August 2002.

Ronnie Rich

The night of the flood, some of us stayed here at the station, but I went home through the roughest part of it. I got up at about five-thirty that morning when I got the call to go to the Brian Center. When I got there, they had already started evacuating and they needed some big trucks. Well, I work with Rich's Heat and Air. My brother owns it and we work together. We had some big trucks down at the shop. So I take off to go down there the way I usually go, but I had to go all around to get there because of the water. I said, "Damn, this is a lot of water!" It still hadn't dawned on me that it was all that bad. When I got down close to my shop and rounded the curve, I looked and saw our business waist deep. It was shocking. My mouth fell open like, what has happened?

Then we got the call to go down to Rockfish Country Club. There was a truck that had washed over, and a boy was stranded hanging on to a pine tree. It was over on [Highway] 41 about two miles out of town. I rode out to where the scene was. It was around eight-thirty or nine in the morning.

When I arrived, the water was just pure gushing across the road. The current was just unreal. Around the corner you could see the young man on the tree. I stepped off in the water, and I noticed that my feet wanted to leave out from under me because the current was so strong. I had to kind of crouch down to the pavement to try to walk heavy to keep my balance, and keep from being knocked [off] my feet. And the depth probably wasn't over my ankles at that point. The current was just that strong, it would knock you off your feet.

The boy was just hanging on that tree. We had called for some boats to come, and Ross Sykes, owner of Dixie General Contractors here in Wallace, he came. We got some lifejackets on and got the boat situated. Ross and I had a rope, and we were debating which way to go, 'cause we couldn't go directly to him. We had to go around by some deeper water and kind of swing out.

We lunged across there and made the swing, and we got up close to the tree. The current was so strong we had to try to get there at first pass. Ross done one heck of a job guiding that boat right up there. I was on the front of the boat. We threw the rope out and wrapped it around the tree, and then we got the boy into the boat. I think the boy was nine or ten years old at the time.

The truck was under the water, and you couldn't see it. The boy had been holding on to this tree, maybe a hundred yards off the road. The truck was swept off the embankment and just rolled over. In questioning the little boy, he said that they had a sliding back glass in the truck. I think he got out first, then his stepfather got out second. They were both hanging on to the tree. When we got to him, we started asking him, "Where's your father?" and he said that he just got tired and turned loose. He said he couldn't hold on no more. He turned loose and went down with the current, and the boy pointed in the direction that he thought he had went. We got the little boy in the boat, wrapped him up, and made a pass to see if he was hanging on a branch or anything. But we didn't see him anywhere. Once we got the boy back on land, we went back and kept looking to try to find the gentleman, but we never had any success.

You couldn't even see the truck. It had rolled, but it ended up on its tires. If I had to guess, I'd say the water was probably twelve or fourteen feet deep in that area. This is the seventeenth fairway on the golf course. The current was very, very strong. Stronger than any mountain water I've ever seen.

There was a Mexican out there on the tree too. I forgot about that. There was a Mexican out there who had jumped in after him and was helping him hold on to that tree. When we got there, we actually got both of them in the boat.

We've got a video of that rescue. I felt real sorry for the kid. Of course losing anybody in that type of situation is bad. I kind of took it upon myself to find him. I wasn't going to quit until I found him. That evening, I even went back out to look again. But we had no success. We tried to figure out which way the water was traveling and where he might have went. Even the next morning, I went back out. It was late the next evening that you could start to see the top of the truck. It was Thursday when we found him. It was a week since the storm, 'cause we had a fire meeting that night.

Afterward the boy would talk about it, but he wouldn't really go into any details. I got to where I was pretty close with him. And even today, when he sees me, we won't talk about that day, but we're pretty good friends.

Some newspapers, like the *News and Observer*, the *Star-News*, and the *Wallace Enterprise*, they went around to the Mexican gentleman's house one day and awarded him some stuff. They got his picture and got him and the boy hugging and all this stuff. This wasn't the first time he had saved somebody. They said he had saved others in a storm before back in Honduras or wherever he's from. He sure was mighty brave to jump in that water that day. No doubt that he was definitely a hero. I don't know that I would have had the strength to fight that water the way he did to get to him. Like I said, it was ankle-deep water that could knock your feet out from under you.

After we got them situated, we got another call to go down to Powers Road. We put the boat in there and went after Buddy Blackman and his wife. They were actually on top of their house at that point. Well, his wife was on top, but he was inside the house and the water was up to his waist. It looked like an ocean out there. I mean there was whitecaps, just like you were on a boat out in the ocean. It was unreal. Houses were to the top of the windows. Some of the mobile homes you couldn't even see.

We do heat and air work, and there were a lot of units that were total losses, and some that were reconditioned and fixed. Slimiest water I've ever encountered in my life. Our business was flooded, and we lost thousands of dollars worth of units, motors, and equipment. I mean nothing was any good. And we didn't have insurance, none whatsoever. It was all flood, and you couldn't get any help from anywhere. All you could do was maybe get a loan.

The economy here has been hurt in a lot of ways. I mean, we don't have a lot of business and industry around here anyway. It set a lot of people back, and they had to start over again. It's been a struggle.

[Authors' note: The boy rescued by Ronnie Rich and Ross Sykes was fifteen-year-old Gary Williams. Erasmo Mencias, a fifty-one-year-old construction worker from Magnolia, was the first to reach Williams. Mencias held the teenager tightly for more than thirty minutes while waiting for rescuers to arrive. Williams's stepfather was Mitchell Piner, one of the fifty-two fatalities reported in North Carolina in the aftermath of Floyd.]

Allan Hoffman

Allan Hoffman is the news anchor for WNCT-TV in Greenville. Following Hurricane Floyd, Allan and the Channel 9 news team provided round-the-clock coverage for almost nine days. Their news broadcast evolved into an information clearinghouse that helped thousands of flood victims find resources and loved ones during the peak of the disaster. For all its staff's hard work, WNCT was awarded the prestigious Edward R. Murrow award for broadcast journalism. Hoffman was interviewed in his Greenville studio in June 2002.

It was just one of those experiences that you go through, and you don't ever want to go through it again. We were on the air continuously for so long. We could see it kind of building that summer. We had one hurricane, and another one came, and it bounced around there sucking up water, and by the time Floyd got to us, I thought, "We can't take much more of this." We'd been on the air for those hurricanes with continuous coverage, too. When the water started rising, everybody looked at each other and went, "Oh, my God, what's happening now?" The decision was made by our news director that we would jump right back into the coverage. We had gone three days before that covering the storm coming through. Then we all got a few hours' break before the

water started rising. Jean called us all back in and said, "Guys, we've got a situation." That's when our continuous coverage started.

I'm a Vietnam veteran. I have seen the best that people can offer under very traumatic situations. And I am so proud of not only the crew here, but the people of eastern North Carolina. You'd have never convinced me that people that weren't affected by the water would stop everything they were doing to go help others who were. Literally thousands of people called us and said, "Where do you want me?" That's all it took—where do you want me. "I want you to go with the Red Cross over here, or to load a truck over there." And I'm talking about doctors with philosophy degrees and Billy Joe Bob who just got his GED working side by side, loading relief supplies by forming a chain of people to move stuff when a helicopter landed.

When we were doing our thing at Sam's Club, loading up all those trucks, people would just show up and hand us money. I took a break from being on the air and went over there for three or four hours. At one point I had ten thousand dollars in my hands that people had just given to me. I turned

Margaret Knight, from the Georgia Southern Baptist Disaster Relief Team, serves hot food to flood victims staying in a shelter at Tarboro High School. Hundreds of volunteers from across the country swarmed to eastern North Carolina to help in the relief effort. (Photo by David Weaver; courtesy of the *Rocky Mount Telegram*)

around to look for someone to hand this money to. I looked at Brian Baily, our sportscaster who was there at the time, and he had a fistful of money, too. He had even more than I did. Checks and cash. You know, from two dollars from a seven-year-old kid who walked up and said, "People need this," to a sixty-year-old man who says, "I don't want anybody to know I gave this five-thousand-dollar check." And they would walk off, wanting nothing more from it than to help. That's the kind of people we have in eastern North Carolina.

In Vietnam I was a helicopter pilot. You'd see war firsthand, and it's not pretty. The flood was a lot like war. It had a mind of its own. It took on its own personality. When the whole thing washed over us like it did, you felt helpless —like a lot of times when the bad guys were shooting at you and there was nowhere you could go. But then there's something you find in yourself that you pull out, and it helps you get through it. I saw that all around us.

Carla Alligood, our reporter, became literally a lifeline for some folks over in the Belvoir area. She would go over there to do stories on them, and they couldn't get their medicines. So she would come back and get medicines for them, go back over there with help from the National Guard, and deliver the medicines to these people. She took food to them, too. People would come by the station and bring us food. We had a room full of volunteers who helped with various things. One lady brought her kid, and this kid sat here for twenty-four hours, drawing pictures of us at work. He would give us our pictures and even sign them for us. He was a little artist. They were terrific little vignettes in time, through the eyes of a nine-year-old. It was just an amazing thing.

Normally we tell stories. We tell stories of the lives of the people around us. That's probably what we do best. And that's what news is really, telling those unusual stories. But during this crisis, it very quickly became clear that people were depending on us to get information to them. I mean not just the normal information about where the flooding was—we literally became a lifeline to people. We would have them call and say, "We've lost track of our cousin, our brother, our mom. We don't know if they're in a shelter on the other side of the river, or what." It got to where we would list names of people that needed to contact emergency officials so they could be accounted for. We would handle phone calls from older people who were sitting in their living rooms wondering if their homes would float away. They looked outside and the water's up to their steps, and they want to know, "Am I safe?" "No, you're not safe. Get out, or let me know where you are, and I'll make sure the National Guard gets to you." We did that for hundreds and hundreds of callers while we were on the air.

My main objective at that point was to make sure that everybody knew where the help was. Then afterward, as it began to subside, they needed help to understand that they'd been through a psychological trauma. I think that's what we provided. And we did a pretty good job.

We had close ties with the National Guard, Red Cross, and emergency management. We had the number for Bobby Joyner's beeper that he wore right on his hip. We had them coming into the station like a round-robin event when the water was at its highest. Especially when the electricity was about to go out. We would send our live units over there and do interviews. That way everybody would know.

You might remember that during this time, the ECU football team was away and beat the Hurricanes, which we thought was real fitting. But there was also a Duke football game during one of these days. We had some viewers that didn't live in the flooded area who were actually cussing at some of our volunteers: "Why don't you goddamn people put the game on?" and that kind of thing. It got so bad that I went on the air and said, "Look, folks, you'll never hear me tell you to go somewhere else, but if you want to watch the game, tune in to WRAL because what we're doing here has to do with life and death, and we're not going to show your football game." The phone calls stopped.

Most of the time you wonder if people are even listening. You know, you wonder if what you're doing is even getting out there. But then in times like that, you know you've made a difference.

It was almost seven days. We had a couch back there, and sometimes I would go and lay down for two or three hours. We'd get some of that bottled water here, and I'd bathe in it. And I shaved with bottled water. I wore a shirt three days once and was pretty raw at the end of that one. People around here not only brought us food, they brought us water and ice and made sure we were taken care of. That made us feel good. They knew we had a job to do, and it was an important job, and that we needed help. They supplied it and were never asked.

The Murrow Award was neat because it's an award that journalists give to each other. It's based on the quality and integrity of work of a man who a lot of people really admire. So that was important to us. We were the only ones with a helicopter up. Here's a station, one-hundred-and-fourth market at the time, I think, and we spent thirty-five thousand dollars on a helicopter. I'm the only helicopter pilot in this whole building, and I never got in it a minute! All that money, and I didn't get to fly! But we had people flying all the time. And we were the only ones with approval to do that. We got in there first, and by the time the other guys realized what was going on, we were it. We had to stay above where the rescuers were working. That was the agreement. We'd stay at one thousand feet, and they would work between ground level and five to eight hundred feet. We saw people on rooftops and animals scattered all over the place. We had video of dead hogs. I mean there were hundreds of dead hogs, and it broadcast over the CBS national news. We started getting e-mails and calls about the hundreds of people who had died. Well, the people who saw the video misinterpreted it and thought that hundreds of people had died.

There were so many rumors. We had one about refrigerated tractor-trailer trucks in Rocky Mount with hundreds of bodies that the government wasn't telling us about. So we would send a reporter out to go find them. And of course, there were none. I mean, we were trying to handle all the misinformation as well as the real information.

My daughter was here from Orlando. When the storm hit, she couldn't fly home to Orlando. She was stranded here along with everybody else. One afternoon, I took about two hours off and was going to try to get her over to somewhere where she could fly out, maybe Wilson or somewhere like that. Well, you couldn't get there, and I got to a little place out in the county. I stopped at a little country store, and there was a guy there with a generator going to keep his soda machine working. I walked in to get a soda for me and my daughter, and he recognized me. I could see that light of recognition. He said, "Aren't you that guy on TV?" And I said, "Yeah, I am." He said, "Why aren't you there?" I explained to him what I was doing, and he said, "Mr. Hoffman, you've got to get us some help. We're without electricity, we can't get any food in, we're surrounded by water, we've got people in houses that can't get out of their houses, and the water's two and three feet in there." I felt helpless. I mean, there was nothing I could do. And I didn't know how to tell him that. So I listened. There were two or three people who came in while we were there, and they all said, "We need help out here. Mention our names on TV and let somebody know we're here." So when I got back, that's what I did.

We had the story of a little eleven- or twelve-year-old boy who climbed up a tree to stay alive. For some reason he got left behind. This was another one where the parents had called us and didn't know where their son was. We broadcast it, and pretty soon somebody called us and said, "Yeah, he's over here." So they were reunited. We did interviews with the kid. Great kid. Tells a heck of a story about hanging on this branch as the water's coming up the tree. Said he tied his dog to the front porch and the dog drowned. But he survived.

I've never cried on TV. I'm just not that kind of guy. Except for once. We were doing a story about a rescue center that had been set up. They were moving equipment to be loaded on helicopters to be sent to people stranded in the water. These two women were working—they were going at one hundred percent. You could see this woman in the back just working as hard as she could work, and Eric would kinda talk with her while she was still working. It was like she didn't really realize the cameras were there. She was so focused on what she was doing. She would answer his questions, but she wouldn't stop working. She was driven to do this because she knew it would help people. At one point, these two women stopped, looked at each other, and started crying. Then they just hugged each other. And that's kind of what I did at the time. It was just a real poignant moment.

There was another moment like that for me. David Sawyer, who is one of our meteorologists, was stranded on this side and his family was in Kinston. The flooding was between here and Kinston, so he couldn't get home. For four days he was stuck here. People would bring him food and clean shirts, and that kind of stuff. Once all of us were on set, and this little boy who I was telling you about started drawing these pictures. He gave one to David. It showed David here, a thing of water, and his wife and four kids over here. And of course, that got David. And almost got me again. So there were a couple of times like that. I'm not prone too much to emotionalism, but those two instances . . .

Carla was just a dynamo. She went and did her thing and was just very interesting in her storytelling. The station realized after several days that we were all worn down. I mean this is a small station. So they started bringing in the best reporters from other stations in the group, as well as live units and that kind of thing. They descended on us to give our people a little relief. Our meteorologists were all up twenty-four hours at a time. We finally got a meteorologist from another station to help them out. But Phillip Williams did just an incredible job. David was sent up in the helicopter and when he'd get back, we'd put just raw video on the air with him telling us what he sees. It was almost real time. Ben Smith was there making sure that the other two had exactly what they needed, and overnight he would do his thing on air. Since Vietnam, that's probably the most sleep-deprived and the most stress I've been under in a long time. Here it is, now going on nearly three years later, and I'll still get, "Hey, you guys did a great job during the flood."

When it started off, there's the immediate facing the storm. Then there's kind of a calm, and then another buildup. And then it's lifesaving. And then it's life-keeping. You make sure people have food, clothing, water. At some point after that, the lifesaving aspect fades and we have to get back to living. How are we going to find you a place to stay, and how are we going to make sure that you get the help you need to rebuild? For weeks we followed these stories about people who needed help.

My son had four feet of water in his little duplex down by the river. He borrowed a canoe to get to his apartment to see if he could rescue anything. There wasn't very much he could rescue. What it did for him was he had a little post-traumatic stress from it. But he bore down and got determined to pass this quarter. I never saw him study that hard. And he got the best grades he'd ever gotten in college.

I put out a call that we're out of eighteen-wheelers, folks. If anybody knows anybody that's got a rig, we need them. Within an hour, they'd call up and say, "We've got another rig in." This was over at Sam's. People would literally go into Sam's, buy what they could buy, and give it to us to put in the trucks. They would spend three, four hundred dollars. It was just an amazing thing. Some of it was so spontaneous that it surprised us. Everybody stepped up so quickly.

The people of this area were truly amazing. I mean, there's an old saying from the Second World War, when a kid asks his dad, "Were you a hero?" And the dad says, "No, but there were dozens of them in the company I served." I served in the company of so many heroes. It was amazing. And it still gets to me this day.

I went home to grab another shirt and stopped at a filling station to get some water. This guy was in there, who says, "You're doing a good job. Keep it up. We need you to do it." That just stuck with me. I thought, "Yeah, they need us to do something. They just don't want it, it's a need." So I drove right back to the station and didn't go to get the shirt. I said, "I can live without a shirt."

Bill Ellis Bill Ellis has operated Bill's Bar-B-Que Restaurant in Wilson for more than forty years. On the Friday morning following Floyd, his restaurant was filled with floodwaters to within six inches of the ceiling. With no flood insurance but a lot of gritty determination, Bill built his restaurant back to be better than ever. He was interviewed there in August 2002.

This is our forty-first year with the restaurant. We did the drive-in bit, and then some people wanted me to cater some stuff for them. I bought me a little station wagon. We were the first to start cooking chicken on the road.

We didn't get the big flood until that Friday. We got all the water we've been getting for years, but we got all the dams too. Our dam is supposed to take two years to fill up. It filled up the next day, and it wasn't even raining. The storm was gone, but the water kept rising because we were getting all the water from up yonder.

There was seven feet of water in the restaurant. We had someone cooking in the barbecue house that was stranded, and we had to come get them in the boat. My neighbor had a boat, and I asked him if he'd bring it down because I had somebody I had to get out of there. So he brought it down and we put it in the water. This guy we rescued comes to work and doesn't even notice the flood, 'cause he's just working at night and knows it's raining. But when the light comes up, he goes, "Oh, we've got a problem here!"

We didn't have flood insurance. We had it before, but when we renewed, they didn't pick it up. We thought we had insurance. We thought we had everything. Come to find out we didn't have any. We owned the whole intersection here. We figured we lost three-and-a-half million dollars, and we spent about two million opening everything back up. So it's about a five-and-a-half-million-dollar loss. But we never cried about it, we just went to work. I never really looked at my loss, I just looked at the next day.

The city was very cooperative. They had their hands full, and I had my hands full. So in essence they turned me loose, and I went to work. I came down here that day, and it was the biggest mess you've ever seen in your life. We had fifteen fryers that lost all their grease everywhere. I was sitting at a table, and I said, "Lord, I'm not gonna ask you why you did it, but I'm gonna tell you one thing right now, you're gonna have to stay with me until I can get this thing back going. I need your help." Then everything just fell in place so good. Everything I did just worked out perfect. This building here, the buffet, used to be a picnic shelter. I was getting ready to remodel here anyway. The old part is still closed, and we basically just built the new part back behind. We

were catering in three days. The truck reopened in October, the walk-in and drive-through opened December, and the buffet opened in January.

None of the employees really had a lot of problems. Maybe one or two of them. We've got a real nice pig farm that's about fifteen minutes from here, and we had nothing down there. No flooding problems. I mean the lagoons didn't even run over. We've got pictures, day by day, of everything that came out of the restaurant. We've even got pictures of the eels that was swimming around in the building. That's when I decided I ain't going in that water no more until it goes down.

This gentleman lived back here behind the lake. He stepped out on his back porch, and the water was already high. He said he looked across the field, and so help him God, there was a tidal wave coming across that field that was four to five foot high. And it wasn't raining or nothing. Something strange. It was just coming right across that field, and that's when he got out. I mean it come through there "sssheeoooom!" and took his house down. I think it's up to the individual, whether he wants to pick up and go on or not or wants to sit down and cry about it.

We had a hundred ten employees when the flood came, and we narrowed it

Bill Ellis (*left*) and Bradley Neal (*right*) navigate the flood-waters as they rescue Henry King (*center*) from Bill's Bar-B-Que and Chicken Restaurant in Wilson. King was at the restaurant all night cooking a pig when water began flooding the building. The pig was being prepared so the restaurant could feed utility workers in the aftermath of the storm. (Photo by Keith Barnes; courtesy of the *Wilson Daily Times*) down to about fifty after the flood. Now we've got it back up to about sixty-five or seventy. We do more volume than we ever did before, with almost fifty people less. This buffet on Mother's Day is a big thing. The line never stops coming in, and there's always a place for them to sit down.

Very shortly after the flood, we went down to TRW in Greenville to feed the employees breakfast. They would airlift them across the Tar River to work by helicopter. Then that afternoon, when they flew them back over, we'd feed them again before they went home. We fed them about three meals a day for about a month. I think it was a couple hundred employees, 'cause we had to send an eighteen-wheeler. We also worked right after the flood to feed the city workers.

Ten years ago, we even went down to Florida for Hurricane Andrew. But I was very disappointed in that. That was the most unorganized thing I've ever seen in my life. We went down there, did our thing, and came home. A guy called us and said, "You better get out of here before dark. They'll steal your wheels and everything you got." It was the most unorganized thing I've ever seen in my entire life. Disasters always bring out the looters.

It's made me a stronger person. I thought I was strong then. In the last five years, I lost a sister, a mother, and I lost my son, my wife, and my brother. All just before or after the flood.

The way I look at it is, you don't make all the rules. You try to go by them, and you do what you have to do. I've never seen a Brinks truck behind a hearse yet, so you can't take anything with you. So, hey, go to work! The Lord made your body to work. You got good pores, you got hair in the right places so it doesn't rub wrong, so he made you to work. So go ahead and work! Just get it done. I believe in honesty, and I believe in hard work. So if you've got those two things in line, and you've got a business, just go to work.

John Morgan   John Morgan is a general contractor and volunteer fireman on Oak Island. He stayed on the island the night Floyd arrived and awoke to find four inches of water in his home. After the storm, he helped repair and rebuild many of the beach cottages damaged by storm surge. He was interviewed by telephone in September 2002.

I moved here from Winston-Salem in 1992. I don't remember the names of all the hurricanes, but I've stayed here through all of them. I haven't left the island since I came. I build houses here. I ain't good at telling stories—I just work.

Before it got here, a lot of people boarded up like they always do. I've got several houses that I board up before hurricanes for people. Then they start evacuating, but there's some who don't. They stay. We've never had any really bad emergency from one of them.

I fixed up several houses on the beach after the storm. We had to put pilings back under them, and decks, and steps. It really came in at night. It came in sometime between ten-thirty and about two o'clock. I was on the pedestrian walk at the end of Middleton Street, and it was up pretty good then. The waves were coming up to my knees when I was out there. I left and went home and laid down to get me a little nap. I woke up at about two o'clock and had about four inches of water in my house. It wasn't from the surge, it was just from where it had rained so much so quickly that it didn't have nowhere to go. Before it went over the crest in the road and into the waterway, it came in my house. It was like a lake all out in the street, and it laid in there a couple of days.

I woke up and put my feet in the water, and I didn't know what had happened. I didn't know if the ocean was there, or what was there. I cut the lights on, and there was just water everywhere. I opened the door, and a little more came in. It looked funny to just look out in the yard and see nothing but water. There weren't a lot of houses that were flooded, but there were a lot of streets with water in them. The water table was so high from the surge and all the rain, it just had nowhere to go.

Well, there wasn't anything I could do, so I just got in the truck. I started down the island and went back to Middleton. It was probably four-thirty, five o'clock or something. When I got to the bridge over Davis Canal, which is probably two blocks off the ocean, I couldn't go down the bridge. I had to stop there 'cause there was steps, gas tanks, and everything else laying up the road there. The house that was where I was standing that night, well, when the surge came in I guess it just picked it up and turned it and set it right back down about three or four feet from the house beside it.

There was stuff washed back to the third row of houses. The beach road was covered with two foot of sand. It was a mess. It was full of washing machines, dryers, televisions, steps, and decks. One house wasn't hurt that bad, but somebody's septic tank floated up out of the ground, came down two or three houses, and hit the corner of it.

I think they condemned about eight houses there, starting about 58th Street down toward 46th Street. Now some of them are back. There's a couple in there that's not back. They're still there, but they're in foul shape. Most of the houses were condemned because they lacked a septic tank. The water was still coming up under the houses at high tide. They had nowhere to put a septic.

At my house, I ran a pump there for a couple of days. I'd pump and pump that water, and then there'd come another rain, and I'd have to pump again to keep it from going back in the house.

I would say the surge was ten feet, from what I've seen. I think it was higher than Fran. Fran had more wind, and I think it did more damage going out than it did coming in. Fran took the sand and the steps, but it didn't take the cement. This one took the cement right out from under the houses and just broke it up in chunks. It was a lot worse. This is the worst one I've seen, as far as the oceanfront.

All of these were older beachfront houses. Some of them had the old pine beams and pine paneling in them. Real old stuff. Some of those old houses were put back after Hazel.

I had a videotape that showed them standing on Long Beach Pier when it was coming in before dark. You could see the waves getting higher and higher. Then they was going over it, then they'd shake it. Then one hit, and it took the end off the pier. It's also got ninety blocks, what it looked like the next morning at daylight. The streets, the houses, everything.

My wife runs a restaurant called Edna's Kitchen. Her business increased because there were so many people down here working. She was the first one to open back up. I had so much work to do. They was standing there wanting to know when I was going to go work on their house. Some of them would come to me every day and ask.

The island was closed almost a week. Edna came back on the third day to the restaurant. I was out there keeping them off the beachfront. It was two weeks before some of them got power back. We had so many people wanting to go back, and we couldn't let them go. We'd let them go if they had the light bill or something to prove they owned the house. I was in the fire department, and I did that for about four or five days. They were upset. There was ladies that would get all over you. You'd tell them that they couldn't go, and they'd cuss you out. They really got upset, a lot of people, because they couldn't go to check on their sister's house, or their dad's house.

I worked out on the beach seven days a week from daylight to dark until April. We had to get all the cement out from under the houses and put it out in the street. This company came down and brought equipment in. They took all the sand and run it through a machine that sifted it, cleaned it, and then it was hauled down to the west end and put back on the beach. All the boards and trash and bad stuff that was in it was hauled to the dump. They had tractors going just day and night for a month. I know there's one house on the second row down there that the sand was a foot up inside the house. I mean you couldn't even get in it.

The beachfront now looks the best I've ever seen it since '92. The piers are built back. A lot of the houses got fixed back better than ever, and they're still building new ones right out on the oceanfront again. Used to, if you walked along at high tide you'd have to go up under people's decks if you didn't want to walk in the water. Now, you're three hundred feet away from the houses. They've just built a whole new beach down here.

This one couple came down, and their house was gone. It wasn't there. They went to town hall and wanted to know what they'd done with it. It was just gone. I know there were maybe eight or ten houses that were gone. You didn't see nothing of them, they were just gone. Maybe you'd find a roof floating a mile down the beach. They just went back to the ocean.

Hurricane Floyd arrived just one month after Robert Egleston began work in the corporate offices of Lowe's Home Improvement Warehouse. Like a number of other corporations, Lowe's quickly launched an effort to provide money and materials to victims of the flood. Robert's work to coordinate this campaign laid the groundwork for what would later become Lowe's ongoing nationwide disaster-assistance program. He was interviewed in his Wilkesboro office in July 2002.

Robert Egleston

I got here on August 12th of that year. The storm hit only one month after I arrived. What we now consider a pretty formalized program of disaster response grew out of what we did with Hurricane Floyd. Floyd was in our backyard. It was a flood of biblical proportions, and it affected areas much further away from the coast than people were used to seeing. We had just signed an agreement with the American Red Cross to do some fund raising for them. We offered to match the first $50,000 of donations given, which at the time we thought was pretty generous. We turned this on in the North Carolina, South Carolina, and Virginia stores. We very quickly got overwhelmed—we ended up raising $624,500 from our customers. So we put a $50,000 match to that, but incredibly the customers just blew the top off of that.

We ended up giving $100,000 to the Governor's Disaster Relief Fund and

Jonathan Hand shoulders two forty-pound bags of ice as he and other employees of Bank of America deliver the much-needed item to flood victims at a Red Cross Shelter in Kinston. The ice was trucked in on two large trailers from Atlanta. Bank of America employees delivered nearly two thousand bags that day. (Photo by Charles Buchanan; courtesy of the *Kinston Free Press*)

made contributions to six of the local United Way chapters down in the flooded area. We gave an $8,000 donation to all the area Red Crosses. We got with our vendors like Quickie Broom and Glo-White Bleach and they sent truckloads of brooms, brushes, bleach, and other things to an old Durham store. I went down there and worked with them to unload these six trucks and then split up the loads and sent them out. They went to each of our eastern North Carolina stores who just passed them out to customers.

We had stores that had individually helped following local disasters, but we had never done much from the corporate angle. We felt like so much damage had been done and so many people were affected that we needed to do it. I think it was neat, Lowe's being a North Carolina–based company, and feeling like it's still a little company, even though it's obviously outgrown that description. We just felt like there were things we should do. In Hurricane Floyd, I think there were something like sixty-seven employees that suffered significant home damage, and some lost everything they had.

We bought $105,000 worth of bottled water to give away. We ended up donating a lot of labor, and a lot of people from our stores were volunteering. We came back in February of the next year and gave $10,000 each to the mayors of six towns—Wilson, Rocky Mount, Greenville, Kinston, Washington, and Goldsboro. We just called up the mayors and said, "We'd like to give you $10,000. What would you like to do?" We also froze our prices for at least ninety days. But clearly, nothing that we did was going to completely repair the damage or fix the problems. So many people were without insurance because they were in places that just never in history had flooded.

Since then, in the three years since Floyd, I've responded to something like seventy-six disasters in twenty-seven states. It doesn't matter whether it's flooding, wildfires, earthquakes, ice storms, tornadoes, or hurricanes. It doesn't matter what the natural disaster is now. But the stuff that we did on the fly after Hurricane Floyd has set the tone for a more systematic way that we respond to disasters. We now have a master plan that did not exist after Floyd. We've had a lot in the last few weeks with the Colorado and Arizona wildfires and the San Antonio flooding. So it kinda seems like we leapfrog from one disaster to another. We've got eight hundred stores in forty-three states, and you don't know where the next disaster's gonna hit. We'll probably respond to thirty or forty disasters this year.

We have the stuff you need to clean up after a disaster, and we have the stuff to repair for the long run. So we know that there are ways Lowe's can benefit or will see sales afterward. But the fact is we're gonna freeze prices and we're gonna offer six months no-pay on our credit card. Sometimes it takes a while before insurance checks come in.

I think all this comes from the small-town southern roots. Lowe's Hardware, as it was then called, was founded in Wilkesboro in 1946. It was just a couple of little hardware stores. It grew up much like the WalMart model, in small towns all across the East and Southeast. We kind of expanded to small towns first.

It was in the fall of 2000 that we made a commitment to help with the rebuilding of Princeville. The one big project we did was to help with a twelve-home Habitat build in what is now called Lowe's Court. We supplied all the building materials and paid for some of the out-of-pocket expenses. Then we used volunteers from a lot of our stores across eastern North Carolina and got some people from here in our corporate office to go down and volunteer, too. It was really rewarding. In the future, what Lowe's will do is help with some things that are on the wish list, like a park and a senior center. We hope that some of that will happen this year. I've had great fun working with Princeville.

At one point, I had gone down with one of these trucks of brooms and brushes. I was in a store talking to one fellow, and I said, "Where do you live?" He said, "Well, actually I live in little Washington. I don't actually work in this store, but I can't get back to my home because the bridge is out. I was over here on this side and can't get back. So I just came in this store and thought maybe one of your employees was having a hard time getting to work, and I'll just work in their place." He'd spent more than a week working at a different store because he couldn't get back to his house. He did that on his own. I get off the phone every day and think we have really got great people in our stores. People that really care.

Power was out in the Greenville area, and our store manager down there went out the day of the flood and bought a couple hundred pounds of hamburger and hot dogs. For the next couple days, he and some associates cooked hot dogs and burgers and just gave them away. He said he figured people are gonna be hungry, they're cleaning up their houses, they don't have electricity, or they don't have time to cook. I thought that was really pretty neat. They just used gas grills in front of the store and passed out food.

We were breaking new ground for Red Cross. This six hundred twenty-five thousand dollars was by far the biggest customer donation program that any retailer had ever run for American Red Cross. Since then, our customers raised a million and a half after nine-eleven. But this six twenty-five three years ago was an all-time record. Lowe's ended up committing about three-quarters of a million all total to Floyd, and then our customers did six hundred twenty-five thousand.

If I was independently wealthy, I would just volunteer all the time. With this work, it's almost like being a volunteer every day. I often say I've got the best job in corporate America. Every day I get to call up stores and help them help other people. It's not always natural disasters. The sad thing is that you have to say no a whole lot more than you say yes. But saying yes is so much fun.

Carolyn Hunt

First Lady Carolyn Hunt was on her family farm in Wilson when Hurricane Floyd swept through eastern North Carolina in 1999. While her husband, Governor Jim Hunt, was busy managing the crisis on a statewide level and lobbying Congress for disaster relief, Carolyn was out in her work boots helping her neighbors haul furniture out of their flooded homes. She was interviewed in her husband's Raleigh office in August 2002.

I think the hurricane was on Tuesday or Wednesday, and the flood came Thursday morning. I decided to go home and stay home. I was on the farm and was the only one in our house. We're off of Highway 42 about ten miles west of Wilson. Jim's dad and stepmother were just a few yards up the path in their house, and we have other family across the lake in another house. So we really have the four generations there. Fortunately, we live on a hill. Contentnea Creek is at the back end of the property.

We were really fearful all night. We've got a multilevel house, so I went down to the basement—but didn't sleep any. We're surrounded by trees, and I was just sure we would have trees come over on the house. We have a lot of glass, so I was afraid crashing limbs would break the glass. I kept checking on his dad and stepmother, and we just sort of got through the night. I don't think I ever went to sleep. We just knew that something really bad was gonna happen.

The next morning, there were lots of limbs and trees down in different places. With Floyd we didn't hear the snapping of trees like we had with Fran. During Fran we could just hear the trees back behind us just snapping and popping. I was just thankful that we got through the night. It seemed like our main buildings were still in one piece.

Immediately, I started checking on everybody and started the cleanup process because there were things everywhere. I don't know when I first heard from Jim, but he got a-hold of me some how. The next couple of days we spent trying to clean up. We had three trees down between our house and the road.

We were thinking about the trees and hadn't even thought about flooding. We got through that day, and it was the next day when we started hearing a lot

North Carolina governor Jim Hunt talks to reporters on Capitol Hill on October 27, 1999, after he and other North Carolina lawmakers met with members of Congress to press for relief in the aftermath of Hurricane Floyd. (Photo by Dennis Cook; courtesy of Associated Press)

about water rising. It was Thursday morning when the water really started to rise. We were still cleaning up in the path when someone told us how much the water was rising down on 42. Well, we all had boots and coveralls, so we got in our four-wheel-drive and went over there. We started down the hill and got partway, and boy, the water was just coming up there like it was an ocean or something. It was just rolling over the highway.

We went to check on my husband's cousins. They lived in a house near the road, and some other cousins lived across the road and down just a little ways. Water was just pouring into both houses. Contentnea Creek was rising. So we did what we could to help them move furniture out of their houses.

The water was coming into the yard when we got there. When we left it was on the top step going into the floor of the house. They had sort of a sunken living room. It was one of those rooms that goes down, and there was a piano in it. Some other people came and helped us get the furniture out of the house —as much as we could. The water was coming up pretty fast. I don't know how long we were there, maybe three or four hours. But it got up to where we knew we had to get out. We moved a lot of stuff just as fast as we could.

In the meantime, a car with two people in it submerged off of 42 right between the two cousins' houses. The car washed over with a man and a woman inside. Two Rock Ridge firefighters came along and tied ropes around these people and saved them. It was all within a hundred yards of where we were working. They would have drowned. I'm serious. They had gotten down into the ditch, and the water was clear over the top of their car.

We didn't stop to watch the rescue. We just kept moving. We worked there as hard as we could. You know you get kind of frantic because you don't know how fast this water's gonna come. It was just roaring over 42, just rolling over that highway. I've never seen anything like this, and I've been here almost forty-five years. I've seen floods where I grew up, but I've never seen anything like that here. I've been through fires, tornadoes, and now I've been through a flood.

There were two other houses that got flooded here, so really it got four houses where we are. Now one's being torn down and another one's being redone. There were several people from our church who had floodwater too. It flooded quite a few homes in Wilson. It was amazing. You should have seen it at Bill's Bar-B-Que. He really had it bad.

It was such a shock. We made it through the hurricane, and I had no idea that we were gonna have this flood. It just caught a lot of people by surprise. You thought, "Well, we're over the worst." We just didn't know what was coming.

It took quite a long while for things to get back to normal in Wilson. There were people suffering for a really long time. It went on a lot longer than a lot of people wanted to think it was going on. People were out of their homes. It just takes so long to get someone to go look, to get these estimates. Then you've got to get over the shock, so you can start rebuilding or whatever you're going to do. Deciding what to do—that was so hard for so many people.

One nearby family that was flooded had gone to stay with someone else, but then they came back to their house. I remember at Thanksgiving we took some food down there. They'd gone back to live there. When we were there, you could look in the doorway—we didn't really go in—but this stuff was just peeling out off the walls. I mean nothing really had been done. They'd gotten some money and gotten some furniture, but they eventually left and now it's gonna be torn down. Most people had to depend on their neighbors, or go to a relative or somebody, and just stay until they could get back in. There are a lot of rental properties that were never fixed up.

I think the flood made everybody realize that if yours wasn't flooded and you were okay, you could help somebody else. That's the feeling I think a lot of people had. A lot of people who maybe didn't give volunteer hours gave money for food or clothing. There was a real effort from the churches and volunteer groups, and just individuals, like any of us who would help other people.

I think we were without power seven or eight days. With Fran it was ten or eleven days. Most of us down on the farm have a freezer full of fresh vegetables and meat. So we got the grill out, and we cooked, and went up and down the road taking food to people all along there. It was gonna spoil, so that was another way to help people. All the wells went bad, and I guess we were drinking it while it was bad.

I think people accept it in different ways, because of their different makeups and past experiences. One family I know, I think it took them a long time before they could even go back to church. I don't know exactly what happened, but when they were hit, they just sort of felt they'd stay away or something. For other people, it worked the other way. I think it's really about your own personal makeup. It really took me back to think about what my parents went through when they lost everything in a tornado. The tornado hit our home a month before I was born. It just went through and took everything. It left the house standing but ripped it apart. So this made me think about that, 'cause I've heard so many tales about it all my life.

This flood was exhausting for a lot of people. I think people were just tired to death. They'd gone days without sleep, they didn't have much to eat, no real food, and everything they saw was depressing. They appreciated people helping—they really did. But they just felt like they weren't sure they could keep going.

Stan Riggs

Stan Riggs is a Distinguished Research Professor at East Carolina University. Through the university's geology program, he has devoted his forty-year career to the study of eastern North Carolina's rivers, coastal plains, estuaries, and barrier islands, giving him valuable insights into the dynamics of the Hurricane Floyd disaster. He also experienced the flood firsthand at his farm on the banks of the Tar River. He was interviewed at his Pitt County home in August 2002.

I started working in North Carolina in 1964. I was hired by Leo Jenkins at East Carolina University in 1967. They needed to beef up their sciences, so they hired a geology department. I was one of the first five people they hired to develop a marine science program. I've worn many hats over the years, but I've always kept one foot in eastern North Carolina. I've had an extensive coastal research program that's involved rivers, the coastal plain, estuaries, the barrier islands, and the continental shelf. I've had fifty or seventy-five theses done by graduate students on various aspects of the rivers and the coast. So I've got almost a forty-year history of research in the coastal plain and marine systems.

Now I'm not teaching anymore. I thought I was too old and cranky for the classroom, so in 1999 I put together a large cooperative coastal geology program that deals with the U.S. Geologic Survey, East Carolina University, and the North Carolina Geologic Survey. It's a big, multidisciplinary program that's ongoing right now. It's very exciting. We're taking the coast apart.

Around 1974 I bought a farm about five miles east of Greenville on the Tar River. It's a small farm, about seventy-seven acres, with a half a mile or more of frontage on the river. A lot of it is beautiful swamp forest. It's on a big meander in the Tar River. We didn't live out here; we lived in town up until about four years ago. We had just moved out here when the flood happened. I've spent a lot of time out here, and I've done a lot of work on the river.

By the time the flood came along, we couldn't get out of here because all the bridges blew out. During that one feeder band of Hurricane Floyd, the state lost probably six hundred bridges, and then some more blew out in a couple of subsequent storms. So we couldn't get out of here. I took my canoe down to the river, and every day we'd go out into the swamp forest and paddle around. My property has a large high bank called Rainbow Banks. It's one of the original King's Grants from back from the 1700s. All of them fronted the river, and they all had a landing, because those were the highways in those days. This one was Rainbow Banks Landing. If you go up and down this river, you've got Yankee Hall Landing, Brown's Ferry Landing, and you've got Blue Banks Landing.

This was called the Chatham Plantation at the time. It's an old piece of property that has a lot of history on it.

We were here when Floyd hit. We live on one of the highest pieces of property in Pitt County, here on a little clay hill. We had just moved in. The person that had built this property had cleared it. We didn't hardly have any vegetation on it, so with the flood it was a pretty awesome sediment event. Because of where the house was, and the winds, I was able to watch water flow uphill. It was pretty dramatic.

When it was out at sea it was a major storm. As it approached, of course, it diminished in size and strength. It slowed way, way down and the storm tide sort of fell out from in front of it. So when it made landfall, it wasn't much of a coastal storm. But it was moving so slow at that point that it took a long time to get over the land.

The big problem was that the river was already in flood stage. Most people don't understand that this was not one rain event, but that at least five different weather events produced that flood. The size, magnitude, and duration of it was a product of not just Hurricane Floyd. In order to appreciate that, you've got to look at the whole dynamic down here in the lower coastal plain. For example, the lower parts of the Tar River and the Neuse River are below sea level. Everything all the way up to Greenville is totally influenced by wind tides out of the estuaries. Fifty percent of the time the Tar River here at my place flows uphill. So if I don't pick the right day to float down the river, I've got to paddle downriver.

The rivers were already in flood stage from Hurricane Dennis. When Floyd started slowing down, the storm winds were blowing water back upstream. We were up at sixteen or seventeen feet above mean sea level at that point. Then you put the winds on top of that holding the water back, and it raises the water level even further.

We had a ten-foot storm surge up around little Washington and New Bern. When you push that much water up in the estuaries, that's like a dam down there. So the water can't flow out, and it just piles up and up. Then on top of that, you put the rain from Floyd itself. It was a major rain event, but it was not that big a storm by itself. But you put that on top of the Dennis river level, along with these storm surges that were driving it, and then other tropical rains that came in a couple days later and a frontal system that came across, and you had at least five different rain events.

It was flash floods that wiped out all the highways and killed most of the people. Those blew out within a half an hour's period of time. The first one blew out maybe three or four hundred road bridges and killed a bunch of people. Then the second one came along. I was in town during the second one, and Ann called me and said, "You better get home. You've got about fifteen minutes to get back across the bridge." I just made it. I was the last car across there before the water just roared through. That took out another whole set of bridges. A lot of the devastation in eastern North Carolina was due to these flash floods in the upper streams.

Some have said that water releases at the dams were to blame, but that's absolutely a myth. The amount of water that was released at the dam did not make a very big difference at all. In fact, my response to those people is very simple —had they not released that water, we would have really gotten a deluge if that dam had busted. The amount they released, in the scheme of things, would have changed the water levels just inches, not feet. It was a very important thing to let that water out. There's nothing worse than to get a big pulse from a broken dam. That would wipe everything out. Nobody knew when all this was going to end. It was sort of a crapshoot.

Comparing this flood with the flood of 1955, I don't have a lot of hard numbers—but I have lots of opinion. The Floyd disaster was pretty much of human making. In the 1950s, for example, there was essentially no development in north Greenville. It was just empty land. A lot of it was farmed, but there were very few people living there. Since the 1970s, north Greenville has developed. It's low-cost land, it's swampy land, and today it's a major growth area for the poor and low-cost industry. Now all the trailer parks are over there, industry's over there, county office buildings, the sewage and water treatment, the power plant, everything's over there. And that's all since the seventies.

This storm was catastrophic because we moved into the floodplain. The north side of the river has all these low terraces that are old braid plains from the glacial maximum. But they're not normal floodplains. Until you get almost down to little Washington or New Bern, the rivers in eastern North Carolina are all incised down into older rocks without a floodplain. The floodplains are these glacial-aged braid plains that are perched up a little bit higher.

All the rivers in eastern North Carolina are what I call asymmetric rivers, with steep banks on the south side. The north side is this low, gentle stairstep. The Tar River, the Neuse River, and the Roanoke River are all asymmetric streams with high banks on the south side. That's where all the early development took place, where the old towns were. That's where eastern North Carolina first built up because these south sides were the high, dry lands. Over time, as development progressed, they looked for land wherever they could and began moving into the floodplain on the north side.

The second thing we started doing, particularly in the sixties and seventies, we began channelizing every stream in eastern North Carolina. We've been ditching and draining for three hundred years to get the water off the land, but there was a massive effort to ditch and drain all the streams on the north sides of these rivers. When you ditch and channelize a stream, what you do is make a pipe out of it. You take all the water that flows in there, ditches into ditches into bigger ditches, and you build a system of pipes to move the water off the land. That idea works well for just that little bit of water, but when you get a big event like we had during Floyd, you put too much water down there too fast. And it has nowhere to go.

Then we did another thing. We built all these road dams across these streams. Wherever you drive in eastern North Carolina, if you pay attention when you go across the big streams, you'll drive over fill, fill, fill across the swamp, a little bridge across the main channel, and then another levee on the other side. For example, at every single bridge on the Tar River, we've dammed the floodplain. Most of them end up being ninety or ninety-five percent dams with just little tiny holes in them. They work fine under low-flow conditions, but in high-flow conditions they hold water back.

The last bridge that was built here in Greenville was built in 1974, and it was built on the downstream side of Greenville. It's a big road dam that actually has three holes in it. But that effectively held the water back. In Greenville they had thirty-foot water at maximum stage. I'm down five miles and I had about twenty-five-foot water. The Grimesland bridge is just below me, and we had about twenty foot of water at that bridge. Once it got below the Grimesland bridge, it went down to five feet of water.

The fourth factor would be all the impervious surfaces that have been built. These increase the amount of water running off. This is an important factor, but I'd put the other three ahead of it as more critical.

The five-hundred-year flood designation is based on a tremendous amount of assumptions, and not necessarily how the real world works. First of all, we only have a hundred-year record of floods, maybe a hundred and ten in some places. The designation of a five-hundred-year flood is a statistical number that's based on your record. Well, your record is only a hundred years old. So how good is it when we start projecting to five hundred years? It doesn't take into consideration the storm patterns—there's a cyclicity to these storms that isn't even on the table in those kind of designations.

Also, the rainfall with this flood, particularly since it was really five different rain events, was extremely variable. The guy with Greenville utilities that runs the water gauge here in Greenville had something like sixteen inches of rain on the north side of the river. He lived on the south side of the river and had his own weather station at his home. He got eight inches of rain in his own gauge. On one side of the river you might have an event that could calculate as a five-hundred-year storm, and on the south side it might only be a one-hundred-year storm. Just the next town down it could be a fifty-year storm. In my opinion, the use of those kind of terms is very, very misleading.

In my experience in dealing with the coast of North Carolina, it's not the big storms. It's when you get three nor'easters in two weeks back to back that brings more damage than does a big nor'easter. It's the second and third punch that does it. In this case, Floyd was the second in a three-punch thing that made this flood last a month and a half. Had Hurricane Irene come in one week earlier, we would have been right back with a Floyd-level flood for another two weeks. It so happened that the water blew out completely and we were back to normal water level when Irene came our way. We lucked out with Hurricane Irene.

I'm not very involved with the public policy part of the floodplain issue. But I'll tell you a few of the things that I saw happen. Everybody in Greenville was on the right page, and they talked about how bad the whole evolutionary development of Greenville was, and how we had to change that. They recognized it. And everybody was in harmony right after the storm. The tears are still flowing, everybody feels bad, and we're going to do something about it. So the town council started to debate this, and they came up with a fairly good set of responses to what should be done differently to prevent this from happening again. They went into public debate session, and everything they put on the table went down the toilet. They finally ended up with an absolutely wimpy, totally nothing change that represented a one-foot raising of all the trailers. It was almost a joke.

Every city had its own thing. From the little bit I saw, most of them went this same way. A few of the towns seemed to have a little better leadership and seemed to take a little stronger stance. Kinston had just gone through two of these in a row, and they seemed to have done a better job. People remembered Hurricane Fran's flooding in Kinston. They seemed to have done a better job than most of the other towns around.

There was a perception that Floyd was just a once-in-a-lifetime event that couldn't happen again. That's what the average person on the street believes. That's the bad part of these five-hundred-year flood designations. The public just does not understand that you could have a five-hundred-year storm every year, three years in a row. They don't understand the statistics behind it at all. I think we do ourselves a great disservice by using that kind of terminology.

On the good side of things, I've noticed a major change in the approach of DOT. You know there's a good reason why they built dams across the floodplains. It's because of costs. It's cheaper to build a road dam than it is to build a bridge. What I've noticed is that DOT is changing their tune. They are now starting to rebuild many of these bridges. We've been working with them and the local people to educate them about some of the dynamics and what the tradeoffs are. If you understand the tradeoffs, then maybe we're willing to spend a little more money in critical places. In the right place, a road dam is good. But you don't put it just downstream of a town.

You remember there were lots of headlines and newspaper articles as this flood was developing, about all the pollution and how severe the consequences were going to be. I never did believe that. My own opinion was that there was such an incredible volume of water that whatever was going into the system was going to be diluted far more effectively than anything is diluted today. There's no water in that river today, except what comes out of all our waste-pipes. That river today is a stinking, rotten river. There's no flow in it at all. Yet we put a billion gallons of wastewater a year into that river. Today, because of the drought, probably ninety percent of that water is wastewater.

After Floyd, the biologists were screaming that this was going to destroy the fisheries, blah, blah, blah. My own opinion is that's not true. These estuaries are tough ecosystems that are dependent on these kinds of floods. To me, the flood was like the great big flush. We were cleaning out the system. We were flushing the river, we were flushing the floodplains, we were flushing the estuary. It's kind of like a fire on land. There are certain kinds of plants and trees that require a fire for reproduction. These estuaries live by the fires of the sea, which in this case are floods and hurricanes. I think that our estuarine system, three years later, is proving this correct. They're healthier today than they've been in a while. Fisheries are coming back up very quickly after the flood. There's no evidence yet that this was an environmental disaster to the estuarine system. The pollutants were just totally diluted and flushed out of the system.

Ever since George Washington dug the first ditch up in Dismal Swamp, we've been ditching and draining eastern North Carolina. We have a three-hundred-year heritage of destroying an incredibly important major freshwater system. And we've essentially destroyed it at this point. We used to have one of the most incredible water systems, maybe next to south Florida, and it's essentially destroyed at this point. The price we're paying now are these extremes. We're running out of groundwater, the rivers are drying up, and when we have these small or moderate rain events, the system overloads very quickly. That's the price we pay for three hundred years of diddling around with them. To undo what we've done will require a tremendous amount of resources that right now nobody has.

During the flood, every day I'd go down and I'd paddle through the swamp, sit on my bank, and watch the river go by. The river was really doing its thing.

If I got down there early enough in the morning, all these rescue helicopters would use the river and it was like being in Vietnam. If I could get down there before they started flying, it was extremely quiet and peaceful. What impressed me more than anything was how peaceful that river was and how it was really doing what it's supposed to do.

The morning the flood was peaking, I was sitting on a bank. I had a cabin down there, and it was underwater. I thought it was going to float down the river. I was sitting on one of my benches, with my legs in the water, and the water was just pouring over the bank. It was before the helicopters started flying, and it was an absolutely crystal-blue, cold north wind sky. There's always cattle over on the north side of the river, and when the wind blows out of the north, I can smell them and hear them and I feel like I'm out west. When I got down there the cattle were mooing, and the river was rising, and I sat there and listened. The intensity of their mooing increased, and by seven o'clock in the morning, maybe, they were all bawling. Just this chaotic bawling. Then by about seven-fifteen, they all went quiet. And I knew then that the world was not at peace, even though the river itself was very peaceful. It shook me back into the reality that things were not well out there in the rest of the world. It was right after that helicopters started flying. It was a very important moment in that flood. It sort of pointed out the fact that rivers really work. They are an important part of our natural system. But we've got to respect that river, and we've got to learn to live with it. We will never manage that river to our specs. And we better back off a little bit.

The Fatalities

The greatest tragedy of Hurricane Floyd was the toll of human lives claimed by the storm and the flood that followed. Some reports suggested that more than seventy-five deaths occurred along the East Coast of the United States. The North Carolina state medical examiner reported fifty-two deaths within the state. That's more than the totals for Hurricanes Fran, Hugo, and Hazel combined. Only one other hurricane, an obscure coastal storm in 1883, is believed to have claimed the lives of more North Carolinians (it caused fifty-three deaths). Tragically, many of the victims of Floyd were motorists who attempted to drive across flooded roadways and were swept into deep ditches by raging currents.

Following is a list of fatalities in North Carolina, taken from a report in the *Raleigh News and Observer*, with additional information from the state medical examiner.

- Eulalia Mills Aldridge, 87, of Spring Hope, drowned when the car she was riding in was swept off a US 64 overpass.
- Sherry Boyer, 54, of Pennsylvania, died of a heart attack when the van in which she was riding was struck with water from a burst dam on I-95.
- Chris Brown, 75, of Rocky Mount, drowned when he fell into a ditch of rushing water in Edgecombe County.
- Paul Buco, 70, of Wilmington, died when floodwaters swept his car off I-40 in Pender County.
- Badger Chandler, 76, of Vanceboro, died when his car sank in deep water on NC 43.
- Aaron Child, 18, of Leland, was found by campus police after he drowned in a stream near East Carolina University.
- Ransom Cole, 70, of Wallace, died when he was swept away by floodwaters near his home.
- Judy Core, 37, of Goldsboro, died fleeing a fire in her home that was ignited by a kerosene lamp.
- Brandon Davis, 8, of Maryland, died when a car driven by his father tried to get around a washed-out bridge.
- Kenneth Denning, 51, of Mount Olive, died when his pickup truck was swept into floodwaters on Steven Mills Road.
- James Driver, 50, of Wilson. Details unknown.
- Destiny Flowers, 3, and Cabrina Flowers, 5, of Pinetops, died when the small boat in which they were being rescued capsized.

Carlos Vines, 24, awaits news of his missing daughter after rains from Hurricane Floyd flooded communities in Pinetops. The news was not good. His daughter, five-year-old Teshika, drowned along with five others after the boat they were riding in capsized. (Photo by Mel Nathanson; courtesy of the *Raleigh News and Observer*)

- Mario Gomez, 26, and Silverio Beltran Gomez, 35, of Grimesland, drowned when their car was swept away in floodwaters on Blackjack-Grimesland Road.
- Linwood Gooding, 54, of Kinston, drowned after he abandoned his stalled car in floodwaters on NC 11.

- Randolph Grandberry, 38, of Harrellsville, died of an apparent heart attack while bailing out his girlfriend's car.
- Benjamin Harrison, age unknown, of Nash County, was the last recorded fatality of the storm. His body was found in a quarry in November 1999.
- Lou Hendricks, 55, of Norlina, died when floodwaters swept the car in which she was riding off SR 1600 in Warren County.
- Gerald Hoke, 63, of Orange County, died of exposure. His body was found after the storm.
- George Jefferson, 43, of Windsor, drowned when his pickup truck ran off a road.
- Ossie Lee Jenkins, 65, of Whiteville, died of a heart attack after being rescued from his car.
- Ernita Edwards Jones, 22, of Greenville, was killed when she lost control of her car on NC 42 and struck an oncoming car.
- George Jones, 72, of Warrenton, died along with Lou Hendricks when the car in which they were riding was swept off a road in Warren County.
- Osseynna Jones, 1, of Robeson County, died of burns suffered in a fire at her home.
- Reginald Jones, 37, of Maxton, died when the car in which he was riding hit a fallen tree.
- William Teague Jones, 31, of Hot Springs, was electrocuted while working as a contractor for Carolina Power and Light in New Hanover County.
- Eusebio Maldonado, 30, of Clayton, died after water swept his vehicle into Little River Creek in Johnston County.
- Ben Mayo, 50, and Vivian Mayo, 45, of Pinetops, died after a small boat being used to escape flooded houses capsized.
- Keisha Mayo, 24, of Zebulon, died in the same boat.
- David Mills, 79, of Spring Hope, drowned along with Eulalia Aldridge when their pickup truck was washed off a US 64 overpass.
- Paul Mobley, 31, and Emily Mobley, 5, of Clayton, drowned when their car was swept into a creek on a back road in Johnston County.
- Marvin Moody, 43, of Maxton, died when the car in which he was riding ran into a fallen tree on a road near Pembroke.
- Reiford Nichols, 55, of Grifton, drowned in a boating accident on the Neuse River while on his way to pick up his son.

- William Nixon, 47, of Currie, drowned after floodwaters swept his truck off a back road north of Burgaw.
- Leon Penland, 22, of Hayesville, a National Guard military policeman, died when the Humvee he was driving overturned on Caswell Beach.
- Richard Phillips, 40, of Nashville, died after his car plunged into floodwaters on Nashville Road.
- Mitchell Piner, 42, of Wallace, died after his truck was pushed from NC 41 into rushing water.
- Charlotte Poythress, 47, of Gaston, drowned while trying to get to safety after her fiancé's van stalled on a flooded roadway near Fishing Creek at the Nash County line.
- Otis Reid, 51, of Pinetops, drowned when his mobile home was flooded during the storm.
- Ronald Russell, 43, of Greenville, drowned after abandoning his car on a flooded road.
- Ather Smallwood, 96, of Windsor, died of an apparent heart attack after being returned to the rest home where she was living before the evacuation.
- Roger Smith, 86, of Grifton, died of complications from a broken hip incurred during the hurricane.
- James Stokes, 65, of Hobgood, was found dead in his car south of Scotland Neck.
- Larry Summerlin, 63, of Mount Olive, drowned on his way to work when his vehicle was swept off NC 11.
- Teshika Vines, 5, of Pinetops, died after a boat used to escape flooded houses capsized.
- Artemus Westry, 46, of Nashville, died when his car was washed off US 64 near Stony Creek in Nash County.
- Cheryl Whitley, 42, of Goldsboro, drowned when her car washed off a two-lane road near Stoney Creek Bridge.
- James Wilder, 60, of Trenton, drowned when he was swept into floodwaters off NC 58 near Trenton. Wilder was a North Carolina Department of Transportation worker who died while trying to help a stranded motorist.
- James Wilson Jr., 33, of Godwin, died when the vehicle in which he was riding struck a fallen tree on a road south of Dunn.

The Next Disaster

Previous page:
Firefighter Bobby Wilson carries Iris Horton on his back away from her rapidly flooding Drake Street home on September 16, less than twenty-four hours after the wrath of Floyd was unleashed on Rocky Mount. (Photo by David Weaver; courtesy of the *Rocky Mount Telegram*)

Throughout many eastern North Carolina communities, the destruction caused by Hurricane Floyd remains a vivid memory. For some people, the pain lingers even while the rebuilding continues. The last thing these flood victims may want to think about is yet another hurricane disaster in their communities. But once the floodwaters subsided, government officials, relief agencies, and emergency planners began doing just that—critiquing their efforts during Floyd and preparing for the next great storm.

Though it may be unpleasant to speculate on the subject, there is little doubt about it—sooner or later, another disastrous hurricane will hammer the Tar Heel State. It could be a category-four monster like Hazel or Hugo, or perhaps it will be a series of weaker storms that drench the state with flooding rains. No one knows when it will come or where it might strike, but hurricanes are a fact of life along the Atlantic coast, and North Carolina is a frequent target of their fury. Future hurricanes will certainly overwash our beaches, blow down our forests, and send our rivers flowing into the streets. It might happen next year, or it might happen any time in the next thirty years. Either way, we all have an obligation to be prepared.

On the heels of two devastating hurricanes, Fran and Floyd, those who work in disaster response and recovery are under the heaviest obligations to continue to hone their plans and to not forget the lessons they've learned. Thankfully, tremendous improvements in communications, shelter planning, supply logistics, and other critical needs had already been implemented on a state-wide level before Floyd rolled through in 1999.

During Floyd, evacuations in every coastal North Carolina county (something never before attempted) went smoothly, thanks largely to the Highway Patrol's newly revised exit plans. Significant changes to the state's shelter plan allowed for the housing of larger numbers of people in safer buildings. Contracts were already in place to prestage such items as generators, cots, blankets, and ice in locations where they were most likely to be needed. Debris-removal contracts with private companies were also in place, so that local governments, with just one phone call, would have a sea of chainsaw operators ready to go to work.

Good communication is perhaps the key to effective disaster management. And just prior to Floyd, the state's Division of Emergency Management had redesigned its communications system, thanks to an extensive grant from FEMA. New software and laptop computers were distributed to county emergency managers to help streamline the processing of requests for assistance. Emer-

Jerry Avery, a Kinston fireman, carries Gerry Starkey from his flooded Kinston home. (Photo by Chris Seward; courtesy of the *Raleigh News and Observer*)

gency Management headquarters were also reorganized and upgraded with new computers that allowed workers to respond more effectively to incoming requests. During the first hours of the flood, every minute counted, and the enhanced communication system clearly saved lives. Without these and other systemic improvements, Floyd's human toll could have been much greater.

Experience is a great teacher, and North Carolina gained more than its share of experience with hurricanes even before Floyd. Emergency managers had learned from each storm they encountered through the 1990s and had revised their programs to better anticipate the needs of their communities. Always, the challenge is to improve the speed and quality of the services provided and to try to foresee the needs to be met.

With Hurricane Floyd and the devastating floods that followed, this was no easy task. No one could have anticipated the breadth and magnitude of the flooding, or its far-reaching consequences. Floyd presented challenges that emergency responders in North Carolina had never faced before: swift-water rescue in the eastern counties (including air rescue); heavy humanitarian airlift operations; disaster mortuary operations; large-scale temporary housing needs; livestock recovery and incineration; and animal rescue. Each of these demands was met in a reactive fashion, but since Floyd, emergency officials have worked to incorporate them into the state's response plan for future disasters. If another major flood does occur, the agencies involved will, it is hoped, be better prepared to move proactively to provide the necessary services.

But every hurricane is different, and the next significant storm that makes landfall in North Carolina will undoubtedly test our readiness and our ingenuity in new ways. To help our state effectively meet these challenges and prepare for what the next hurricane might bring, we have compiled the following list of recommendations.

• *Maintain a focus on statewide vulnerability.* There was a time when almost everyone viewed hurricanes as coastal phenomena. Though coastal communities certainly must be diligent in their preparations, history has proved that no corner of North Carolina is immune to the deadly effects of hurricanes. The state's three costliest storms—Hugo, Fran, and Floyd—all devastated noncoastal cities like Charlotte, Raleigh, and Rocky Mount. Another of the state's greatest flooding disasters occurred in 1916, when a dissipating tropical storm dumped record rainfall on the eastern slopes of the Blue Ridge Moun-

Yolanda Keyes huddles with her granddaughter, Shybre Stallworth, as she tries to figure out what she is going to do. Keyes had paid off her 1987 Toyota and was working on buying her house when the flood arrived and she lost everything. Welcome Middle School became her temporary home after her residence on Old River Road in Greenville was flooded. (Photo by Jessica Mann; courtesy of the *Winston-Salem Journal*)

tains and swamped the city of Asheville. Every community across the state should recognize its vulnerability and prepare accordingly.

• *Nurture and expand partnerships.* One of the signal achievements of the post-Floyd recovery was the wonderful collection of partnerships that emerged. Federal, state, county, and city governments, relief organizations, private corporations, interfaith agencies, local churches, and squadrons of nonprofits built an impressive network of cooperation and assistance following the flood. In many cases, these partnerships extended far beyond the state's borders to include national organizations and volunteers from other regions of the country. If another major disaster should befall the Tar Heel State, these same partnerships will be vital components of the response and recovery.

We must also guard against erosion of these great networks. If we are fortunate, we could see a prolonged period of hurricane inactivity—we've had similar periods in the past. Government at all levels—city, county, and state —will be tempted to downsize or eliminate disaster response capabilities. Don't do it!

• *Foster and support nontraditional programs that aid recovery.* As we saw in the aftermath of Floyd, government programs will never be able to meet all the needs of victims of large-scale disasters. We are fortunate that a broad array of faith-based organizations, nonprofits, and corporate citizens stepped up to the plate. In future disasters, these programs will continue to be critical players. Innovative programs that blend resources beyond the scope of government often are able to meet needs that might otherwise go unfulfilled.

One example of this was the Church2Church initiative, which was born out of the realization that churches were anchors for many communities after Floyd, especially in rural North Carolina. They functioned not only as distribution centers for food, water, and clothing, but also as spiritual outposts of the recovery. In many instances churches are uninsured or underinsured and are not eligible for government assistance. Many of these churches had themselves been flooded, and the Church2Church program brought in willing churches from outside the flood zone to help the local churches rebuild so they could resume their vital role in helping their communities heal.

• *Promote personal and community responsibility.* Unfortunately, the vast majority of homes and businesses flooded by Hurricane Floyd were not protected by national flood insurance. Consequently, the financial burden on individual homeowners was great, and federal grants and loans could offer only limited assistance. Aid from FEMA programs did not totally replace the personal losses from Floyd, and in the future the emphasis on individual responsibility will likely expand.

Homeowners must take steps to better understand their own vulnerability and to know the elevations of their homes in relation to floodplains. Those who own homes at risk should consider flood insurance; new, more accurate flood maps will help determine which properties fall into that category. Local governments have already begun taking various actions to mitigate disasters, and in the future more of these mitigation programs should become mandatory.

• *Develop programs for smart growth.* Scientists generally agree that even though Floyd was a great natural flood event, the land-altering practices of humans made the flooding more extreme than it might have been. Across eastern North Carolina, farmlands had been ditched and drained, streams had been channelized, homes had proliferated in low-lying areas, and the construction of roads and highways had essentially blocked the natural flow of water. Though it might be unrealistic and cost-prohibitive to try to undo all of these changes, sensible planning and strong zoning for future growth could make a great difference in future floods.

New initiatives within the Department of Transportation are already addressing some of these concerns. Highway planners are now working closely with researchers to design new bridges and roadways that will allow floodwaters to move downstream more quickly, thus preventing the destructive backup of water into nearby neighborhoods. We may not be able to eliminate all the obstacles immediately, but new and replacement highway projects should incorporate better designs.

Other measures to reduce future losses seem only logical. Building codes that relate to wind-loads should enforce a high standard, especially in the vulnerable coastal counties. New construction in floodplains must be limited, and problem elements like junkyards should be removed from those areas. Hog lagoons and dams need to be inspected regularly and redesigned or relocated if necessary. We should continue to move, elevate, or buy out the most vulnerable homes within the floodplain. Laws that protect coastal habitats and affect construction practices through the Coastal Area Management Act should not be weakened.

North Carolina's population will certainly continue to grow, and new construction projects will spread throughout all of our state's river basins. But with wise planning and strong zoning, we can substantially reduce losses in the next big hurricane.

• *Expand swift-water rescue training and resources.* Immediately following Floyd, this was a hot topic among emergency planners and local officials. Though the response from military units and local fire and rescue personnel was rapid

Tipper Gore, wife of Vice President Al Gore, visits Rocky Mount during its recovery from Hurricane Floyd. Here, she offers comfort to a young girl. (Photo by David Weaver; courtesy of the *Rocky Mount Telegram*)

and effective in 1999, specialized training is already under way to improve the effectiveness of rescue operations should another flood occur. For example, the North Carolina Highway Patrol launched a training program that ultimately could result in every officer across the state being prepared for swift-water rescue. Volunteer fire departments in countless small communities are also investing in boats, equipment, and training in order to be ready if another flood should come. These responders must guard against reducing their readiness, even if many years pass before their skills are tested.

• *Maintain readiness and coordination of military assets.* North Carolina is fortunate to be home to thousands of men and women who serve in the nation's armed forces. During Hurricane Floyd, they went to work in many different capacities and were true heroes of the disaster. During the next big event, we will likely call on them again, so maintaining high levels of coordination and strategic placement of resources will be keys to the effective use of our military assets.

• *Continue to partner with* FEMA. The Federal Emergency Management Administration's role in every disaster is significant, and the professionals who work through the complexities of an event like Hurricane Floyd bring a bounty of resources, experience, and financial support down to the state level. Though FEMA's programs are not always clearly understood by victims during the stressful period following a disaster, the resources that flow into the affected areas significantly speed the recovery process. In future disasters, streamlining the assistance application process and expanding the use of application coaching would ensure a higher percentage of participation by qualified applicants.

FEMA is also involved with each disaster in ways that most people never realize. Long before a hurricane strikes the coast, their agents are busy assisting state officials with the prestaging of such commodities as ice, fuel, blankets, and bottled water. FEMA provides grants to states to reduce their exposure to disasters—for example, the extensive flood mapping initiative that is now under way in North Carolina. After Fran and Floyd, we learned just how outdated and inaccurate our flood maps were, but with this new program North Carolina will eventually have the best flood maps in the country. The new maps will help guide local governments in planning and zoning and will better define the flooding risk for millions of North Carolinians.

Another FEMA-supported program that will make a world of difference in the next great flood is the buyout of thousands of properties that fall below the floodplain. This program, which began after Hurricane Fran in 1996, has already removed thousands of families from vulnerable areas. Some homes have been relocated or elevated, but many have simply been torn down. By purchasing both the house and the land, FEMA ensures that homes won't be rebuilt in the same location, only to be destroyed in turn by some future flood.

• *Preserve the Department of Crime Control and Public Safety.* It makes a lot of sense to have one person, a cabinet secretary, ready at a moment's notice to communicate with the governor and coordinate with the leaders of the North Carolina National Guard, the State Highway Patrol, the Civil Air Patrol, and the Division of Emergency Management. Any redistribution of the management authority of these critical agencies could hamper the state's ability to effectively coordinate their activities when time is of the essence.

• *Maintain a high standard of fiscal accountability and budgetary management.* Major hurricane disasters involve billions of dollars in property losses, and the flow of money through various public and private assistance programs is significant. Just a few publicized reports of mishandled relief funds could be enough to sink an effective program. The opportunity for fraud and misuse is always there, but most programs now have adequate measures in place to minimize that risk.

The high cost of disasters like Fran and Floyd also requires wise budgetary planning and diligent lobbying for federal assistance. Again, the concept of partnership is critical, as the costs of response and recovery are ultimately shared by many different groups. But the largest burden will always fall to federal and state governments that must muster huge sums of cash very quickly, even during periods of economic downturn.

Governor Hunt made multiple trips to Washington in the months following Floyd in an effort to garner relief from Congress. In an interview conducted in August 2002, he described his use of visual aids on Capitol Hill:

> When I started to work on Washington, they said, "Well, it's too late. We're about to adjourn. You'll have to come back next year." Well, if I had done that, there would never have been any money. I took a yardstick. And I'd get in there in those meetings with those senators, congressmen, and White House folks, and I'd put the yardstick up on top of the table, "slap," and I'd show them thirty-two inches. We got twenty inches to start with where I live. And then we got these other rains on top of that over the next two weeks. So when they saw the yardstick, it really made an impression. We ultimately got about four billion out of them.

• *Understand that the next five-hundred-year flood won't necessarily be five hundred years in the future.* Though Floyd was viewed by many as a once-in-a-lifetime event, we must recognize that flooding of that magnitude in eastern North Carolina could happen again soon. No one can say with certainty that it will, but we can't assume that it won't. A series of heavy rainfall events triggered the disastrous flood, and North Carolina has been hit by similar storm sequences in the past. Statistically, the chances remain low for any given year, but communities across the state would be wise to prepare, just in case.

Previous page: Associate pastor Willis Pearson of First Pentecostal Holiness Church in Kinston and Woodrow Wilson of Bonneau, South Carolina, cut up onions for yet another huge vat of the "best home-made soup in the world" as praised by those being served by the church's relief organization members. (Photo by Donna Hardy; courtesy of the *Kinston Free Press*)

Faces from the Flood was created with the participation and guidance of dozens of individuals and organizations. The authors express their sincere gratitude to all of the people who helped with the development of this project.

First and foremost are the fifty-some people who agreed to sit down and talk about their experiences during Hurricane Floyd. Thanks go to all for their time, their candor, and their willingness to relive what were sometimes painful memories. These include: Janice Bailey, Kurt Barnes, Cynthia Burnett, Steve Burress, David Cummiskey, Todd Davison, Robert Egleston, Bill Ellis, Bo Fussell, Chris Hackney, Steve Harned, J. C. Heath, Allan Hoffman, Carolyn Hunt, Bobby Joyner, Jewel Kilpatrick, Billy Kornegay, Diane LeFiles, Buster Leverette, Ed Maness, James Mercer, Clifton Mills, John Morgan, Ken Mullen, Annice Narcise, Drew Pearson, Delia Perkins, Lindy Pierce, Al Price, Ronnie Rich, Stan Riggs, Hazel Sorrell, Barbara Stiles, Faye Stone, Charlotte Webb, and Bob Williams.

We would also like to thank those whose interviews ultimately were not used, including Derek Ayscue, David Campbell, Robin Corbett, Martha Daniel, Malcolm Green, Diane Hardison, Bill Hogan, Gerald Hoover, Steve Johnson, Pete McGee, Marian McLawhorn, Corey Mercer, Warren Moore, Robert Mullett, Bobby Nimmo, James Smith, Thomas Townsend, Carolyn Tyler, and Elizabeth Wilder.

A wide range of individuals and organizations assisted with the book in other ways, and we thank them for their support, direction, and content. They include Bob Barnhill, Terry Carlyle, Robert Carver, Darren Clark, Tom Ditt, William Dudley, Joe Gurley, Wes Hester, Renee Hoffman, Bob Jordan, David Kelly, Bill Massey, April Moore, Susan Murphy, Vicky Storm, Charles Thompson, Eric Tolbert, Skip Waters, Phillip Williams, and John Williamson. Also helpful in various ways were FEMA, the National Climatic Data Center, the National Hurricane Center, the National Weather Service, the North Carolina Department of Transportation, the North Carolina Division of Emergency Management, the North Carolina National Guard, the North Carolina State Highway Patrol, UNC Public Television, UNC Sea Grant, the U.S. Coast Guard, the U.S. Geological Survey, and the U.S. Marine Corps. We gathered much useful information from reports and articles in the *Charlotte Observer*, the *Jacksonville Daily Times*, the *Raleigh News and Observer*, and, for background, *North Carolina's Hurricane History* (University of North Carolina Press, 2001).

The photographs used in *Faces from the Flood* were collected from many newspapers, agencies, and individuals. These included the Associated Press, the *Charlotte Observer*, FEMA, the *Goldsboro News-Argus*, the *Jacksonville Daily News*, the *Kinston Free Press*, NOAA, the *Raleigh News and Observer*, the *Rocky Mount Telegram*, United Press International, the *Virginian Pilot*, the *Wilson Daily Times*, and the *Winston-Salem Journal*. Individuals who provided special assistance include Don Bryan, Charles Buchanan, Cynthia Burnett, Ginny Hauswald, Davie Hinshaw, Carolyn McMann, Jay Price, Hal Tarleton, David Weaver, Drew Wilson, and Karinne Young. We are grateful to all of them.

In addition to those mentioned above, the authors extend special thanks to their loving families, especially Noel, William, Charles, and Mary Eleanor Moore, Heather Leonard, and Robin and Lindsey Barnes. Also deserving special thanks are Billy Ray Cameron, Billy Davenport, Governor Jim Hunt, Mark London, David Perry, Stephanie Scott, and Pam Upton.

Index

Page numbers in italics refer to illustrations.